OXFORD WORLD'

THE EXPEDITIO

XENOPHON was born in the early 420s BC to a wealthy Athenian family. He associated in his youth with the philosopher Socrates. In 401 BC, three years after Athens' defeat in the Peloponnesian War, he accepted an invitation to serve with a mercenary army (the famous Ten Thousand) raised by Cyrus, brother of the king of Persia. Cyrus led his army in an unsuccessful attack on his brother. After Cyrus' death Xenophon was one of the leaders of the Ten Thousand in their retreat to the sea. He was later exiled from Athens and settled by the Spartans in the Peloponnese. It was there that he started writing the extraordinarily wide variety of works for which he is now famous: a didactic historical fiction (the *Cyropaedia*), a contemporary history of Greece (the *Hellenica*), as well as Socratic dialogues and treatises on economics, hunting, horsemanship, and the Spartan constitution. His most famous work is *The Expedition of Cyrus*, his account of the march of the Ten Thousand. He died in the late 350s BC.

ROBIN WATERFIELD is a self-employed writer, whose books range from philosophy and history to children's fiction. He has previously translated, for Oxford World's Classics, Plato's *Republic*, *Symposium*, *Gorgias*, *Phaedrus*, and *Meno and Other Dialogues*, Aristotle's *Physics*, Herodotus' *Histories*, Plutarch's *Greek Lives* and *Roman Lives*, Euripides' *Orestes and Other Plays* and *Heracles and Other Plays*, and *The First Philosophers: The Presocratics and the Sophists*.

TIM ROOD is Fellow and Tutor in Classics at St Hugh's College, Oxford. He is the author of *Thucydides: Narrative and Explanation* and *The Sea! The Sea! The Shout of the Ten Thousand in the Modern Imagination*, as well as of a number of articles on Greek historiography.

OXFORD WORLD'S CLASSICS

*For over 100 years Oxford World's Classics have brought
readers closer to the world's great literature. Now with over 700
titles—from the 4,000-year-old myths of Mesopotamia to the
twentieth century's greatest novels—the series makes available
lesser-known as well as celebrated writing.*

*The pocket-sized hardbacks of the early years contained
introductions by Virginia Woolf, T. S. Eliot, Graham Greene,
and other literary figures which enriched the experience of reading.
Today the series is recognized for its fine scholarship and
reliability in texts that span world literature, drama and poetry,
religion, philosophy and politics. Each edition includes perceptive
commentary and essential background information to meet the
changing needs of readers.*

OXFORD WORLD'S CLASSICS

XENOPHON

The Expedition of Cyrus

Translated by
ROBIN WATERFIELD

With an Introduction and Notes by
TIM ROOD

OXFORD
UNIVERSITY PRESS

OXFORD

UNIVERSITY PRESS

Great Clarendon Street, Oxford OX2 6DP

Oxford University Press is a department of the University of Oxford.
It furthers the University's objective of excellence in research, scholarship,
and education by publishing worldwide in

Oxford New York

Auckland Cape Town Dar es Salaam Hong Kong Karachi
Kuala Lumpur Madrid Melbourne Mexico City Nairobi
New Delhi Shanghai Taipei Toronto

With offices in

Argentina Austria Brazil Chile Czech Republic France Greece
Guatemala Hungary Italy Japan South Korea Poland Portugal
Singapore Switzerland Thailand Turkey Ukraine Vietnam

Oxford is a registered trade mark of Oxford University Press
in the UK and in certain other countries

Published in the United States
by Oxford University Press Inc., New York

Translation © Robin Waterfield 2005
Editorial material © Tim Rood 2005

British Library Cataloguing in Publication Data

Data available

Library of Congress Cataloging in Publication Data

Data available

ISBN 978-0-19-955598-7

Typeset in Ehrhardt
by RefineCatch Limited, Bungay, Suffolk
Printed in Great Britain by
Clays Ltd, Elcograf S.p.A.

16

CONTENTS

CONTENTS

THE EXPEDITION OF CYRUS

INTRODUCTION

Darius and Parysatis had two sons, of whom Artaxerxes was the
elder and Cyrus the younger, and when Darius was ill and
suspected that he was dying, he wanted them both by his side . . .

XENOPHON's *Expedition of Cyrus* starts with the beguiling simplicity of a fairy tale. The story Xenophon unfolds is itself beauti-
fully simple—and the most exciting adventure to survive from the
ancient world. Xenophon tells the story of a young Persian prince,
Cyrus, who rose in revolt in 401 BC against his brother Artaxerxes,
the king of Persia, and gathered a large army—among them about
thirteen thousand Greek soldiers, including Xenophon himself.
Cyrus marched from Sardis (in what is now western Turkey) to
Mesopotamia. To the north of Babylon, he finally encountered the
royal army and died in an impetuous attack on his brother. The
Greek mercenaries in his army were left stranded in the desert a
thousand miles from home. When the Persians demanded that they
hand over their weapons, the Greeks refused and set off northwards
on their long march home. For some days they were shadowed by a
section of the Persian army. Their generals were then invited to a
conference with the Persians, and seized and killed. It was at this
moment of crisis that Xenophon himself rose to prominence. He
inspired the despondent Greek soldiers and led them through the
mountains of Kurdistan and the snowy Armenian plateau to the
sight of 'The sea! The sea!', and then along the coast of the Black Sea
to the fringes of the Greek world.

The march of Cyrus' Greek troops—known to posterity as the
Ten Thousand—has long been admired. The Greek biographer
Plutarch tells the story that Mark Antony, during his own disastrous
retreat from Parthia in 36 BC, 'would often cry out loud "Oh, the
Ten Thousand!"', in awe at Xenophon's men, whose march back
from Babylon to the sea had been even longer and who had won their
way to safety fighting far greater numbers of enemies' (*Antony*
45.12). John Macdonald Kinneir, an early nineteenth-century
explorer who travelled through much of the same terrain, thought
that the achievement of the Ten Thousand was 'unparalleled in the

annals of war' and 'a memorable example of what skill and resolution
are able to effect',[1] while a modern archaeologist who also crossed
the same formidable mountain passes—'in the comfort of a modern
Land Rover on a modern road from Bitlis to Erzerum in summer'—
has written of 'the almost incredible discipline, high morale and
almost superhuman powers of endurance of this force'.[2]

The Expedition of Cyrus (Greek *Anabasis Kyrou*—literally *Cyrus'
March Up Country*) has been admired as much as the march it
describes. Xenophon wrote an extraordinarily wide variety of works
besides *The Expedition of Cyrus*: the *Cyropaedia*, a pseudo-historical
account of the upbringing and leadership of the founder of the
Persian empire, Cyrus the Great, after whom the prince Xenophon
served was named; the *Hellenica*, a work on contemporary Greek
history; the *Apology*, a version of the defence speech of his one-time
mentor Socrates, as well as other philosophical conversations involving Socrates (*Memorabilia*, *Symposium*) and the poet Simonides
(*Hiero*); the treatises *On Hunting* and *On Horsemanship*, and others
on household management (the *Oeconomicus*, another Socratic
work), military leadership (the *Cavalry Commander*) and politics (the
Constitution of the Spartans); an encomium of the Spartan king
Agesilaus; and an economic pamphlet (*Ways and Means*). At some
periods of history his more didactic and philosophical works have
been more popular, but for the last two centuries *The Expedition of
Cyrus* has generally been regarded as his masterpiece. It can be
enjoyed in its own right as a gripping narrative that offers a glimpse
of Greek soldiers encountering a foreign world—hunting gazelle in
the desert, stumbling on the almost deserted cities of Nimrud and
Nineveh, confronting wild mountain tribes who block their way
by rolling rocks down steep slopes, sheltering against the harsh
Armenian winter in underground homes while restoring their spirits
with the local 'barley wine'. Xenophon's narrative also offers a
unique insight into the character of a Greek army on the march. We
see at first hand the soldiers at leisure, holding athletic competitions
amongst themselves. We meet a world marked by the particular

[1] J. M. Kinneir, *Journey through Asia Minor, Armenia, and Koordistan, in the Years 1813 and 1814, with remarks on the Marches of Alexander and the Retreat of the Ten Thousand* (London, 1818), 396.
[2] R. D. Barnett, 'Xenophon and the Wall of Media', *Journal of Hellenic Studies*, 83 (1963), 1–26, at 26.

forms of Greek religion: vows and sacrifices are frequently made to the gods, seers are constantly consulted, a sneeze is thought to be a favourable omen. This world permeated by the divine is also a world permeated by the particular forms of Greek political life. The propitious sneeze occurs at a meeting where the troops elect their own generals and debate what steps they should take next. The troops manage to create among themselves a sense of common purpose and a readiness to accept discipline, but that hard-won sense of unity comes increasingly to be threatened by internal tensions as they draw nearer to Greece itself. The life of the Greek cities from which these soldiers came was marked by a similar blend of co-operation and rivalry.

Xenophon's account tells us much about the character of Greek soldiers and of Greek political life, but it also offers insight into a broader human experience. The sense that Xenophon's narrative is somehow archetypal was well expressed by the French critic and philosopher Hippolyte Taine. Taine found that, just as he first learnt what a battle was like when he read Stendhal's account of the battle of Waterloo in *The Charterhouse of Parma*, so too he felt when he read the retreat of the Ten Thousand that he was 'learning for the first time what the march of an army is'.[3]

The Expedition of Cyrus has had an extraordinary afterlife. Xenophon himself was much admired in antiquity. The second-century AD historian Arrian drew from Xenophon the title of his *Expedition of Alexander* (*Anabasis Alexandrou*); he also imitated Xenophon by writing philosophical memoirs and a work on hunting. Rhetoricians praised the grace and purity of Xenophon's style (it earned him the names 'the Attic Muse' and 'the Attic bee'—bees were proverbial for elegance) while many other writers of prose history and fiction copied it.

The fame of Xenophon's account in the modern world comes in large part from its use as a school text. Xenophon's fairly simple style had always made him a suitable author for beginners in Greek to read, but it was the greater formalization of examinations in the nineteenth century that led to *The Expedition of Cyrus* becoming entrenched as *the* school text. In a lecture delivered in the 1850s, John Henry Newman imagined a university interview in which a

[3] H. Taine, 'Xénophon: *L'Anabase*', in his *Essais de critique et d'histoire* (11th edn.; Paris, 1908; orig. pub. 1858), 150–87, at 166.

tutor tests a dim pupil on a single word—'anabasis'. The choice of
the *Anabasis* for this mock-interview allows Newman to have
some fun at the poor candidate's expense ('now where was Sardis?
[*Candidate.*] In Asia Minor? . . . no . . . it's an island . . . *a pause, then*
. . . Sardinia'), but it is still a revealing comment on the position
Xenophon's text had gained within the Victorian educational system.[4]

For many schoolchildren, the way *The Expedition of Cyrus* was
taught made their lessons in Greek uncomfortable. The folklorist
Andrew Lang recalled how 'ten lines of Xenophon, narrating how he
marched so many parasangs and took breakfast, do not amount to
more than a very unrefreshing sip of Greek. Nobody even tells the
boys who Xenophon was, what he did there, and what it was all
about. . . . The boys straggle along with Xenophon, knowing not
whence or whither.'[5] Nonetheless, the school editions that pro-
liferated to help hapless schoolchildren through Xenophon's text
could come to be endowed with the charm of nostalgia. A character
in one of George Gissing's novels recalls 'the little Oxford edition
which I used at school, with its boyish sign-manual on the fly-leaf, its
blots and underlinings and marginal scrawls . . . a school-book,
which, even as a school-book, was my great delight'. He remembers
The Expedition of Cyrus as 'an admirable work of art, unique in its
combination of concise and rapid narrative with colour and pictur-
esqueness': 'Were this the sole book existing in Greek, it would be
abundantly worth while to learn the language in order to read it.'[6]

At the same time as *The Expedition of Cyrus* established itself in
schools, the wild areas through which the Ten Thousand had passed
started to be explored by European travellers. Travel writers would
often recount dangers similar to the ones that the Ten Thousand had
surmounted, and observe with a patronizing fascination how oriental
customs had not changed since Xenophon's day. On one page alone,
John Macdonald Kinneir noted that the habit of holding a black
cloth before the eyes against the glare of the snow was 'still practised
in Armenia and Koordistan'; that the villages in Armenia were 'still
built in exactly the same manner'; that cattle, men, women, and

    [4] J. H. Newman, *The Idea of a University: Defined and Illustrated*, ed. I. T. Ker
(Oxford, 1976; orig. pub. 1873), 276–8.
    [5] A. Lang, 'Homer and the Study of Greek', in his *Essays in Little* (London, 1891),
77–92, at 81–2.
    [6] G. Gissing, *The Private Papers of Henry Ryecroft* (London, 1964; orig. pub. 1903), 92.

children 'all live in the same apartment in this country at the present day'; and that wheat and barley were 'still cultivated'. Only one thing had changed: Kinneir was struck by Xenophon's description of barley wine, but he 'could never discover any liquor of this kind whilst in Armenia'.[7]

Another sign of the growing fame of Xenophon's story was that its Greek title, 'anabasis', came to be applied to other long marches. *Deutsche Anabasis 1918* was the title of a short memoir by a German soldier describing a retreat inland through the Balkans at the end of the First World War. He drew attention to many parallels with the retreat of the Ten Thousand, and concluded with an appeal for the Germans to take heart and prove themselves worthy of the German name: 'Anabasis means ascent. If German hearts are again strengthened and raised to Duty, Faith, and Honour, then from the collapse the German people will have another great Anabasis: Escape, Ascent, Resurrection!'[8] At that same time the appeal of Xenophon's story was also seen in the 'Anabasis' of the Czech Legion in Siberia— an army that had been fighting behind Russian lines against the Austro-Hungarian empire, and then, when it found itself stranded after the Treaty of Brest-Litovsk, refused a Russian command to disarm and set off towards Vladivostok with the plan of joining the newly formed Czech national army fighting on the Western Front. This Czech Anabasis even had some practical benefits: the achievement was used to promote the Czech claim for a nation state. Xenophon was used to support another battle for freedom at the climax of the evacuation from Dunkirk in June 1940, when *The Times* ran a lead editorial headed 'ANABASIS'. Here the retreat to Dunkirk was aligned with the retreat of the Ten Thousand, and it was claimed that 'British soldiers look on blue water as did the Greek army of XENOPHON, whose cry of θάλαττα, θάλαττα! was the climax of the Anabasis, and marked the successful completion of the most famous march of the ancient world'.[9] The myth of the *Anabasis* lives on in the personal narratives of participants in the invasion of Iraq in

---

[7] Kinneir, *Journey through Asia Minor*, 487.
[8] F. von Notz, *Deutsche Anabasis 1918: Ein Rückzug aus dem bulgarischen Zusammenbruch in Mazedonien* (Berlin, 1921), 63–4.
[9] *The Times* (London), 4 June 1940, p. 7.

2003. One of the first such accounts was entitled *The March Up*, and said to be 'inspired by the classic story of the *Anabasis*'.[10]

The heading of the *Times* editorial reflects the particular appeal of one section of the Ten Thousand's long trek—the march to the sea. 'Anabasis' means a march up country, away from the coast, but at the time of the Dunkirk evacuation the word was used of a retreat to the sea. The achievement of the Greeks in adversity was far more glamorous than Cyrus' fratricidal ambitions. And no scene in the Greeks' long march to the sea was more appealing than the climax evoked that day in June 1940—the scene where the Greeks reach a mountain from which they catch sight of the Black Sea:

When the first men got there, a huge cry went up. This made Xenophon and the rearguard think that the van too was under attack from another enemy force . . . But the cry kept getting louder and nearer, as each successive rank that came up began to sprint towards the ever-increasing numbers of those who were shouting out. The more men who reached the front, the louder the cry became, until it was apparent to Xenophon that something of special significance was happening. He mounted a horse, took Lycius and the cavalry, and rode to lend assistance; and before long they could make out that the soldiers were shouting 'The sea! The sea!' and passing the word along.

That shout of 'The sea! The sea!' (*'Thalatta! Thalatta!'*) has become proverbial (it is the only phrase from Xenophon in the *Oxford Dictionary of Quotations*). It gives a ringing start to the second cycle of Heinrich Heine's *North Sea* poems: 'Thalatta! Thalatta! | Greetings to you, o eternal sea! | Greetings to you ten-thousandfold.' It is evoked towards the start of one of the most renowned twentieth-century novels, James Joyce's *Ulysses*, when Buck Mulligan looks out over Dublin Bay: 'Ah, Dedalus, the Greeks. I must teach you. You must read them in the original. *Thalatta! Thalatta!*' And it has been quoted by writers as diverse as Shelley, Louis MacNeice, and William Carlos Williams, and quoted, too, in many less illustrious works—in poems and articles in Victorian periodicals, in popular romantic novels, in works of travel and adventure. It has been as readily transformed into a symbol of national freedom and of triumph

---

[10] R. L. Smith and F. J. West, *The March Up: Taking Baghdad with the 1st Marine Division* (London, 2004), 2.

over adversity (as at the time of the retreat to Dunkirk) as into an emblem of the romantic longing for a return to the primal sea.[11]

It is the apparent simplicity of Xenophon's narrative as it builds up to the climactic shout of 'The sea! The sea!' that has made that shout so appealing to readers of *The Expedition of Cyrus*. It is dangerous, however, to succumb too readily to the impression of simplicity created by Xenophon's account. T. E. Lawrence—who saw parallels between himself and Xenophon—knew better when he told George Bernard Shaw that he found *The Expedition of Cyrus* 'charming'—but also 'cunningly full of writing tricks' and even 'pretentiously simple'.[12] Much as Lawrence's own *Seven Pillars of Wisdom* was written at a time when the consequences of his military campaigns in the Middle East during the First World War were controversial, so too Xenophon's *Expedition of Cyrus* was written at a time when the exploits of the Ten Thousand and his own role during their retreat were open to debate. To appreciate why he wrote his account as he did we must look in more detail at the goals he had in writing about his adventures in Asia. Like Andrew Lang, we must ask who Xenophon was, what he did there, and what it was all about.

Xenophon

Xenophon was born, probably in the early 420s BC, to a wealthy Athenian family. Little is known either about his father Gryllus, who does not seem to have achieved political prominence at Athens, or about Xenophon's own early life. We do know, however, that Xenophon was among the well-off young men who associated with the philosopher Socrates, and it is likely that he remained in Athens during the reign of the Thirty Tyrants (404–403 BC), the junta imposed by the Spartans after Athens' defeat in the Peloponnesian War, and that he fought against the exiled democrats as a cavalryman.

The Expedition of Cyrus is the main source of our knowledge of

[11] 'Sea-Greeting': *The Complete Poems of Heinrich Heine*, trans. H. Draper (Oxford, 1982), 145 (I have restored 'Thalatta! Thalatta!' for the translator's 'Thalassa! Thalassa!'). Mulligan: J. Joyce, *Ulysses* (Paris, 1922), 5. See, in general, T. C. B. Rood, *The Sea! The Sea! The Shout of the Ten Thousand in the Modern Imagination* (London, 2004), on the modern reception of this shout.

[12] Quoted in J. M. Wilson, 'T. E. Lawrence and the Translating of the *Odyssey*', *Journal of the T. E. Lawrence Society*, 3. 2 (1994), 35–66, at 37.

Xenophon's life, but it covers only his two exceptional years of service with the Ten Thousand—and it reveals only how Xenophon wanted his role to be perceived. Even so, the account is selective. Xenophon says very little about his experiences during the march up country and the early stages of the retreat. It is only after their generals have been treacherously slain by the Persians that he comes to the fore in the narrative. He reports how he stirred up the dejected soldiers and was elected one of the two commanders of the rearguard. He continued to provide moral and strategic leadership during the march to the sea: as the army encountered one difficulty after another, he would devise ways for the army to get through. Xenophon presents himself as a model leader: accessible, sharing the toils of the common troops, keeping the tired soldiers on the move, even taking the initiative in chopping up firewood. After the Greeks' arrival in Byzantium, he led the remaining troops during a winter's campaigning for the Thracian dynast Seuthes and then into service with the Spartans in Asia as they embarked on a campaign against the Persians (399 BC).

Xenophon also included in *The Expedition of Cyrus* one flashback to his earlier life and one section looking ahead to his later life. The flashback—inserted at the point when Xenophon first rouses up the spirits of the dejected soldiers—tells how he had been invited by Proxenus, a Boeotian guest-friend (*xenos*), to join Cyrus. Modern scholars tend to suppose that his reasons for accepting the invitation were his distaste for the restored democracy at Athens and his desire for an exciting adventure. What Xenophon himself says is that his ambition was to become a friend (*philos*) of Cyrus. The Greek term implies that he wanted to enter into a relationship with the Persian prince defined by an ethic of equality and reciprocity, not by service for cash: he insists that he had come along 'not as a general, nor as a company commander, nor as a soldier' (3.1.4)—that is, not in one of the positions whose differing rates of pay he has earlier recorded.

Xenophon also reports that he consulted Socrates about his proposed expedition with Cyrus (3.1.5–7). Socrates told him to consult the Delphic oracle to see whether or not he should go, since he 'thought that friendship with Cyrus might well be actionable in the eyes of the Athenian authorities, because Cyrus was widely believed to have wholeheartedly supported the Spartans in their military operations against the Athenians'. But instead of posing the question

Socrates had suggested, Xenophon asked for the names of gods to whom he should sacrifice in order to achieve a successful return.

Socrates' advice hints that following Cyrus would prove dangerous to Xenophon, and so it turned out. At various points in the march along the Black Sea coast and after the arrival at Byzantium, Xenophon reports that he wanted to return home to Athens, but towards the end of the work he looks ahead to the event that prevented his return—a decree of exile: 'Xenophon . . . made no secret of the fact that he was getting ready to go home—for there was no sign yet in Athens of any proposal that he should be officially banished' (7.7.57). It is not, however, certain that it was serving with Cyrus that led to Xenophon's exile, as Socrates had feared. The date and circumstances of his exile remain controversial. It may be that it was not so much joining Cyrus' army as marching against Artaxerxes that got Xenophon into trouble. Marching against Artaxerxes could have been held against Xenophon during the early stages of the Corinthian War in Greece (395–387 BC), when the Persians were subsidizing the anti-Spartan coalition, or even before that, when Athens was looking to win Persian help. There remains a third possibility. Xenophon went on to serve with the Spartan king Agesilaus in Asia and to accompany him on his return to Greece in 394 BC. It may have been Xenophon's presence with Agesilaus at the battle of Coronea in that same year, when the Athenians were part of the anti-Spartan coalition, that led to his exile.[13]

What happened to Xenophon after his exile emerges from a flash forward placed in *The Expedition of Cyrus* at the point where the Greeks have reached Cerasus on the Black Sea coast (5.3). At Cerasus it was decided to divide up among the troops the money received from the sale of prisoners captured during the retreat, to set aside a tithe for Apollo and Artemis of Ephesus, and to give this sacred money to the generals for safe keeping. Xenophon then reveals that

[13] For discussion of Xenophon's exile, see P. J. Rahn, 'The Date of Xenophon's exile', in G. S. Shrimpton and D. J. McCargor (eds.), *Classical Contributions: Studies in Honour of Malcolm Francis McGregor* (New York, 1981), 103–19; C. J. Tuplin, 'Xenophon's Exile Again', in M. Whitby, P. R. Hardie, and M. Whitby (eds.), *Homo Viator: Classical Essays for John Bramble* (Bristol and Oak Park, Ill., 1987), 59–68; P. Green, 'Text and Context in the Matter of Xenophon's Exile', in I. Worthington (ed.), *Ventures into Greek History* (Oxford, 1994), 215–27. The broader theme of displacement is discussed by J. Ma, 'You Can't Go Home Again: Displacement and Identity in Xenophon's *Anabasis*', in R. Lane Fox (ed.), *The Long March: Xenophon and the Ten Thousand* (New Haven, 2004), 330–45.

after his exile he was settled by the Spartans at Scillus, not far from the great panhellenic sanctuary of Olympia, and that with his own portion of the tithe he bought a piece of land for Artemis, built a temple, and founded a festival in her honour.

Many readers have admired the brief vignette Xenophon presents of his life at Scillus: neighbours would come to the festival and feast on the sacrificial victims and on the other goods that the goddess provided, and the young men—Xenophon's sons among them—would hunt stags and boars. But there also seems to be a hint of nostalgia in Xenophon's description of his country estate. The description is cast in the Greek imperfect tense. This verbal form could denote recurrent action, but it could also mean that Xenophon was describing a way of life that he was no longer in a position to enjoy. And that suspicion is reinforced by the nostalgic way in which he quotes the inscription he set up at the sanctuary of Artemis. The inscription proclaimed that the possessor of the sacred land should offer a tithe each year to the goddess and keep the temple in good repair, and 'neglect of these duties will not go unnoticed by the goddess' (5.3.13).

If there is an elegiac tone in the Scillus description, an explanation lies readily to hand. Xenophon was forced to leave his estate at Scillus at some point after the Spartan defeat at Leuctra in 371 BC. According to some ancient sources, he spent the rest of his life in Corinth, but later in antiquity, at least, the locals at Scillus claimed that Xenophon was buried there. There is no evidence that he ever returned to Athens, though a decree rescinding his exile is attested and his son Gryllus was killed fighting for the Athenian cavalry at the battle of Mantinea in 362 BC. Xenophon himself probably died in the late 350s BC.

Xenophon the man has been admired as much as his works. The eighteenth-century translator Edward Spelman saw him as a 'universal Man' whose various works show that he 'possess'd, in a Sovereign Degree, the Art of Government', and that he was 'a compleat General', 'an entertaining, an instructive, and a faithful Historian', 'an Orator', 'a Sportsman', 'a Friend and a Philosopher'—and 'all of them, that he was a good Man'.[14] This universal man could also resemble a familiar national stereotype—or so a reviewer in the

---

[14] E. Spelman, 'Introduction', *Xenophon: The Expedition of Cyrus* (2 vols., London, 1740–2), vol. i, pp. xxii–xxiii.

Times Literary Supplement thought in 1930: 'Xenophon's *Anabasis*, made a chopping-block for generations of schoolboys, has served to conceal from many people a noble character—soldier, country gentleman, philosopher, sportsman, in whom, risking a charge of smugness, we may venture to claim a resemblance to a not uncommon English type.' The book under review, appropriately, was entitled *Sport in Classic Times*.[15]

Not everyone has been so willing to be accused of smugness. Indeed, since the second half of the nineteenth century there has been a strong reaction against idealizations of Xenophon. A common assumption has been that all of his writings are narrowly self-serving. In the case of *The Expedition of Cyrus*, it has been supposed that he was looking to defend himself against charges brought against his leadership during the retreat.[16] The image of Xenophon that emerges from his narrative can appear too good to be true: as Italo Calvino wrote, 'on occasions Xenophon appears to be one of those heroes from children's comics, who in every episode appear to survive against impossible odds'.[17] Hence the suspicion that Xenophon was trying to manipulate his fellow Athenians, who had exiled him; or the remnants of the Ten Thousand, who had found his leadership a bit rough; or the Spartans, who had difficult dealings with Xenophon and the Ten Thousand on their arrival at Byzantium. Another suggestion is that Xenophon wrote his memoir in order to demonstrate the weakness of the Persian empire and so encourage the Greeks at large to attack the Persians. But even advocates of this view have accused Xenophon of advertising his own military credentials for leadership of a panhellenic expedition.[18]

Crucial to determining Xenophon's purpose in writing *The Expedition of Cyrus* is discovering the date at which he composed the work. Dates have been proposed ranging from the 390s BC, very soon after the events described (it's so 'fresh'), to the late 360s or even

---

[15] Review of A. J. Butler, *Sport in Classic Times*, *Times Literary Supplement*, 1478 (29 May 1930), 455.

[16] F. Durrbach, 'L'Apologie de Xénophon dans l'"Anabase" ', *REG* 6 (1893), 343–86, remains one of the most forceful proponents of this view.

[17] I. Calvino, 'Xenophon's Anabasis', in *Why Read the Classics?*, trans. M. McLaughlin (London, 1999; Ital. orig. 1991), 19–23, at 20.

[18] F. Robert, 'Les Intentions de Xénophon dans l'Anabase', *Information littéraire*, 2 (1950), 55–9.

350s BC (old men forget the odd river or two).[19] The problem is that there is very little evidence within the text that helps determine the date it was written. And in the absence of any such firm data arguments about its date of composition tend to be connected with views about the audience the work was addressed to. Critics who think that Xenophon was promoting a panhellenic expedition often date the work to the early 360s BC, a time when Athens and Sparta were co-operating against Thebes and keen to dissociate the new Arcadian confederacy from Thebes, and when Thebes was looking to Persia for help. It has also been proposed that the work was written in two parts, with the first part written as a protest against the King's Peace of 386 BC and the second part written to bolster the tottering power of Sparta.[20] The nostalgic tone of the Scillus digression does perhaps make a date in the 360s BC the most likely, but this dating does not in itself offer a firm clue as to Xenophon's intentions in writing his account.

Two pieces of ancient evidence may offer a clue to Xenophon's aims. The Byzantine lexicographer Stephanus gives four extremely short citations from another *Anabasis* written by one of the Ten Thousand's generals, Sophaenetus of Stymphalus. The fragments themselves tell us almost nothing about Sophaenetus' work. But it has been argued that Sophaenetus' account was a source for the fourth-century BC historian Ephorus, and through Ephorus for the epitome found in the history of the first-century BC Sicilian Diodorus, where Xenophon is first mentioned, not in the retreat to the sea, but only when the army is in Thrace. Perhaps Xenophon was responding to an earlier account in which his own role had been undervalued.[21] It is dangerous, however, to argue that a work about which we know a lot was written in response to a work about which we know very little. It may be noted that no other general in Diodorus plays the role of saviour that Xenophon allots himself—and it is likely in any case that most of Diodorus' account stems from

---

[19] Whether or not Xenophon used some sort of diary is open to debate: see note to p. 5.

[20] E. Delebecque, 'Xénophon, Athènes et Lacédémones: Notes sur la composition de l'Anabase', *REG* 59–60, (1946–7), 71–138.

[21] See e.g. G. L. Cawkwell, 'Introduction', in *Xenophon: The Persian Expedition*, trans. R. Warner (Harmondsworth, 1972), 9–48; Cawkwell's arguments have now been re-stated in his chapter 'When, How, and Why did Xenophon Write the *Anabasis*?', in Lane Fox (ed.), *Long March*, 47–67.

Xenophon's own memoir. It is even possible that Sophaenetus did not write an *Anabasis* at all. It is disturbing that the work is attested only at so late a date. The citations may derive from oral narratives that were preserved in military handbooks. Or perhaps the account of Sophaenetus was a later fiction—a rhetorical exercise produced at a time when Xenophon was an established classic. What better persona to adopt for a rewriting of *The Expedition of Cyrus* than that of the oldest general—who is presented by Xenophon as overly cautious and tactically weak?[22]

The other piece of ancient evidence is perhaps the oddest passage in the whole of Xenophon—his summary of Cyrus' expedition in the *Hellenica*: 'How Cyrus collected an army and marched up country against his brother, and how the battle happened, and how he died, and how afterwards the Greeks came through in safety to the sea—this has been written by Themistogenes of Syracuse' (3.1.2). Why refer to the obscure Themistogenes rather than to his own work? Perhaps because Xenophon published *The Expedition of Cyrus* under the pseudonym of Themistogenes—an inference that was already made in antiquity by Plutarch (*On the Fame of Athens* 345 E), who saw the pseudonym as a device used by Xenophon to make his rosy account of his own actions more acceptable.

Some aspects of Xenophon's self-presentation do not fit well the specific target audiences that have been proposed for *The Expedition of Cyrus*. If Xenophon was wanting to win a recall to Athens, for instance, it is odd that he stresses how he considered not returning to Athens at all: at one point he planned to found a city on the coast of the Black Sea, and later he was tempted by Seuthes' offer of some strongholds on the Thracian coast. He also makes no secret of his service with Sparta. And he even says that his friend Proxenus wooed him to go on the expedition by describing Cyrus as 'more important to him than his homeland'.

On the other hand, it would be a pity to return to the image of Xenophon as country squire, the retired general fondly writing his memoirs. Xenophon was a strikingly innovative writer—one of the great generic experimenters of antiquity. *The Expedition of Cyrus*

[22] Oral Sophaenetus: P. J. Stylianou, 'One *Anabasis* or Two?', in Lane Fox (ed.), *Long March*, 68–96. Sophaenetus as later 'forgery': H. D. Westlake, 'Diodorus and the Expedition of Cyrus', *Phoenix*, 41 (1987), 241–55. Stylianou convincingly argues for the general dependence of Diodorus on Xenophon.

itself can claim to be the first known military memoir, but it is also a work that eludes easy classification. It has no formal prologue. Parts of it have contact with geography and ethnography. And while much of it is written from Xenophon's perspective, it is not formally a memoir at all: Xenophon conceals his authorship by using third-person forms to refer to his own actions during the retreat. Xenophon the man is no easier to pin down than Xenophon the writer. Supposedly a model of conventional Greek values, Xenophon was willing to abandon Athens in favour of Athens' great enemy, Sparta. Even before that he had been willing to abandon Greece in favour of a Persian prince. How had it come about that this aristocratic Athenian was drawn to serve with a barbarian in a battle for the vast Persian empire?

Cyrus

Cyrus first came into contact with the Greek world in 407 BC, when he was appointed by his father, Darius II, to a special command in western Asia Minor. His arrival proved to be the turning point in the Peloponnesian War (431–404 BC). At the start of the war, the two protagonists, Athens and Sparta, had both sought help from Persia, but the Persians had been reluctant to intervene. The Persians took more interest in the war after the Athenian defeat in Sicily (413 BC). But at first the satrap Tissaphernes was content to play the two sides off against each other. It was only with the arrival of Cyrus that the Persians began supporting one side wholeheartedly: Persian gold financed the Spartan fleet and won the war for Sparta.

As well as a new policy, Cyrus brought with him a new and more charismatic style of leadership. He told the Spartan admiral Lysander that if he used up the money the king had sent for the Spartans he would finance them from his own resources—and that if he used those up too he would even cut up his gold and silver throne (*Hellenica* 1.5.3). Cyrus also overturned Greek assumptions about oriental effeminacy. In his *Oeconomicus*, Xenophon tells the story that when Lysander met Cyrus at his 'paradise' at Sardis (the Persian term includes both gardens and hunting grounds) he noticed that Cyrus was wearing fine clothes, jewellery, and perfume—and was then astonished to discover that this seemingly soft prince had laid out his own garden and planted some of the trees himself (4.20–5).

Cyrus' keen support for Sparta may have been prompted by his own dynastic ambitions: the Spartans repaid him for his support by backing his bid to overthrow his brother Artaxerxes. Xenophon does not expressly mention this official Spartan support in *The Expedition of Cyrus*. He does allude to it, however, in the *Hellenica*, his history of contemporary Greek affairs (3.1.1), and even in *The Expedition of Cyrus* he mentions the progress and arrival of ships sent by the Spartans (1.2.21, 1.4.2). It is also possible that Clearchus, the exiled Spartan general who Xenophon says was the only one of the generals who knew that Cyrus was planning to attack the king, was acting with the support of the Spartan authorities.

The Spartans' victory in the Peloponnesian War made them willing to help Cyrus when the request came. Cyrus may also have been encouraged to strike when he did by a revolt against Persian rule in Egypt. But why did Cyrus rebel against Artaxerxes in the first place? Unlike some other sources, Xenophon does not mention any dispute about the inheritance of the Persian throne itself. The story Xenophon presents is a story about suspicion. When Darius fell ill, he summoned Cyrus back home. When Darius died and Artaxerxes became king, Tissaphernes spread allegations that Cyrus was plotting against his brother, and Artaxerxes had Cyrus arrested. His fear turned out to be self-fulfilling: as soon as Cyrus' mother won him his release, Cyrus resolved never to put himself in his brother's power again and began to make preparations for his great march inland.

Xenophon's account of the origins of the quarrel between the two brothers prepares for the stress on suspicion found later in the work. He brings out later the mutual suspicion between the Greek and Persian armies after Cyrus' death, and also the tensions that arose between the Ten Thousand and the Greek cities along the Black Sea coast confronted by their sudden arrival. An atmosphere of uncertainty also pervades the account of the Ten Thousand's dealings with the Spartans after their arrival at Byzantium.

A sense of the fraternal hatred underlying Cyrus' ambitions does emerge at some points in Xenophon's account. During the march towards Babylon, when the royal army has still not appeared and Cyrus is asked if he thinks his brother will fight him, Cyrus replies: 'If he really is the son of Darius and Parysatis, if he really is my brother, I won't gain this empire without a fight' (1.7.9). In the battle that soon follows, Cyrus launches a direct assault on his brother with the words 'I see him!' (1.8.26). Cyrus' brazen acknowledgement of his fratricidal desires has something of the chilling quality of Eteocles' decision to fight his brother Polynices in Aeschylus' *Seven against Thebes*. But while the later historian Diodorus of Sicily made a passing comparison between Cyrus' fight with his brother and the tragic fratricide of Oedipus' sons (14.23.6), Xenophon's account does not focus the reader's attention on the moral problems of fratricide.

The prize at stake in Cyrus' impetuous attack on his brother is best revealed by some words of encouragement that Cyrus delivers to the Greek soldiers: 'My father's empire extends south to a region where men cannot live because of the heat and north to a region where they cannot live because of the cold. All the territories between these two extremes are governed by my brother's friends, but if I'm victorious, I am bound to put *my* friends in charge of them' (1.7.6–7). Those words—for all their hyperbole—capture well the Greeks' perception of the vast extent of the Persian empire—the largest empire known to the Greeks up to that time.

The Persian empire had expanded rapidly under the rule of Cyrus the Great (559–530 BC). He defeated the Medes and Lydians, conquered Babylon, and expanded Persian rule in the east towards modern Afghanistan. His conquest of the Lydians brought under his sway the Greek cities in Asia Minor which had been subjected by the Lydian king Croesus. Cyrus' son Cambyses extended the empire further by conquering Egypt in 525 BC. Cambyses' death was followed by some political disorder which was resolved when Darius seized power and founded the Achaemenid dynasty (Darius sought to connect his own family with Cyrus' by claiming a common ancestor, Achaemenes). Darius' reign saw the first major clashes between Greeks and Persians. The Greek cities in Ionia revolted from Persian rule in 499 BC. They received help from Athens, and in the course of one expedition inland the residential parts of the satrapal capital Sardis were burnt. Darius sought revenge by sending an expedition against mainland Greece, but his army was defeated by the Athenians at Marathon in 490 BC. His son Xerxes sent a larger expedition ten years later which was defeated at sea at Salamis (480 BC) and on land at Plataea (479 BC). The Persians made no more attempts against mainland Greece but they retained control of the Greek cities in Asia Minor.

The promises Cyrus made to his Greek followers came to nothing when he was killed at Cunaxa. Xenophon seems to put some of the blame on Cyrus' own rashness in the heat of battle. More contro-versial is an incident at the start of the battle. Cyrus' Greek hoplites (heavily armed troops) were positioned on the right of the battle line, next to the Euphrates and well away from the Persian king who was in the centre of the royal army outflanking the left wing of Cyrus' army. Cyrus ordered the Greek general Clearchus to lead the Greeks across the battlefield directly against the king, but Clearchus refused, afraid that they would be encircled. Already in antiquity he was criticized for his refusal (Plutarch, *Artaxerxes* 8.3–7)—but many have thought his caution justified.

It is tempting to speculate on what would have happened had Cyrus won the day at Cunaxa. The historian J. B. Bury presented an alarming picture of what the dynamic Cyrus would have been able to achieve: 'Perhaps the stubborn stupidity of Clearchus on the field of Cunaxa . . . saved Hellas from becoming a Persian satrapy'—but thanks to Cyrus' death Greece was 'little affected by the languid interventions of Artaxerxes'.[23] Bury's speculation is tainted both by the lingering appeal of orientalism and by his reliance on Xeno-phon's characterization of Cyrus. The image of Persia as weak and effeminate derives from contemporary Greek sources driven more by ideology than by reality, and the praise Xenophon heaps on Cyrus in his obituary notice is no more reliable.

The problem with Xenophon's panegyric of Cyrus is that it justi-fies his own decision to leave Greece and follow Cyrus. There is a strong element of apology in the claim that 'of all the successors of Cyrus the Elder, no Persian was a more natural ruler and none more deserved to rule' (1.9.1). Xenophon substantiates this claim by stressing Cyrus' skill at handling horses and at archery and javelin— traditional Persian pursuits—and his maintenance of order through harsh punishments ('one could often see, by the side of busy roads, people who had lost feet, hands, or eyes'). He also praises Cyrus' generosity and fair-mindedness in distributing gifts—a practice that struck several other Greek observers of the Persian monarchy: 'No single individual, in my opinion, ever received more gifts than he did . . . but he gave them away again, chiefly to his friends, taking into consideration each individual's character.' Xenophon praised Cyrus

[23] J. B. Bury, *A History of Greece to the Death of Alexander the Great*, 3rd edn., rev. R. Meiggs (London, 1956), 523.

further in his *Oeconomicus*, where he makes Socrates claim that vast numbers of people deserted from the king to Cyrus but that no one deserted from Cyrus to the king—a claim that is not borne out by *The Expedition of Cyrus*. In fact, one of the reasons for Cyrus' failure was that he did not receive the backing of the Persian nobility.

There may be more than meets the eye to Xenophon's obituary of Cyrus. The traditional aspects of the Persian education, according to Herodotus, were learning to ride, to shoot, and to tell the truth (1.136). Xenophon, as we have seen, attributes to Cyrus the first two qualities—but not truth-telling. And in his narrative it emerges that Cyrus first told the Greek soldiers that he was planning to lead them against the Pisidians, a troublesome mountain tribe in Asia Minor, and later, when it became clear that the Pisidians could not be his aim, that he was leading them against a rebel on the Euphrates. It was only when the Greeks had gone too far to turn back that he revealed that he was leading them to Babylon. Cyrus is presented as a clever manipulator.

Xenophon's portrayal of a manipulative Cyrus may also have an apologetic aspect. He states that the real object of Cyrus' expedition was known to only one of the Greeks—the general Clearchus. Diodorus, by contrast, says that all the generals knew that Cyrus was leading the Greeks against the king. Xenophon could be offering a defence of his conduct to the Athenians, who may have exiled him for marching against Artaxerxes. But Xenophon was not in any case one of the original generals—and it may be true that Clearchus was the only Greek in Cyrus' confidence. There is a certain plausibility to Xenophon's shrewd account. Cyrus' manipulation is more than matched by the manipulation of Clearchus himself, who pretends to have the Greeks' welfare at heart while all the time serving his own and Cyrus' interests.

A different image of Cyrus is found in a passage interpolated in Xenophon's *Hellenica* (2.1.8–9) and perhaps derived from the sensational *Persica* (*Persian Affairs*) of the Greek doctor Ctesias. This passage claims that Cyrus once killed two of his cousins because they did not push their hands through the *korē* (a kind of long sleeve) when they met him—an honour normally reserved for the king alone; and that Cyrus' father feigned illness and summoned him back to court because of this ruthless act of violence. The Cyrus Xenophon presents also assumes the prerogatives of the Persian king, but he does not behave with conspicuous villainy. It is not necessarily the case, however, that the image of Cyrus as a reckless murderer is more true to the real Cyrus than Xenophon's largely flattering picture. Ctesias—who was present with the Persian king at the battle of Cunaxa—had as good a reason to damn Cyrus as Xenophon had to praise him. The real Cyrus remains impossible to recapture.

While it seems fruitless to speculate on what would have happened to the Greek world had Cyrus defeated his brother, Cyrus' expedition did turn out to have important and unexpected consequences for relations between Greece and Persia. Seventy years later the Persian empire fell to the invasion of Alexander the Great, and when later Greek writers looked back to explain Alexander's success they tended to start by praising the remarkable achievements of the Greek soldiers Cyrus had enlisted—the famous Ten Thousand.

The Ten Thousand

The title of Xenophon's work, *The Expedition of Cyrus*, applies properly only to the first of its seven books. It is at the end of the first book that Cyrus is defeated at the battle of Cunaxa. His Greek mercenaries are victorious in their part of the field, however, and the rest of the work traces their fortunes after they have been left stranded by Cyrus' death.

The fourth-century BC Athenian orator Isocrates used the performance of the Ten Thousand at the battle of Cunaxa as proof of the weakness of the Persian empire: 'Everyone agrees that they won as complete a victory in battle over all the forces of the king as if they had come to blows with their womenfolk, but that at the very moment when they seemed to be masters of the field they failed of success, owing to the impetuosity of Cyrus' (5.90). More commonly, it was what happened after the battle that was taken as proof of Persian weakness: Polybius, the second-century BC historian of the rise of Rome, claimed that the origin of Alexander's war against Persia lay in 'the retreat of the Greeks under Xenophon from the upper satrapies, in which, though they traversed the whole of Asia, a hostile country, none of the barbarians ventured to face them' (3.6.10).

The achievements of Cyrus' Greek mercenaries were not uncontroversial. In another work, the *Panegyricus* (composed in 380 BC), Isocrates referred to these soldiers as 'six thousand Greeks who were not picked troops, but men who, owing to circumstances, were unable to live in their own countries' (4.146). It suited Isocrates' purpose to lower both the number and the social standing of the troops who accompanied Cyrus: by stating that they were fewer than they in fact were and by stressing their lowly status, he could make their achievement in escaping from Mesopotamia more striking and the weakness of Persia more blatant. But Isocrates' comments also reflect a growing anxiety about the use of mercenaries in the fourth century BC. Mercenaries became more important as campaigns became longer, as military skills became more specialized, and as the system of alliances fostered by the bipolar world of the fifth century started to fall apart. At the same time, the use of mercenaries was lamented by political thinkers who thought that their growing importance marked a decline from the old *polis* morality under which cities were defended by their own citizens, not by paid troops.

Xenophon himself was alive to the potential hostility aroused by mercenary service. As we have seen, he was keen to define his own position in the army in terms of the ethic of reciprocity: he went to Asia to become Cyrus' friend, not for the sake of the cash payments received by the ordinary soldiers. But it is not just his own service with Cyrus that he defends. When he relates how he considered founding a city on the shores of the Black Sea, he makes a broader claim about the motivations of Cyrus' Greek soldiers. He explains that most of the troops wanted to return home rather than settle by the Black Sea, as they 'had set sail and undertaken this mercenary service not because they were hard up, but because they had heard of Cyrus' magnanimity' (6.4.8). Xenophon seems here to be responding to the attacks made on the Ten Thousand by Isocrates (and doubtless by others).[24]

How plausible is Xenophon's defence of the quality of the Ten Thousand? The size and timing of Cyrus' expedition make it tempting to assume that he was able to enlist so many Greek mercenaries because the long and destructive Peloponnesian War had recently ended. Was Cyrus exploiting a sudden availability of soldiers from

---

[24] On the ideology of mercenary service, see V. Azoulay, 'Exchange as Entrapment: Mercenary Xenophon?', in Lane Fox (ed.), *Long March*, 289–304.

cities afflicted by the war? Almost two-thirds of his hoplites came from the relatively poor regions of Arcadia and Achaea in the Peloponnese. Xenophon does not, however, specifically state why many of the troops decided to serve with Cyrus. There were troops who were escaping trouble at home: the Spartan Dracontius 'had been banished from his home while still a boy for having accidentally stabbed another boy with his dagger and killed him' (4.8.25). Another Spartan who could not have considered returning home was the exiled general Clearchus—but he was long dead by the time the army reached the Black Sea. Xenophon's comment about the motivation of the troops who sailed out to join Cyrus must be an over-simplification. There were in any case many members of the Ten Thousand who came originally from mainland Greece, but who were already serving as mercenaries in Asia Minor when Cyrus recruited them. These troops were following a long tradition of mercenary service in Asia Minor. The sixth-century Lesbian poet Alcaeus refers to his brother serving in Asia, and sizeable forces are attested in Persian service in the fifth century (in 440 BC the Samians were provided with seven hundred Greek mercenaries by the satrap Pissuthnes).

Even the troops who were enlisted in Asia Minor may not have been driven to mercenary service by extreme poverty or by the effects of the Peloponnesian War. Arcadia and Achaea had not been hit particularly hard by the war, and Arcadians were famous for mercenary service even before Cyrus' expedition. It has been estimated that at least 8 per cent of the adult male population of Arcadia was serving with Cyrus.[25] This proportion does not reflect a sudden crisis at the end of the fifth century, but a conscious decision by families within Arcadia to raise sons in the expectation that some of them would go abroad to serve as mercenaries.

The conditions of service also suggest that the mercenaries were not driven by extreme poverty. A recent study concludes that 'the hoplites who took service with Cyrus were in large part from the hoplite class in their own community, trained as hoplites at home and

[25] J. Roy, 'The Ambitions of a Mercenary', in Lane Fox (ed.), *Long March*, 264–88, at 276.

xxviii   *Introduction*

probably able to supply their own equipment'.[26] Many of them were also wealthy enough to bring servants with them to carry their equipment. The rate of pay was not particularly high by comparison with the known rates of pay for other types of employment, though pay was at least given for each day of service. The troops also had to buy food for themselves and for their servants from local villages or from the merchants who accompanied the expedition. They were sometimes allowed to plunder slaves as well as other goods, and one or two of them enjoyed windfalls—the seer Silanus, who was rewarded by Cyrus for a correct prophecy with a gift of 3,000 darics, or the general Timasion, who acquired an expensive Persian carpet.

Xenophon's claim that the troops who sailed out were eager to return home is not borne out by his narrative. Some—like the wealthy Silanus—certainly did want to return home. Others slipped away from the army but not necessarily in order to go home. The majority of the survivors were happy to join the Spartans at the end of the expedition—to resume a career of mercenary service in Asia Minor.

Why did Cyrus decide to hire so many Greek hoplites (10,600 in all) for his great march up country? Early in *The Expedition of Cyrus*, Xenophon illustrates the advantages of hoplites in a striking scene that the American historian V. D. Hanson chose as the epigraph of his 2001 bestseller *Why the West has Won*. Cyrus wants to display his troops before the wife of the ruler of Cilicia. He holds a review in the plain and orders the Greeks to form up as if for battle. The hoplites line up, each equipped with a spear for thrusting, a sword, a round wooden shield faced with bronze, a bronze helmet, greaves, and body-covering. As Cyrus inspects the Greeks, he stops his chariot in the middle of their line and orders the whole line to advance with weapons raised for battle. The trumpet sounds, and the Greeks raise their spears and advance. They quicken their pace and start shouting, and then keep on running towards the assembled crowd. Cyrus' other troops are all afraid, and the wife of the Cilician ruler even flees in her covered carriage. Finally the Greeks return to their tents, laughing. The scene is a paradigmatic display of hoplite warfare.

---

[26] Roy, 'Ambitions', 276. On the question of the supply of equipment, see P. McKechnie, 'Greek Mercenary Troops and their Equipment', *Historia*, 43 (1994), 297–305, and D. Whitehead, 'Who Equipped Mercenary Troops in Classical Greece?', *Historia*, 40 (1991), 105–13.

The troops are on level ground—classic hoplite terrain. As they cross the plain, the troops maintain cohesion as they shout and charge in line—a terrifying spectacle for troops who are more lightly armed.

The display the Greeks put on for Cyrus is not a demonstration of every aspect of hoplite warfare. The authors of *The March Up* (the account of the 2003 invasion of Iraq, mentioned earlier) praise the Ten Thousand as 'tough characters bound by an unflinching warrior code' who 'hacked their way through every army that challenged them'; in the Roman army, by contrast, 'manoeuver replaced the headlong charge'.[27] This historical overview does not do justice to Xenophon's text. Throughout their retreat the Ten Thousand proved able to adapt to the difficult terrain that confronted them. At one point they organized small mobile units to fill gaps as the line contracted and expanded. On another occasion they formed in columns rather than in a broad line, and spaced out the columns to outflank the enemy and to cope with the roughness of the ground.

The image of the Ten Thousand hacking their way through hostile armies also ignores the presence of many non-hoplites in their number. In addition to the hoplites, Cyrus hired 2,300 of the lightly armed troops known as peltasts. Peltasts carried light, crescent-shaped wicker shields, long javelins, and short swords. They tended to come from mountainous areas on the fringes of the Greek world, and were far more mobile than hoplites in mountainous terrain. Another sign of the variety of troops within the Ten Thousand are the two hundred Cretan archers whom Clearchus hired on Cyrus' behalf. The value of variety was further shown when a volunteer force of slingers was constituted from the Rhodian contingent in the army. Throughout the retreat, it was 'the integrated operation of the different elements in the expedition'—together with the skill with which they were deployed—that enabled the Ten Thousand to fight through to the sea.[28]

Xenophon often alludes to the Ten Thousand as 'the Greeks', but it emerges at some moments in his account that there were non-Greeks ('barbarians', to use the Greek term) among them. Among the troops enlisted by Clearchus, for instance, were eight hundred

---

[27] Smith and West, *March Up*, 2.
[28] M. Whitby, 'Xenophon's Ten Thousand as a Fighting Force', in Lane Fox (ed.), *Long March*, 215–42, at 239.

Thracian peltasts. Three hundred of this troop deserted to the king soon after the battle of Cunaxa and so did not take part in the retreat to the sea, but a stirring vignette soon before the army arrives at the sea makes it clear that the Ten Thousand contained other non-Greeks apart from those Thracians. The army finds itself confronted by a deep ravine with hostile troops on the opposite bank. They can see no way forward—until a peltast who had once been a slave at Athens approaches Xenophon and says that he can recognize the language the men across the ravine are talking: 'I think . . . that this is my native land' (4.8.4). This peltast has come home to the land of his fellow Macronians. He is able to negotiate a safe passage for the army, but what happened to him afterwards Xenophon does not reveal.

It is not just the non-Greek element among the Ten Thousand that Xenophon tends to neglect. He also pays little attention to the camp followers—who included many women. The only women who appear as individuals are two bedmates of Cyrus who are taken prisoner at the battle of Cunaxa when Cyrus' camp falls into the king's hands (one of them manages to escape, naked, back to the Greeks). Elsewhere Xenophon mentions how some soldiers sneak gifts for a good-looking boy or woman, how the women join in the cry at a favourable sacrifice, and how some of the tribesmen along the Black Sea want to have sex with the women—in public.[29]

Xenophon's stress on the Greekness of the army and his neglect of the camp followers is ideological. At stake in the experience of the stranded soldiers is the sense of what it is to be a Greek. At a meeting of the surviving officers after the murder of five of the generals, a man named Apollonides, who speaks in the Boeotian dialect, insists that they must try to win the favour of the king. When Xenophon breaks in and calls him 'an embarrassment not just to his homeland but to the whole of Greece', he is told that this man 'doesn't belong in Boeotia or anywhere in Greece', since 'he has both ears pierced, Lydian-style'—and 'this was true' (3.1.30–1). Apollonides is then driven away from the meeting. As with the Macronian peltast, Xenophon does not tell what happened to Apollonides afterwards. He has served his role—as a scapegoat who serves to unify the remain-

---

[29] See 1.10.2–3; 4.1.14; 4.3.20, 30; 5.4.33; also note to p. 105.

ing officers and to define the masculinity of the Greeks by contrast with the supposedly effeminate Lydians.

Xenophon's representation of the Ten Thousand has often been seen as having a practical aim. As we have seen, their performance at Cunaxa and during the retreat was thought in the Greek world to have shown the weakness of Persia and to have paved the way for the conquests of Alexander. Xenophon himself was aware that the performance of the Ten Thousand could be used to highlight the possibility of an attack on Persia. In his *Hellenica* he claims that the Spartan admiral Lysander and the ambitious tyrant Jason of Pherae drew inspiration from their achievements (3.4.2, 6.1.12). Did he write *The Expedition of Cyrus* to promote a different sort of expedition—a united Greek expedition against the old enemy?[30]

There is much in Xenophon's account that could be taken to support a grand panhellenic scheme. The military skill of the Greek mercenaries is stressed. They are unbeaten at Cunaxa, they refuse to submit to the king's demand that they hand over their weapons, they overcome all the obstacles that lie in their way, they get through to the sea. At one point Isocrates' claim that the Greeks' victory at Cunaxa was as easy as if it had been a battle against women is given a slight twist: at a banquet amongst the Paphlagonians, one of the army's slave-girls does a dance with a light shield, and 'the Paphlagonians asked whether the women fought alongside them, and the Greeks said that these were the very women who had put the king to flight from his camp' (6.1.13). Many of the speeches inserted by Xenophon—including some spoken by Xenophon himself—contain appeals to the Greek spirit and to the memory of earlier Greek victories against Persia. In one of his speeches Xenophon even raises the possibility that the army could settle in Mesopotamia and live independently of Persian rule—but he goes onto warn:

I'm afraid that once we've become accustomed to a life of idleness and luxury, and to the company of Median and Persian women and girls, who are tall and beautiful, we'll become as oblivious of our homeward journey as the lotus-eaters were. So I think it right and proper that our main efforts should be put towards getting back to Greece and our families, so that we can prove to the Greeks that their poverty is self-inflicted. They

[30] For a more detailed discussion, see T. C. B. Rood, 'Panhellenism and Self-Presentation: Xenophon's Speeches', in Lane Fox (ed.), *Long March*, 305–29.

could bring here those who are now living a hard life there and watch them prosper. (3.2.25–6)

The opposition between poor, virtuous Greeks and luxurious, decadent easterners is found in contemporary panhellenic discourse. But Xenophon is not actively promoting a scheme of colonization in Mesopotamia: he is warning of the danger that the Greeks, too, could be softened by the abundant natural resources of the region. Underlying his warning is the concept of environmental determinism elaborated in Herodotus and in the Hippocratic treatise *Airs, Waters, Places.*

Crucial to the issue of Xenophon's attitude towards panhellenism is his presentation of the workings of the Ten Thousand as a political unit. Cyrus' Greek mercenaries have often been celebrated as a walking city, a *polis* on the march. Hippolyte Taine saw the army as a 'sort of Athens wandering in the middle of Asia'.[31] Edward Gibbon was similarly effusive: 'Instead of tamely resigning themselves to the secret deliberations and private views of a single person, the united councils of the Greeks were inspired by the generous enthusiasm of a popular assembly: where the mind of each citizen is filled with the love of glory, the pride of freedom, and the contempt of death.'[32] This united and democratic force would seem to have the right qualities for an assault on Persia. Was Xenophon presenting a model of the type of army required to fulfil the panhellenic dream?

Xenophon does not consistently portray the army as a *polis* on the march. The Ten Thousand were not originally a united force, but a collection of smaller units. Cyrus carefully tried to avoid suspicion by raising small groups in different areas. His garrison commanders in Asia Minor hired troops as if for use against the satrap Tissaphernes, who was contesting with Cyrus control over the Ionian cities. Clearchus raised troops in the Thracian Chersonese, while another section came from Thessaly. During the march with Cyrus, there were tensions among the leaders of the different contingents—above all, Clearchus and Meno—as they vied to win Cyrus' favour. The first assembly held by the army increased those

---

[31] Taine, 'Xénophon: *L'Anabase*', 151.

[32] E. Gibbon, *The History of the Decline and Fall of the Roman Empire*, ed. D. Womersley (3 vols.; Harmondsworth, 1994; orig. pub. 1776–88), i. 951. For the idea of the army as city, see S. Hornblower, ' "This was Decided" (*edoxe tauta*): The Army as *polis* in Xenophon's *Anabasis*—and Elsewhere', in Lane Fox (ed.), *Long March*, 243–63.

tensions as many troops decided to desert their original leaders and serve under Clearchus. Nor is Xenophon uncritical of the way the large military assemblies formed decisions: at this first assembly Clearchus used deceit to persuade the army to carry on with Cyrus.

It is after the death of the generals that the political capabilities of the army are seen in their best light. Xenophon uses speech to good effect to persuade the troops that their position is not hopeless, and the army elects new generals to replace the ones who have been lost. Xenophon claims, however, that it was thanks to his own insistence and encouragement that the remaining captains and generals decided to convene a meeting of the whole army. And no further meetings take place as the army fights its way to the coast. Strategic and tactical decisions are made by the generals.

The Ten Thousand most resemble a walking city when they arrive at the Black Sea coast and start negotiating with the Greek cities and the tribes along the coast. But the picture Xenophon paints of this walking city is far from positive. The appeals to Greek identity made in speeches stand in tension with the army's increasingly difficult dealings with the Greek cities along the coast and with the imperial power of Sparta. Near the city of Cerasus some of the troops attack some local traders, kill their envoys, and pursue into the sea a market official and some of the other local Greeks. Those who cannot swim drown. Free of the danger of the interior, the soldiers give in to greed and indiscipline. At one point they even decide to elect a single leader because they think it will lead to swifter decision-making—and to more profit for themselves. They also quarrel among themselves: an Arcadian group splits off from the main army and has to be rescued by Xenophon. The position does not improve when the Spartans are persuaded by the local Persian satrap to transport the army across the Bosporus: the Ten Thousand are only prevented from sacking Byzantium by a cunning speech from Xenophon, and then Xenophon himself falls under suspicion and narrowly escapes arrest and execution at the Spartans' hands.

The increasing pessimism of the final books of *The Expedition of Cyrus* militates against simple interpretations of the text as a panhellenic tract. Xenophon's romantic adventure story turns out to be a powerfully analytical work. Xenophon explores how order is created in the army—and how that order disintegrates. His analysis of the fragility of the attempt to create order recalls the concerns of some of his other works: the *Hellenica* closes with Greece in a worse state of confusion than ever before, and the *Cyropaedia* and the *Constitution of the Spartans* both end with controversial codas which trace the decline of once solid social institutions.

The Expedition of Cyrus does not sit altogether well with the triumphalist readings that have been thrust on the exploits of the Ten Thousand. A rather different approach is suggested in a short essay on *The Expedition of Cyrus* by Italo Calvino. Calvino stresses not the triumph of the Greeks' arrival at the sea, but their sense of isolation when they are stranded far from home. When they agreed to serve with Cyrus they had not imagined that they would ever find themselves cut off so far from the sea. Somehow they have to find a way out even if it means harming people who have done them no wrong. Isolated in an alien landscape, this ancient army becomes, in Calvino's vision, an emblem of modernity:

The Greek army, creeping through the mountain heights and fjords amidst constant ambushes and attacks, no longer able to distinguish just to what extent it is a victim or an oppressor, and surrounded even in the most chilling massacres of its men by the supreme hostility of indifference or fortune, inspires in the reader an almost symbolic anguish which perhaps only we today can understand.[33]

[33] Calvino, 'Xenophon's Anabasis', 23.

TRANSLATOR'S NOTE

THE most recent edition of the Greek text of Xenophon's *Expedition of Cyrus* is the 1998 revision by John Dillery of Carleton L. Brownson's old Loeb. I have used this as my primary text for this translation, though I have also consulted the fuller apparatuses of the Oxford Classical Text, the Budé and the Teubner editions. Those few places where I differ from Brownson/Dillery have been marked in the text with an obelus. An asterisk indicates a note in the Explanatory Notes.

The tripartite references to the text in the Introduction and Explanatory Notes are to book, chapter (numbered in square brackets in the translation), and section divisions within the original Greek text. They also appear in the running headlines.

SELECT BIBLIOGRAPHY

Xenophon

Anderson, J. K., *Xenophon* (London, 1974).

Breitenbach, H. R., 'Xenophon von Athen', *Real-Encyclopädie der classischen Altertumswissenschaft*, IX A2 (1967), cols. 1567–1928.

Dillery, J., *Xenophon and the History of his Times* (London, 1995).

Higgins, W. E., *Xenophon the Athenian: The Problem of the Individual and the Society of the* Polis (Albany, NY, 1977).

Tuplin, C. J. (ed.), *Xenophon and his World* (Stuttgart, 2004).

The Expedition of Cyrus

Briant, P. (ed.), *Dans les pas des Dix Mille: Peuples et pays du Proche-Orient vus par un grec = Pallas*, 43 (1995).

Calvino, I., 'Xenophon's Anabasis', in *Why Read the Classics?*, trans. M. McLaughlin (London, 1999; Ital. orig. 1991), 19–23.

Cawkwell, G. L. 'Introduction', in *Xenophon: The Persian Expedition*, trans. R Warner (Harmondsworth, 1972), 9–48.

Erbse, H., 'Xenophons *Anabasis*', *Gymnasium*, 73 (1966), 485–505.

Gauthier, P., 'Xénophon et l'odyssée des "Dix-Mille" ', *L'Histoire*, 79 (1985), 16–25.

Lane Fox, R. (ed.), *The Long March: Xenophon and the Ten Thousand* (New Haven, 2004).

Lendle, O., *Kommentar zu Xenophons Anabasis* (Darmstadt, 1995).

Manfredi, V. M., *La Strada dei Diecimila: Topografia e geografia dell'Oriente di Senofonte* (Milan, 1986).

Nussbaum, G. B., *The Ten Thousand: A Study in Social Organization and Action in Xenophon's Anabasis* (Leiden, 1967).

Parker, R. C. T., 'One Man's Piety: The Religious Dimension of the *Anabasis*', in R. Lane Fox (ed.), *The Long March* (New Haven, 2004), 131–53.

Rood, T. C. B., *The Sea! The Sea! The Shout of the Ten Thousand in the Modern Imagination* (London, 2004).

Roy, J., 'Xenophon's *Anabasis*: The Command of the Rearguard in Books III and IV', *Phoenix*, 22 (1968), 158–9.

—— 'Xenophon's Evidence for the *Anabasis*', *Athenaeum*, 46 (1968), 37–46.

Soesbergen, P. G. van, 'Colonisation as a Solution to Social-economic Problems: A Confrontation of Isocrates with Xenophon', *Ancient Society*, 13–14 (1982–3), 131–45.

Taine, H., 'Xénophon: *L'Anabase*', in his *Essais de critique et d'histoire* (11th edn.; Paris, 1908; orig. pub. 1858), 150–87.

Tuplin, C. J., 'On the Track of the Ten Thousand', *Revue des études anciennes*, 101 (1999), 331–66.

—— 'Xenophon in Media', in G. B. Lanfranchi, M. Roaf, and R. Rollinger (eds.), *Continuity of Empire (?): Assyria, Media, Persia* (Padua, 2003), 351–89.

—— 'Heroes in Xenophon's *Anabasis*', in A. Barzanò, C. Bearzot, F. Landucci, L. Prandi, and G. Zecchini (eds.), *Modelli eroici dell'antichità alla cultura europea* (Rome, 2003), 115–56.

Westlake, H. D., 'Diodorus and the Expedition of Cyrus', *Phoenix*, 41 (1987), 241–55; repr. in his *Studies in Thucydides and Greek Historiography* (Bristol, 1989).

Mercenary Service

Dalby, A., 'Greeks Abroad: Social Organisation and Food among the Ten Thousand', *Journal of Hellenic Studies*, 112 (1992), 16–30.

Krasilnikoff, J. A., 'The Regular Pay of Aegean Mercenaries in the Classical Period', *Classica et Mediaevalia*, 44 (1993), 77–95.

Parke, H. W., *Greek Mercenary Service from Earliest Times to the Battle of Ipsus* (Oxford, 1933).

Perlman, S., 'The Ten Thousand: A Chapter in the Military, Social and Economic History of the Fourth Century', *Rivista storia dell'antica*, 6–7 (1976–7), 241 84.

Roy, J., 'The Mercenaries of Cyrus', *Historia*, 16 (1967), 292–323.

—— 'The Ambitions of a Mercenary', in R. Lane Fox (ed.), *The Long March* (New Haven, 2004), 264–88.

Persia

Briant, P., *From Cyrus to Alexander: A History of the Persian Empire*, trans. P. T. Daniels (Winona Lake, Ind., 2002; Fr. orig. 1996).

Brosius, M. (trans. and ed.), *The Persian Empire from Cyrus II to Artaxerxes I* (LACTOR, 16; London, 2000).

Hirsch, S. W., *The Friendship of the Barbarians: Xenophon and the Persian Empire* (Hanover, New Haven, and London, 1985).

Lewis, D. M., *Sparta and Persia* (Leiden, 1977).

Tuplin, C. J., 'Modern and Ancient Travellers in the Achaemenid Empire: Byron's *Road to Oxiana* and Xenophon's *Anabasis*', in H. Sancisi-Weerdenburg and J. W. Drijvers (eds.), *Achaemenid History VII: Through Travellers' Eyes* (Leiden, 1991), 37–57.

—— 'The Persian Empire', in R. Lane Fox (ed.), *The Long March* (New Haven, 2004), 154–83.

xxxviii   *Select Bibliography*

Wiesehöfer, J., *Ancient Persia: From 550 BC to 650 AD*, trans. A. Azodi (London, 1996; Ger. orig. 1993).

Thrace

Archibald, Z. H., *The Odrysian Kingdom of Thrace: Orpheus Unmasked* (Oxford, 1998).
Stronk, J., *The Ten Thousand in Thrace: An Archaeological and Historical Commentary on Xenophon's Anabasis, Books VI.iii–vi–VII* (Amsterdam, 1995).

War

Anderson, J. K., *Military Theory and Practice in the Age of Xenophon* (Berkeley, 1970).
Hanson, V. D., *The Western Way of War: Infantry Battle in Classical Greece* (2nd edn; Berkeley and London, 2000).
Hutchinson, G., *Xenophon and the Art of Command* (London, 2000).
Pritchett, W. K., *Ancient Greek Military Practices* (Berkeley, 1971; vol. i of *The Greek State at War*, 5 vols., Berkeley, 1971–91).
Wees, H. van (ed.), *War and Violence in Ancient Greece* (London, 2000).
Whitby, M., 'Xenophon's Ten Thousand as a Fighting Force', in R. Lane Fox (ed.), *The Long March* (New Haven, 2004), 215–42.

Further Reading in Oxford World's Classics

Herodotus, *The Histories*, trans. Robin Waterfield, ed. Carolyn Dewald.
Plutarch, *Greek Lives*, trans. Robin Waterfield, ed. Philip A. Stadter.
—— *Roman Lives*, trans. Robin Waterfield, ed. Philip A. Stadter.

OUTLINE OF EVENTS

[3] The king sends envoys about a truce; the Ten Thousand agree terms of withdrawal with Tissaphernes.

[4] The retreat begins. Ariaeus joins Tissaphernes. Suspicion between the Ten Thousand and the Persians; a messenger alleges that the Persians plan to attack the Ten Thousand. The Ten Thousand cross the Tigris.

[5] Clearchus holds a meeting with Tissaphernes; he goes to meet Tissaphernes a second time, with four other generals; the five Greek generals are seized and executed.

[6] Obituaries of the five Greek generals.

BOOK THREE

[1] Despair in the Greek camp. How Xenophon came to serve in Cyrus' army. Xenophon stirs himself and Proxenus' captains; meeting of the surviving generals and captains; election of new generals.

[2] Meeting of the whole army.

[3] The Ten Thousand destroy their waggons and tents. The Persians spy on the Ten Thousand's actions. The retreat starts again. The Ten Thousand are pressed by cavalry and archers; changes in the order of march.

[4] Slingers and archers beat off the Persians' attack; the Ten Thousand mutilate enemy corpses as a deterrent. They march past Larisa and Mespila; skirmishes with the Persians; they reach the hills.

[5] Tissaphernes' scorched-earth policy. The Ten Thousand are caught between the Tigris and mountains; a Rhodian proposes that they cross the Tigris on animal skins. They decide to head into the mountains.

BOOK FOUR

[1] The Ten Thousand enter the mountains of the Carduchians; they remove unnecessary animals and slaves. The Carduchians abandon their villages and head for the heights; they press the Ten Thousand from above.

[2] Xenophon leads the baggage animals by a side route; fighting against the Carduchians.

[3] The Ten Thousand reach the plain and the Centrites river; they force a crossing of the river.

[4] Marching through Armenia. Truce with Tiribazus. The Ten Thousand lodge in villages in the snow. They sack Tiribazus' camp.

[5] Marching through snow; suffering on the march; arrival at well-stocked villages.

[6] The Ten Thousand capture a mountain pass blocked by the native inhabitants.

[7] The Ten Thousand assault and capture a stronghold of the Taochians. They march through the land of the Chalybians and the Scythenians. A guide leads the Ten Thousand from Gymnias to a sight of the sea.

[8] The Ten Thousand negotiate their passage through the land of the Macronians. They drive the Colchians back from a mountain pass, arrive at Trapezus, and sacrifice and hold games.

BOOK FIVE

[1] Chirisophus leaves the army to fetch ships. The Ten Thousand try to procure ships.

[2] The Ten Thousand are led against the Drilae; they capture a fort but face a difficult retreat.

[3] The Ten Thousand march from Trapezus to Cerasus. Xenophon's later life on his estate at Scillus.

[4] The Ten Thousand enter the land of the Mossynoecians; they help one Mossynoecian faction attack another.

[5] Marching through the land of the Chalybians and the Tibarenians. The Ten Thousand arrive at Cotyora and receive envoys from Sinope. Xenophon defends the army's conduct.

[6] The Sinopeans advise the Ten Thousand to travel by sea. Xenophon thinks about founding a colony but is denounced.

[7] Xenophon defends himself against the allegation that he wanted to lead the army back to Phasis; he warns the army about its increasing lack of discipline.

[8] Inquiry into the generals' conduct; Xenophon defends his use of violence in the march through Armenia.

BOOK SIX

[1] Truce and feasting with the Paphlagonians. The Ten Thousand decide to elect a supreme commander; Xenophon refuses to stand and the Spartan Chirisophus is elected.

[2] The Ten Thousand sail to Heraclea and are shut out. The Arcadians split from the rest of the army. The Ten Thousand march or sail in three separate units.

[3] The Arcadians are pressed by the Bithynians and saved by Xenophon.

[4] The Ten Thousand are reunited at Calpe Harbour; unfavourable sacrifices and trouble with supplies. A Greek contingent is defeated by Pharnabazus' cavalry; Xenophon saves the survivors.

[5] A Greek contingent moves out to bury their dead. The Ten Thousand cross a ravine and defeat Pharnabazus' cavalry.

[6] The Ten Thousand defend themselves before Cleander, the Spartan governor of Byzantium. The Ten Thousand march through Bithynia and arrive at Chrysopolis.

BOOK SEVEN

[1] The Ten Thousand cross the Bosporus; they are ordered out of Byzantium; Xenophon restrains the army's assault on the city. Coeratadas offers to lead the army as general. The Ten Thousand leave Byzantium.

[2] Anaxibius wants to lead the Ten Thousand back into Asia. The Ten Thousand are wooed by Seuthes.

[3] The Ten Thousand decide to join Seuthes; feast at Seuthes' camp; the Ten Thousand raid Thracian villages with Seuthes.

[4] Thracian night attack on the village where Xenophon is posted. Seuthes subdues the rebels.

[5] Dispute with Seuthes over pay. The Ten Thousand raid more Thracian villages.

[6] The Spartans offer to employ the army. Xenophon defends himself against the charge that he was bribed by Seuthes.

[7] Xenophon answers Seuthes' complaint that the army is living off his land; he makes Seuthes pay the army.

[8] The Ten Thousand sail across to Lampsacus; they march to Pergamum. Xenophon leads a raid on Asidates. The Ten Thousand join the Spartan general Thibron.

THE MARCH OF THE TEN THOUSAND

THE EXPEDITION OF CYRUS

THE EXPEDITION OF CYRUS

BOOK ONE

[1] Darius and Parysatis had two sons,* of whom Artaxerxes was the elder and Cyrus the younger, and when Darius was ill and suspected that he was dying, he wanted them both by his side. The elder son was in fact already there, but Cyrus was summoned from the province where Darius had made him satrap* and also commander of all the forces whose place of assembly was the Plain of Castolus.* So Cyrus travelled up country,* and he took with him Tissaphernes, whom he believed to be a friend. He was also accompanied by three hundred Greek hoplites* under the command of Xenias of Parrhasia.

After Darius' death and Artaxerxes' accession to the throne, Tissaphernes accused Cyrus, to his brother's face, of plotting to kill Artaxerxes. The king believed this lie, arrested Cyrus, and was intending to kill him, but his mother interceded and got him sent back to his province. Cyrus had been humiliated and had come close to losing his life, so once he was back in his province he began to make plans; he wanted never again to be in his brother's power, and he wanted, if he could, to rule in his place. His mother, Parysatis, was on his side (because she loved him more than Artaxerxes, the one who had become king), and he treated any visitors who came to him from the king in such a way that by the time they returned home they were closer to him than they were to the king. He also made sure that the barbarians* on his staff were competent soldiers and were loyal to him, and he did all he could to conceal the fact that he was assembling his corps of Greeks, because he wanted to give the king as little opportunity as possible to prepare.

This is how he went about gathering the corps. He instructed every officer in charge of a garrison in one of the cities of his province to hire as many Peloponnesian troops as he could of the highest possible calibre, on the pretext that Tissaphernes had designs on the cities—which was plausible because the Ionian cities had originally been given to Tissaphernes by the king,* but by this time all of them except Miletus had seceded and gone over to Cyrus. Miletus was the exception because, forewarned that the inhabitants there were planning to do the same (to go over to Cyrus), Tissaphernes had had some of them put to death and others sent into exile. Cyrus took in the exiles, assembled an army, and besieged Miletus by both land and sea in an attempt to restore those who had been banished—all of which gave him another excuse for assembling an army. He also sent a message to the king in which he insisted that, as the king's brother, these cities should be given to him rather than have Tissaphernes as their ruler, and his mother supported this demand of his. Consequently, the king had no idea that Cyrus was targeting him and believed that he was spending money on his forces because he was at war with Tissaphernes. As a result, he did not find the fact that they were fighting at all disturbing—not least because Cyrus carried on sending the king the tribute raised from those of Tissaphernes' cities which he now controlled.

In the part of the Chersonese that lies opposite Abydus, another army was being assembled for Cyrus, in the following way. Clearchus, a Spartan exile* who was a valued acquaintance of Cyrus and the recipient of 10,000 darics* from him, was using the money to form an army and to make the Chersonese the base for a war against the Thracians who lived beyond the Hellespont. This helped the local Greeks, and so the Hellespontine communities were glad to contribute money towards the upkeep of the troops. So this army was also being secretly maintained for Cyrus.

Aristippus of Thessaly, a guest-friend* of Cyrus who found himself hard pressed by political opponents at home, came to Cyrus and asked for about 2,000 mercenaries and enough money to pay them for three months, so that he could overcome his opponents. But Cyrus gave him about 4,000 mercenaries and pay for six months, and asked him not to settle his dispute with his opponents without first consulting him. So this army was also being secretly maintained for him in Thessaly. He told Proxenus of Boeotia, a guest-friend of his, to bring as many men as he could for an expedition he alleged he wanted to make against the Pisidians, who were, he claimed, disrupting his territory, and he told further guest-friends of his, Sophaenetus of Stymphalus and Socrates of Achaea, to bring as many men as they could for a war he claimed he was going to fight alongside the Milesian exiles against Tissaphernes. And they did what he told them to do.

[2] When the time seemed right for the march up country, the excuse he gave was that he wanted to drive the Pisidians out of his territory once and for all, and he claimed that he was assembling his

troops, barbarian and Greek, for a campaign against them. At this point he also told Clearchus to bring all his men, and he ordered Aristippus to come to terms with his opponents at home and to send him the troops he had under his command. And he told Xenias of Arcadia, who had been put in command of the mercenaries in the cities, to leave behind only as many men as were needed to garrison the acropolises* and to bring the rest. He also summoned the troops who were besieging Miletus and urged the exiles to join him on his campaign, with the promise that, if the expedition achieved its objectives, he would not stop until he had restored them to their native city. They were happy to go along with his suggestion, because they trusted him, and they came to him, armed and ready, at Sardis.

So Xenias arrived in Sardis with about 4,000 hoplites from the cities, while Proxenus came with about 1,500 hoplites and 500 light-armed troops, Sophaenetus of Stymphalus with 1,000 hoplites, and Socrates of Achaea with about 500 hoplites; and Pasion of Megara— who along with Socrates had been among those campaigning at Miletus—also came with 300 hoplites and 300 peltasts.* These were the men who joined Cyrus at Sardis.

All this, however, came to Tissaphernes' attention, and Cyrus' measures struck him as too extensive for a campaign against the Pisidians. So he travelled to the king as quickly as he could, with an entourage of about 500 horsemen, and when the king heard from Tissaphernes about Cyrus' army, he began to prepare to meet him. Cyrus, meanwhile, was setting out from Sardis with the troops I have mentioned, and he marched for three days through Lydia up to the Meander river, a journey of twenty-two parasangs.* The river was two plethra wide and there was a bridge over it consisting of seven boats joined together. Once he had crossed the river, a day's march of eight parasangs through Phrygia brought him to Colossae, an inhabited city, prosperous and large.* He stayed there for seven days and Meno of Thessaly arrived with 1,000 hoplites and 500 peltasts from Dolopia, Aeniania, and Olynthus.

The next leg was a three-day march of twenty parasangs that brought him to Celaenae, an inhabited Phrygian city, large and prosperous, where Cyrus had a palace and a large park* filled with wild animals which he used to hunt on horseback when he wanted to exercise himself and his horses. The Meander river flows through the middle of the park. The river rises beneath the palace and flows through the city of Celaenae too. Celaenae also has, at the base of the acropolis and by the springs of the Marsyas, a fortified palace belonging to the Great King.* The Marsyas, twenty-five feet in width, also flows through the city, and discharges into the Meander. This is the place where, the story goes, Apollo flayed Marsyas after Marsyas had challenged him to a contest of skill and had lost,* and hung the skin in the cave where the river rises—which is why the river is called the Marsyas. And it is the place where, in the course of his retreat from Greece after defeat in the famous battle,* Xerxes is generally held to have built the palace I mentioned and the city's acropolis. During Cyrus' thirty days there, Clearchus, the Spartan exile, arrived with 1,000 hoplites, 800 Thracian peltasts, and 200 Cretan bowmen;* and Sosis of Syracuse and Agias†* of Arcadia arrived at the same time, the former with 300 hoplites and the latter with 1,000 hoplites. While he was there Cyrus held a review in his park, and counted the Greeks: there were altogether 11,000 hoplites and about 2,000 peltasts.

The next leg was a two-day march of ten parasangs that brought him to the inhabited city of Peltae, where he stayed for three days while Xenias of Arcadia sacrificed for the Lycaea and organized an athletic contest.* The prizes were golden crowns* and Cyrus himself was a spectator at the games. The next leg was a two-day march of twelve parasangs that brought him to the inhabited city of Pot-market, the Phrygian city which is closest to Mysia. The next leg was a three-day march of thirty parasangs that brought him to the inhabited city of Cayster-basin, where he stayed for five days.

By then he owed the troops over three months' pay, and they often came to his tent to ask for it, only to hear him repeat his hopes for the future. But he was obviously upset, because it was not in Cyrus' nature to refuse to pay a debt when he had the money. At this point Epyaxa, the wife of Syennesis,* king of the Cilicians, came to visit Cyrus and, it was rumoured, gave Cyrus plenty of money. At any rate, he paid the men four months' wages. The Cilician queen had a bodyguard of Cilicians and Aspendians, and it was generally believed that she and Cyrus were lovers.

The next leg was a two-day march of ten parasangs that brought him to Thymbrium, an inhabited city. Here, by the side of the road, there is the so-called Spring of Midas where, the story goes, the

Phrygian king caught the satyr by adding wine to the spring water.*
The next leg was a two-day march of ten parasangs that brought him
to Tyriaeum, an inhabited city, where he stayed for three days.

The Cilician queen, it is said, asked Cyrus to display the army to
her. Cyrus was happy to do so and arranged for a review to take place
on the plain, of both the Greek and barbarian corps. He told the
Greeks to form lines and take up positions in their usual way for
battle, with each officer organizing his own men, and they formed
themselves into a phalanx four lines deep, with Meno and his men on
the right wing, Clearchus and his troops on the left, and the other
senior officers in the centre. Cyrus first inspected the barbarian
troops, who paraded past him with the horsemen formed into
squadrons and the foot soldiers in companies. Then he inspected the
Greeks, all of whom wore bronze helmets, red cloaks,* and greaves,
and had their shields uncovered,* by driving his chariot past them,
while the Cilician queen rode in a carriage. When Cyrus had driven
past them all, he halted his chariot in front of the middle of the
phalanx, and sent his translator, Pigres, to convey to the Greek generals his request that they should have the entire phalanx move
forward with levelled weapons. The generals passed these orders
on to their men, and when the trumpet sounded they advanced with
their weapons levelled. Soon they were moving faster and faster,
until with a shout the soldiers spontaneously broke into a run and
charged towards the camp. This terrified the barbarians:† the Cilician queen fled in her carriage and the merchants in the market*
abandoned their wares and ran away, while the Greeks, hugely
amused, dispersed to their tents. But the Cilician queen was very
impressed by the brilliance and the discipline of the army, and Cyrus
was delighted to see how frightened the barbarians were by the
Greeks.

The next leg was a three-day march of twenty parasangs that
brought him to Iconium, the last city in Phrygia, where he stayed for
three days. There followed a five-day march of thirty parasangs
through Lycaonia, where Cyrus gave the Greeks permission to turn
to plunder, since it was hostile territory.* Next he sent the Cilician
queen back to Cilicia by the shortest route, with an escort of some of
Meno's troops and Meno himself in command, while he himself
marched with the rest of the army for four days, a distance of
twenty-five parasangs, through Cappadocia to the inhabited city of

Dana, large and prosperous, where he stayed for three days. While he was there Cyrus executed a Persian called Megaphernes, who was a royal secretary,* and another high-ranking officer, on the charge of plotting against him.

Next they set about trying to enter Cilicia. The way in was a cart-track which was so steep that no army could get through against the slightest opposition—and a rumour in fact circulated that Syennesis was on the heights, guarding the pass. Cyrus therefore waited for a day on the plain, but the next day a messenger arrived with the news that Syennesis had abandoned the heights, since he had found out that Meno's men were already in Cilicia, on his side of the mountains, and also because he had been getting reports about triremes* belonging to the Spartans and to Cyrus himself sailing round from Ionia to Cilicia under the command of Tamos. At any rate, Cyrus climbed up into the mountains without meeting any opposition and saw the camp where the Cilicians had been keeping guard.

The plain he came down to on the other side was large and beautiful: well watered, covered with a wide variety of trees and with vines, and rich in sesame, millet, panic, wheat, and barley. It was completely surrounded, from coast to coast, by tremendous, tall mountains. Once down from the mountains, he marched across the plain for four days, a distance of twenty-five parasangs, to Tarsus, a large and prosperous Cilician city. This was where Syennesis, the king of the Cilicians, had his palace. A river called the Cydnus, two plethra wide, flows through the middle of the city. Only stall-holders remained: the rest of the inhabitants had abandoned the city and fled, along with Syennesis, to a stronghold in the mountains. However, the inhabitants of the coastal cities of Soli and Issus stayed where they were.

Syennesis' wife, Epyaxa, had reached Tarsus five days before Cyrus, but two companies from Meno's force had perished during the passage over the mountains and down to the plain. Some said they had been annihilated by the Cilicians while they were out foraging, others that they had fallen behind and got lost, and died without being able to find the rest of the army or the roads. Whatever the facts, each company had consisted of 100 hoplites.† When the survivors reached Tarsus they were so angry about the deaths of their comrades that they looted not only the city, but the palace too. Once Cyrus had marched into the city he sent repeated messages summoning Syennesis to his presence, but Syennesis replied that he had never previously put himself in the hands of anyone stronger than himself and that on this occasion too he would not come to Cyrus until his wife had won Cyrus over and had been given pledges of his good intentions. Later, when they met, Syennesis gave Cyrus a great deal of money for the army and Cyrus gave Syennesis gifts which are regarded as tokens of honour at the king's court*—a horse with a gold-studded bridle, a golden torque and armlets, a dagger of gold, Persian clothing, the guarantee that his land would not be plundered any more, and permission for his people to take back any of the men captured as slaves they could find.

[3] Cyrus and the army stayed at Tarsus for twenty days, because the soldiers refused to carry on; they already suspected that they were going against the king and they said that this was not the job for which they had been hired. Clearchus was the first to try to force the men under his command to go on, but they threw stones at him and his yoke-animals every time they started off. Clearchus only just avoided being stoned to death then, but later he realized that coercion was going to get him nowhere and he convened his men for an assembly. At first he stood and wept for a long time, while his men watched him in silent astonishment, but then he spoke as follows:

'Comrades in arms, don't be surprised if the present situation causes me grief. Cyrus is my guest-friend. When I had been banished from the land of my birth, he showed me honour in various ways, and not least by giving me 10,000 darics. And what did I do when I had been given this money? I did not bank it for my own personal use or waste it on luxurious living; I spent it on you. First, I made war against the Thracians and with your help, in defence of Greece, I punished them by driving them out of the Chersonese and denying them the land of the Greek settlers there which they wanted to steal. Then, when Cyrus sent for me, I set out with you in order to repay him for the favours he had done me by helping him in his hour of need. Since you are reluctant to continue this journey with me, I must either let you down and continue to enjoy Cyrus' friendship, or stick with you and prove myself false to him. I have no idea whether this will be the right thing to do, but I shall choose you and suffer the consequences along with you. It will never be said of me that I led Greeks into barbarian lands and then betrayed those Greeks by pre-ferring the friendship of the barbarians.* So, since you are refusing to

stay with me as ordered, I shall stay with you and suffer the consequences. For I think of you as my homeland,* my friends, and my
allies. With you behind me, I think I shall receive honour wherever
in the world I may be, but without you I doubt my ability either to
help a friend or to defend myself against an adversary.* So rest
assured of this: I shall go wherever you go.'

After this speech the soldiers—not just those under his command,
but all of them, when they heard that he was refusing to carry on to
the king—applauded his stance, and more than two thousand of
them, from Xenias' and Pasion's divisions, gathered up their
weapons and baggage carts and joined Clearchus' camp. Cyrus did
not know how to cope with all this and in his distress he sent for
Clearchus. Although Clearchus publicly refused to go, he sent word
to Cyrus, without the soldiers knowing anything about it, telling him
to bear up, because things would turn out fine, and to keep sending
for him, even though he would refuse to go.

Next, Clearchus called together his own men, along with those
who had joined him and anyone else who wanted to come, and spoke
as follows: 'Comrades in arms, Cyrus' situation with regard to us is
obviously the same as ours with regard to him: we are no longer his
troops, since we're refusing to stay with him, and he is no longer our
paymaster either. However, I'm sure he thinks we have done him
wrong, and this means that, although my continuing refusal to obey
his summons is prompted largely by the shameful awareness that I
have proved myself utterly false to him, I'm also afraid that he will
arrest me and punish me for the wrong he thinks I have done him. It
seems to me, then, that this would not be a good time for us to sleep
or to stop thinking about what's best for us; no, we should be weighing
up possible courses of action. As long as we stay here, we should, I
think, be considering how best to reduce the risks of staying; and if
we decide to leave straight away, we should be considering how to do
so with as little risk as possible to ourselves, and how we will get hold
of provisions—without which neither officers nor rank and file are
any good. As a friend, Cyrus is worth a great deal to anyone who is
loyal to him, but he's a terrible enemy to anyone who goes against
him. We're all equally well placed to see the resources he has at his
command—the foot soldiers, horsemen, and warships—and we
understand what he's capable of. After all, our camp is not too far
from his, I think. And so this would be a good time for people to

bring up any ideas they have about what it would be best for us to do.'

That was the end of his speech, and afterwards some men got to their feet of their own accord to propose this or that plan of action, while others, primed by Clearchus, stood up to point out the impossibility of either staying or leaving without Cyrus' consent. In fact, one of them, who made out that he was in an inordinate hurry to set out for Greece, proposed that they should immediately elect new generals, if Clearchus was unwilling to lead them home. He went on to say that they should buy their provisions (even though the market was in the barbarians' camp), pack up their baggage, and go and ask Cyrus for ships for their voyage home. If he refused to give them ships, he suggested that they should ask for a guide to take them home through friendly territory; and if he refused to give them a guide as well, he said they should immediately form up for battle and send men to occupy the high ground before Cyrus did—or before the Cilicians did, 'since we have seized as booty many of the Cilicians' men and a great deal of their livestock'.

Once this speaker had finished, Clearchus said only: 'None of you should think of me as your general for this; I can see many reasons why I should not have the job. But think of me as one who will do his best to obey whoever you choose as your general, and then you will appreciate that I know as well as anybody in the world how to take orders as well as give them.'

Next, someone else got up to point out the stupidity of the suggestion that they should ask Cyrus for ships as if he were on a homeward voyage, and also pointed out how stupid it was to ask for a guide 'from the very man whose project we're damaging. If we're to trust a guide given us by Cyrus, we might as well ask Cyrus to occupy the high ground for us as well. I for one', he went on, 'would hesitate to board any ships given by him, for fear that he might sink us with triremes from the very same fleet, and I'd be afraid to follow any guide given by him, for fear of being led into a trap. Since I'm leaving without Cyrus' permission, I'd rather leave without his knowing anything about it—which is impossible. No, these ideas are rubbish, in my opinion. Here's what I think we should do. A delegation of suitable men, including Clearchus, should go to Cyrus and ask him what he wants us for, and if the project is more or less the same as the one for which he was using mercenaries before,* we should not desert him and prove ourselves more cowardly than those who went on his previous journey up country. On the other hand, if the project turns out to be more important, more physically demanding, and more dangerous than the earlier one, we should insist that he either gives us good reasons for following him or listens to our reasoning and lets us go in friendship. In this way, if we stay with him we do so as friends who are committed to the project, and if we leave we leave safely. But his response, whatever it may be, must be reported back here and then we'll discuss what to do.'

This proposal was carried and, once they had chosen a delegation to accompany Clearchus, they sent the men off to Cyrus. They asked him the questions approved by the troops, and he replied that, according to information he had received, Abrocomas,* an enemy of his, was at the Euphrates river, twelve days' march away, and that it was Abrocomas against whom he wanted to march. If Abrocomas was there, he said, he wanted to punish him, 'and if he has fled, we will discuss the future there'. The delegation reported Cyrus' response to the troops, and although they suspected that he was leading them against the king, they decided to stay with him. But they did ask for a pay rise, and Cyrus promised to give them all half as much again as they had been getting before—one and a half darics a month for each soldier instead of just one. But on this occasion no one heard anything—or any plain words, at least—about his taking them against the king.

[4] The next leg was a two-day march of ten parasangs that brought him to the Psarus river, which was three plethra wide. The next leg was a one-day march of five parasangs that brought him to the Pyramus river, which was a stade wide. The next leg was a two-day march of fifteen parasangs that brought him to Issus, a coastal city, large and prosperous, which was the last city in Cilicia. During their three days there the ships arrived from the Peloponnese to join Cyrus—thirty-five of them, under the command of Pythagoras of Sparta.* They had been shown the way from Ephesus by Tamos of Egypt, who brought in addition twenty-five of Cyrus' ships, with which he had been blockading Miletus, when it was loyal to Tissaphernes, and generally supporting Cyrus' campaign against Tissaphernes. Chirisophus of Sparta also arrived on board the fleet, in response to a summons from Cyrus, with 700 hoplites, whose general he remained after joining Cyrus. The ships lay at anchor

next to Cyrus' tent. It was also while Cyrus was at Issus that the 400 Greek hoplites who had been mercenaries in the service of Abrocomas joined Cyrus' service for his war against the king.

The next leg was a one-day march of five parasangs that brought him to the Cilician-Syrian Gates. These gates consist of two forts. The one on the western side, defending Cilicia, was held by Syennesis and a garrison of Cilicians, while the one on the eastern side, defending Syria, was reported to be held by the king's garrison. Between these two forts flows a river called the Carsus, a plethron wide. The total distance from one fort to the other was three stades, and it was impossible to force a crossing because the entrance was narrow, with fortifications reaching down to the sea on the one side and sheer rocks above the entrance on the other side. Both forts were also equipped with gates.

This defile was the reason Cyrus had sent for the ships. With their help, hoplites could be put ashore between the gates and on their further side, and these hoplites could effect a passage by force if there did in fact turn out to be a garrison defending the Syrian side. Cyrus expected that Abrocomas would use his vast military resources to do just that, but instead, on hearing that Cyrus was in Cilicia, Abrocomas had turned around and was marching from Phoenicia to join the king with an army reported to consist of 300,000 men.*

The next leg was a one-day march of five parasangs that brought him to Myriandus, a coastal city inhabited by Phoenicians. It was a trading port, with a lot of merchant ships lying at anchor. Cyrus stayed in Myriandus for seven days, and during this time Xenias of Arcadia and Pasion of Megara boarded a ship with their most valuable possessions and sailed away. Most people believed that they did so out of injured pride, because when their men had gone and joined Clearchus, with the intention of returning to Greece instead of marching against the king,* Cyrus had let Clearchus keep them. After they had disappeared, the rumour spread that Cyrus had sent triremes after them; while some prayed that the 'cowards', as they put it, would be caught, others felt sorry for what would happen to them if they were caught.

Cyrus summoned the generals to a meeting and said: 'Xenias and Pasion may have left, but they should be fully aware that they have not slipped away unseen, since I know the direction they took, and they have not outdistanced me either, because I have triremes that could catch up with them. But I swear by the gods that I will not pursue them, and it will never be said of me that I make use of people while they are with me, but, when they want to leave, I arrest them, do them harm, and rob them of their possessions. No, let them go. They know that they have treated me worse than I have treated them. It is true that I have their children and their wives under guard at Tralles, but they will not lose even them: they will get them back, in recognition of the good they did me before.' This speech by Cyrus revealed his calibre so well that even those Greeks who had been disheartened by the prospect of the march up country became happier and more committed to the expedition.

The next leg was a four-day march of twenty parasangs that brought him to the Chalus river, which was one plethron wide and teemed with large, docile fish. The Syrians regarded these fish as gods and did not let anyone harm them, or doves either.* The villages where they bivouacked had been given to Parysatis for her girdle-money.* The next leg was a five-day march of thirty-five parasangs that brought him to the sources of the Dardas river, which is a plethron wide. Here there was the palace of Belesys,* the former ruler of Syria, and a very large and beautiful park, which bore the fruits of every season. But Cyrus devastated the park and burnt down the palace.

The next leg was a three-day march of fifteen parasangs that brought him to the Euphrates, which was four stades wide. On this part of the river there was a large and prosperous city called Thapsacus, where they stayed for five days. Cyrus sent for the Greek generals and told them that they were to march in the direction of Babylon, against the Great King. He told them to inform their men of this and to persuade them not to abandon him. They convened an assembly at which they gave the troops the news. The soldiers were angry with the generals and accused them of having known this for a long time and having kept the information from them. They said that they would not go without the kind of financial inducement received by the earlier force that had accompanied Cyrus on his journey up country to his father, even though these men had not been going to war, but Cyrus had only been responding to the summons from his father. When the Greek generals told Cyrus the soldiers' terms, he promised to give each man five mnas of silver* when they reached Babylon, and to pay the Greeks their full wages right up until he got them back to Ionia.*

This was enough to win over most of the Greeks, but before it was clear what they would do—whether or not they would go with Cyrus—Meno called his own troops to a separate meeting and spoke along the following lines: 'Men, if you do as I suggest, Cyrus will think more highly of you than of all the rest of the troops, and you will win this respect from him without any danger or hardship. Here's my idea. At the moment, Cyrus is asking the Greeks to accompany him against the king. The course of action I recommend is that you should cross the Euphrates before the rest of the Greeks have made up their minds how to respond to Cyrus. Then, you see, if they vote to accompany him, this decision will be held to have been your doing, since you were the first to make the crossing, and Cyrus will be grateful for your commitment and will recompense you for it—and there is no one better at recompensing than he is. On the other hand, if the others vote against accompanying him, we'll join them on their return journey, but Cyrus will regard you as the only Greeks capable of obeying orders, and so he will treat you as his most reliable troops and will use you for garrison duty and as his company commanders; and if there's anything else you want, I'm sure you'll find Cyrus amenable.'

The troops found Meno's argument convincing and crossed the river before the rest of the Greeks had formulated their reply. Cyrus was delighted at the news that they had made the crossing and sent Glous to Meno's contingent with the following message: 'Men, at the moment it is I who am pleased with you, but I will see to it that you are pleased with me too, as sure as my name is Cyrus.' So Meno's troops had high hopes for the future and prayed for Cyrus' success, while Meno himself, it was said, was handsomely rewarded. Then Cyrus crossed the river, and every single one of the rest of the troops went with him. As they were crossing the river, none of them got wet above the level of his chest, but the people of Thapsacus said that the river had never before been fordable. In the past, a pontoon of boats had always been used, but on this occasion Abrocomas had been there first and had burnt the boats to prevent Cyrus from crossing. And so this was held to be a miracle; it seemed clear that the river had yielded before Cyrus since he was destined to be king.*

The next leg was a nine-day march of fifty parasangs through

Syria that brought him to the Araxes river, where there were many villages which were well stocked with grain and wine. They stayed in the region for three days and replenished their supplies.

[5] The next leg was a five-day march of thirty-five parasangs through the Arabian desert, keeping the Euphrates on his right. In this region, the land was completely flat and as level as the sea, except that it was covered with wormwood. All the other species of shrub or reed there were as fragrant as spices. The desert was treeless, but had a wide variety of animals; wild asses were the most common, but there were also plenty of ostriches, and bustards and gazelles as well. The horsemen sometimes chased these creatures, and the asses, when chased, ran on ahead—they were much faster than horses— and then stopped; then, when the horses got close, they did the same thing all over again. They were impossible to catch, unless riders took up positions at intervals and then took turns to chase them. The flesh of those that were caught tasted like a more tender version of venison. No one managed to catch an ostrich, and any horseman who set off after one soon stopped; the bird would pull a long way ahead by using not only its feet, to run away, but also by hoisting its wings, as if it were using a sail. But bustards can be caught if one puts them up quickly, because they fly only a short way, like partridges, and soon give up. Their flesh was very tasty.

Their march through this land brought them to the Mascas river, which was a plethron wide, where they found a large, deserted city called Corsote, inside a bend of the river. They stayed there for three days and stocked up on provisions. The next leg was a thirteen-day march of ninety parasangs, keeping the Euphrates on his right, which brought him to the Gates.* During these thirteen stages many of the yoke-animals died of starvation, because the land was abso- lutely bare, without grass or any trees either. The local inhabitants made a living by quarrying and manufacturing millstones by the side of the river, which they took to Babylon and sold in exchange for grain. The troops ran out of grain and were unable to buy it except from Lydian traders attached to Cyrus' barbarian corps, where it cost four *sigloi* for one *kapithē* of wheat flour or barley meal—a *siglos* being the equivalent of seven and a half Attic obols and a *kapithē* that of two Attic choenixes. The soldiers therefore survived by eating meat.* Moreover, whenever Cyrus wanted to reach water or fodder, he made the stages of the march very long.

Once in particular they came across a narrow, muddy place where the going was difficult for the carts. Cyrus halted with his entourage of wealthy noblemen and told Glous and Pigres to take some men from the barbarian corps and extricate the carts. But he thought they were taking too long over the job, and so, feigning anger, he told the Persian noblemen in his entourage to help the carts to get a move on. It then became possible to witness a fine bit of discipline. They let their outer robes of purple drop to the ground without caring where they stood and sprinted, as if they were competing in a race, down a very steep hillside in their expensive tunics and colourful trousers, with some of them even wearing torques around their necks and bracelets on their arms.* As soon as they got there, they leapt into the mud in all their finery and lifted the carts free of the mud more quickly than one would have thought possible.

On the whole, Cyrus was obviously in a hurry throughout the journey and never delayed except when he called a halt for some essential purpose such as replenishing supplies. His thinking was that the faster he went, the less prepared the king would be for battle, and that every delay would allow the king to assemble a larger force; and in fact it was obvious to anyone who thought about it that although its size and the enormity of its population gave the king's empire strength, the length of the journeys involved and the fact that its forces were scattered made it weak and vulnerable to a sudden offensive.*

On the other side of the Euphrates during these desert stages of the march was a prosperous, large city called Charmande, where the soldiers bought supplies. They crossed the river on rafts which they made by filling the animal skins which served as their tents with dried grass, and then joining the skins together and sewing them up to stop the water reaching the hay. They used these floats to cross the river and get their supplies—wine made from dates and bread made from millet, which was very plentiful in this region.

A dispute arose while they were at Charmande between a soldier from Meno's contingent and one of Clearchus' men. Clearchus judged the case and in his opinion Meno's man was the wrongdoer, so he had him flogged. The man's fellow soldiers were indignant, when he returned to his own contingent and told them what had happened, and their feelings were running high against Clearchus. Later that same day Clearchus went to the river-crossing. After inspecting the market there he rode back to his tent, with a small retinue, through Meno's encampment. Cyrus was still on the march and had not yet arrived. One of Meno's soldiers was chopping wood when he saw Clearchus passing by, and he threw his axe at him. He missed, but someone else threw a stone, and then another stone flew, and soon the air was thick with stones and shouts.

Clearchus sought the safety of his own camp and immediately called his troops to arms. He told his hoplites to wait with their shields resting against their knees, while he took the Thracians and the horsemen he had in his unit—there were more than forty of them, mostly Thracians—and advanced against Meno's men. The upshot was that Meno's troops, and Meno himself, were terrified and ran to collect their weapons, although there were others who just stood still in bewilderment. But Proxenus, who happened to have fallen behind and to be approaching the Greek encampment along with a unit of hoplites, immediately led his men between the two sides, halted them with their weapons at the ready, and asked Clearchus to stop what he was doing.

Clearchus was angry that Proxenus was talking in a mild-mannered way about what had happened to him, when he had only just escaped being stoned to death, and he ordered him out of the way. Just then Cyrus came up too and was told what was going on. He immediately seized his javelins and rode between the two sides with those of his trusted advisers who were on hand. 'Clearchus,' he said, 'and Proxenus, and all you Greeks here, you have no idea what you are doing. If you fight one another even for a moment, you should know that I shall be cut down today and not long afterwards you will be annihilated too. For if things go wrong for us, all the barbarians you can see here will be more hostile towards us than those fighting for the king.' These words brought Clearchus back to his senses, and both sides stood down and returned to their quarters.

[6] As they went on from there they began to come across hoof-marks and droppings; it looked as though they were on the trail of about 2,000 horsemen who, as they advanced, were burning fodder and anything else that might have been useful. Orontas, a Persian who was related to the king and was said to be as good as any Persian at warfare, hatched a plot against Cyrus. He had been Cyrus' enemy before, but they had become reconciled. He now asked Cyrus for 1,000 horsemen, with which, he said, he would either ambush and

kill the cavalry detachment which was burning everything ahead of them, or capture enough of them to stop them burning things as they advanced; and he also said that he would do this in such a way that they would never catch sight of Cyrus' forces and report back to the king. Cyrus thought this was a useful idea and he told Orontas to take a detachment from each of his cavalry commanders.

Thinking that the horsemen were his for the taking, Orontas wrote a letter to the king in which he said that he would come and would bring as many horsemen as he could, and he urged the king to tell his cavalry to receive him as a friend. He also included in the letter reminders of his former loyalty and reliability. He gave this letter to a man he considered trustworthy, but the man took it and gave it to Cyrus. After reading it, Cyrus arrested Orontas, summoned to his tent seven of the Persian noblemen from his entourage, and told the Greek generals to bring up their hoplites and have them stand at the ready around his tent. In accordance with his instructions, the generals brought up about 3,000 hoplites. Cyrus also asked Clearchus to join him inside as one of his advisers, since both he and the rest of the Persians thought that Clearchus was the most highly regarded of the Greeks.

When Clearchus emerged from the tent, he informed his friends, since he had not been forbidden to do so, what had happened in Orontas' trial. He said that Cyrus began the proceedings by speaking as follows: 'I have invited you here, my friends, because I want with your help to decide what both gods and men would consider the right way to deal with Orontas here. Once we have reached a decision, I will carry it out. My father first gave him to me as my subordinate. Later, acting, he claims, on my brother's orders, he occupied the acropolis of Sardis and made war on me, but I fought back so successfully that I made him decide to end his hostility towards me, and we shook hands on it. Subsequently,' he said, turning to Orontas, 'did I wrong you in any way?'

'No,' Orontas replied.

Cyrus then asked him a further question: 'Later—although, as you yourself admit, you had not been wronged by me—did you not go over to the Mysians and do all you could to harm my territory?'

'Yes,' said Orontas.

'And,' Cyrus continued, 'once you had come to realize the limits of your powers, did you not go to the altar of Artemis* and say that you were sorry? And, when I believed you, did we not once again exchange pledges?'

Orontas agreed to this too.

'What wrong have I done you, then,' said Cyrus, 'that you should now be caught red-handed in a third conspiracy against me?'

When Orontas agreed that Cyrus had not done him any wrong, Cyrus said: 'So you admit that you have done me wrong?'

'I am bound to admit it,' said Orontas.

Then Cyrus asked him a further question: 'Will you in the future be an enemy of my brother and a loyal friend to me?'

'Cyrus,' he replied, 'even if I were, you would never believe it.'

Cyrus then turned to those present and said: 'You've heard what this man has done and what he has said. Clearchus, I want you to be the first to tell us what you think.'

Clearchus spoke as follows: 'My advice is that you should get rid of this man as soon as possible, so that we can stop taking precautions against him. Then, so far as this fellow is concerned, we can have the time to do good to those who have chosen to be our friends.' And Clearchus said that everyone else agreed with his point of view.

Next, at Cyrus' command, everyone stood up, even Orontas' relatives, and took hold of Orontas' belt, to indicate that they voted for his death. Then the appointed men took him outside. When those who had previously paid homage to Orontas saw him, they did so even then, although they could see that he was being taken to his death. He was taken into the tent of Artapatas, the most loyal of Cyrus' staff-bearers, and no one ever again saw Orontas alive or dead, nor could anyone say with certainty how he died, although people came up with various conjectures. No one ever saw his grave either.

[7] The next leg was a three-day march of twelve parasangs through Babylonia. In the course of the third day Cyrus conducted a review of both Greeks and barbarians on the plain. The review took place in the middle of the night, because he expected the arrival of the king at dawn the following day, along with his army, to do battle. He put Clearchus in charge of the right wing and Meno of Thessaly in charge of the left wing, while he deployed his own troops. At daybreak the following day, after the review, deserters from the Great King arrived with information about the king's army.

Cyrus summoned the Greek generals and company commanders

to a meeting to consider with their help how the battle should be fought. He also tried to raise their morale and their determination by speaking somewhat as follows: 'Men of Greece, it is not because I am short of barbarian troops that I have brought you here to fight on my side; it is because you are, in my opinion, braver and better than hordes of barbarians. That's why I got you to join me. Endeavour, then, to prove yourselves worthy of the freedom you possess. I envy you this freedom. Why? I assure you that I would choose freedom over all my wealth,* even if I was far better off than I am now. Now, there are aspects of the coming conflict of which you are ignorant but I am not, and so I shall explain them to you. The enemy army is vast and as they advance they will raise a terrific clamour. As long as you are not put off by this—well, as for the rest, I feel ashamed when I think how feeble you will find the people of this land of mine to be. If you are men and if my business here goes well, I will make any of you who wants to return home an object of envy to his neighbours; but I think I shall make many of you choose to stay with me rather than return home.'

At this point Gaulites, a Samian exile who was one of the company, and was a trusted adviser of Cyrus, said: 'And yet, Cyrus, there are those who say that you're making generous promises now because of the situation you're in, a situation of imminent danger, but that if things go well you will forget the promises you made. And there are others who say that even if you do remember them and want to keep them, you won't have the resources to pay everything you are promising.'

Cyrus replied: 'Well, my friends, my father's empire extends south to a region where men cannot live because of the heat and north to a region where they cannot live because of the cold. All the territories between these two extremes are governed by my brother's friends, but if I'm victorious, I am bound to put *my* friends in charge of them. So there's no reason for you to worry that, if things go well, I may not have enough to give to each of my friends; it would make more sense for you to worry that I may not have enough friends to reward. And I will also give each of you Greeks a crown of gold.'

These words of Cyrus had the effect of increasing the resolution of the Greeks, and when they passed the news on to everyone else, some of the other Greeks too went to Cyrus and asked him to tell them what they would get if they were victorious. Before dismissing them, he satisfied the desires of each and every one of them. In conversation with him, everyone urged him not to take part in the fighting, but to assign himself a position in the rear. This was the context of a question Clearchus put to Cyrus, phrased more or less as follows: 'Do you think your brother will fight you, Cyrus?' 'He most certainly will,' Cyrus answered. 'If he really is the son of Darius and Parysatis, if he really is my brother, I won't gain this empire without a fight.'

When the Greeks were counted, while under arms on the third day of this leg, there were found to be 10,400 hoplites and 2,500 peltasts.* Cyrus' barbarian troops numbered 100,000, and there were about 20 scythe-bearing chariots. The enemy force was said to number 1,200,000,* with 200 scythe-bearing chariots; in addition there were 6,000 horsemen under the command of Artagerses, who were deployed in defence of the king himself. The king's army had four commanders—Abrocomas, Tissaphernes, Gobryas and Arbaces— each of whom was responsible for 300,000 men. But only 900,000 of the king's troops and 150 scythe-bearing chariots took part in the battle because Abrocomas, marching from Phoenicia, arrived five days too late. This was the information given Cyrus by deserters from the Great King before the battle, and enemy prisoners gave the same facts and figures after the battle too.

The next leg was a one-day march of three parasangs. During this march all the troops, both Greek and barbarian, were drawn up in battle order, because this was the day on which Cyrus expected the king to join battle. About halfway through this stage there was a deep artificial trench, five fathoms wide and three fathoms deep, which extended inland over the plain for twelve parasangs and ended at the Median Wall.* By the side of the Euphrates there was a narrow gap, about twenty feet wide, between the river and the trench. The Great King had constructed this trench as a means of defence when he found out that Cyrus was marching against him.

Cyrus and his army passed through this gap and found themselves beyond the trench. The king did not offer battle that day, but the tracks were visible of many men and horses who had withdrawn before them. Cyrus summoned Silanus, his diviner from Ambracia, and gave him 3,000 darics because ten days earlier Silanus had pre-dicted, as a result of his sacrifices, that the king would not fight within ten days. At the time Cyrus had said: 'Then he won't fight at all, if he won't fight within ten days. But if you're right, I promise you ten talents.' So this was the money he paid him then, since the ten days had passed.

The king's failure to obstruct the passage of Cyrus' army at the trench made Cyrus and everyone else think that he had abandoned the idea of fighting, and so the next day Cyrus took fewer precautions as he marched on, and on the day after that he travelled on a chariot with only a few men in battle order in front of him, while the bulk of the army made their way forward in a chaotic fashion, with much of the soldiers' weaponry and armour being carried on carts and yoke-animals.

[8] Late in the morning,* when the staging area where Cyrus was intending to halt was near by, Pategyas, a Persian who was one of Cyrus' trusted advisers, came into view. He was riding at full speed, with his horse all covered in sweat, and he lost no time in shouting out to everyone he met, in Greek and other languages, that the king was approaching with a vast army, ready for battle. Considerable turmoil was the result of this news, because the first thought that occurred to the Greeks—to everyone, in fact—was that the king would fall on them while they were in disarray.

Cyrus leapt down from his chariot. He put on his breastplate, mounted his horse, and was handed his javelins; then he told everyone else to arm themselves and instructed each man to take up his proper position in battle order. Everyone rushed to do so. Clearchus, with the right wing, was by the Euphrates; Proxenus was next to him, and then came the rest, while Meno and his troops held the left wing of the Greek corps. As for the barbarians (apart from a Paphlagonian cavalry unit of about 1,000, who were stationed beside Clearchus on the right wing, along with the Greek peltasts), on the left wing there was Ariaeus, Cyrus' second-in-command, and the rest of the barbarian foot soldiers, while Cyrus and his horsemen, about 600 in number, occupied the middle. These Persian horsemen wore breastplates and cuisses, and all of them except Cyrus, who rode into battle bare-headed, wore helmets as well. All the horses in Cyrus' squadron were equipped with protective armour on their foreheads and chests, and their riders also carried Greek-style swords.

Midday came and still there was no sign of the enemy, but early in the afternoon a cloud of dust appeared, looking at first like a white cloud in the sky. Some time later, however, it was as if there was a huge black smudge on the plain. Before long, as the enemy drew nearer, there were flashes of bronze, and then the tips of their spears and the divisions of the enemy army became apparent. On the left wing there were cavalrymen in white cuirasses, reported to be under the command of Tissaphernes; next to them were foot soldiers with wicker shields and then heavily armed troops, rumoured to be from Egypt, with wooden shields which reached down to their feet. Then there were further cavalry units and more archers. All of them marched in serried squares, with a different people making up each square. In front of them, and at some distance from one another, were the scythe-bearing chariots, as they are called; they were equipped with scythes which projected out sideways from their axles and faced the ground under the chariots as well, so as to cut to pieces anything or anyone they met. The plan was to use these chariots against the Greeks as they advanced in formation to break up the enemy lines. But one thing Cyrus said at the meeting he had convened turned out to be wrong: he had urged the Greeks to stand firm against the barbarians' clamour, but in actual fact they made no noise, but advanced slowly and steadily, in all possible silence.

Just then Cyrus rode along the line accompanied only by Pigres (his translator) and three or four others and, shouting out loud, ordered Clearchus to lead his men against the centre of the enemy formation, because that was where the king was. 'If we win there,' he said, 'we'll have accomplished all we came for.' But although Clearchus had seen how compact the enemy's centre was, and although he had been informed that the king was beyond Cyrus' left wing—for the king's troops so far outnumbered Cyrus' that the king's centre was beyond Cyrus' left wing—nevertheless, Clearchus was reluctant to open up a gap between the right wing and the river, which would have made him vulnerable to being outflanked on both sides, and so he told Cyrus that he would make sure that things went well.*

At that moment, then, the barbarian army was steadily drawing closer and the Greeks were staying put while latecomers were still taking up their positions in the battle lines. Some way in front of the army, Cyrus was riding past, looking in both directions—at both his enemies and his friends. Xenophon of Athens* spotted him from the Greek lines, rode to meet him, and asked him whether he had any instructions. Cyrus reined in his horse and told Xenophon to spread the news that the sacrifices and the omens were favourable. Just as Cyrus was speaking, he heard a noise running through the Greek lines and he asked what it was. When Xenophon said that the watchword* was now being passed back through the lines, Cyrus asked, in surprise, who had authorized it and what it was. Xenophon replied: 'Zeus the Saviour and Victory.' On hearing the watchword, Cyrus said: 'That's perfectly acceptable; let it stand.' And with these words he rode back to his own position.

Only three or four stades separated the two phalanxes when the Greeks struck up the paean* and began to advance against the enemy. As they were advancing, a part of the phalanx surged forward, so those who were falling behind broke into a run. Then all the soldiers cried out their usual war-cry to Enyalius* and began to run. Some say that they also clashed the shafts of their spears against their shields to frighten the enemy horses. Before they were within bow-shot, the barbarians caved in and fled. The Greeks then set out after them at full speed, but called out to one another not to make it a race, but to keep their formation. The enemy chariots, abandoned by their drivers, hurtled through the ranks of both the enemy and the Greeks. When the Greeks saw them coming, they opened up a gap to let them through. One man, behaving like someone caught panic-stricken on a horse-racing track, was actually run down by a chariot, but the report said that even he was not hurt, and neither was any other Greek, except for someone on the left wing who was said to have been wounded by an arrow.

Cyrus saw that the Greeks had defeated the unit opposite them and had set out in pursuit. He was pleased, and some of his entourage were already doing homage to him as king,* but even so he was not tempted to join in the pursuit. Instead, he kept his squadron of 600 horsemen in close formation and watched to see what the king would do. He was sure that the king held the centre of his army—and in fact it is the universal practice of barbarian rulers to hold the centre when they are in command, because they think it the safest position, since they have forces to either side of them and their troops can receive any messages they need to send in half the time. So on this occasion too the king held the centre of his army. Despite this, he found himself beyond the left wing of Cyrus' army and so, since there was no one straight ahead to offer battle to him or the men deployed in front of him, he had his men change direction with the intention of outflanking his opponents.

Cyrus, worried that the king might get behind his forces and annihilate the Greeks, rode to meet him. The attack was successful. He and his 600 men defeated the 6,000 deployed in front of the king and put them to flight—and he even killed their commander, Artagerses, with his own hand, it is said. But after the enemy had been turned, Cyrus' 600 set out after them and also became scattered, until Cyrus was left with only a very few men around him, mainly his so-called 'table-companions'.* This was his situation when he caught sight of the king and the compact troop around him. Without hesitating for a moment, he cried out, 'I see him!', and charged at him. He struck the king on the chest and wounded him through his breastplate. This is on the authority of Ctesias the doctor,* who adds that it was he who healed the wound.

As he was striking the blow, however, a javelin struck him hard under the eye.* There followed a fight between Cyrus and the king, and their respective retinues. Ctesias, who was with the king, reports the number of the casualties on the king's side; but Cyrus himself was killed, and eight of the bravest men from his retinue lay dead on his body. It is said that when Artapatas, the most loyal of his staff-bearers, saw that Cyrus had fallen, he leapt off his horse and threw himself on the body. Some say that the king ordered one of his men to butcher Artapatas on Cyrus' body, but according to others Artapatas drew his dagger and did the deed himself. For he carried a golden dagger, and also wore all the usual accoutrements that noble Persians wear, such as a torque and armlets, which had been given to him by Cyrus as rewards for his loyalty and reliability.

[9] This is how Cyrus died. Of all the successors of Cyrus the Elder,* no Persian was a more natural ruler and none more deserved to rule. This was the view of all who were held to have been close to Cyrus. In the first place, even while he was still a child, at school with his brother and the other boys, he was regarded as the best of his generation at everything. All the sons of Persian noblemen are educated at court, where they gain a thorough grounding in self-discipline, and where there is no harsh sound to be heard or ugly sight to be seen. The boys see and hear about those who are highly regarded by the king, and those who receive no honour from him, which means that from their earliest years they are learning how to

rule and how to be ruled. In this context, Cyrus was thought, first, to be more respectful than any of his peers and more obedient to his elders even than his inferiors in rank. Second, he adored horses and was particularly good at handling them. Third, there was reckoned to be no one who was more keen to learn the military skills of archery and javelin, and no one who practised them more assiduously.

Moreover, when he reached the appropriate age, he was not only very fond of hunting, but also relished the risks involved in facing wild creatures. A she-bear once charged him, but he engaged the creature without flinching and was dragged from his horse. He received some injuries, the scars of which remained plainly visible, but in the end he killed the beast. Moreover, he made the first man to come to his assistance a general object of envy.

Then again, when he was sent down to the coast by his father to be satrap of Lydia, Greater Phrygia, and Cappadocia, and was also appointed commander of all the forces whose ordained place of assembly was the Plain of Castolus, he demonstrated, first, that the quality he held most important when he was making a treaty or entering into a contract or making a promise was his own personal integrity. This is why the cities there trusted him and put themselves into his hands, and why individuals trusted him too. Even former enemies who later entered into a treaty with Cyrus trusted that the terms of the treaty would be adhered to. This explains why, during his war with Tissaphernes, all the cities of their own accord preferred Cyrus to Tissaphernes. The only exception was Miletus, but the Milesians were frightened of him because he refused to abandon the exiles. For he constantly made it plain, by his actions as well as his words, that he would never abandon them, now that he had become their friend, not even if their numbers declined still further and their situation further deteriorated.

It was also clear that he always tried to go one better than anyone who did him either good or harm. In fact, there was a story in circulation of how he used to pray to live long enough to repay with interest both those who had done him good and those who had injured him. This is why more people wanted to entrust their money, their cities, and even their lives to him than to any other person of our times. At the same time, however, no one could say that he allowed criminals and wrongdoers to mock him. No, he punished them with unstinting severity, and one could often see, by the side of busy roads, people who had lost feet, hands, or eyes. The upshot was that it became possible for any innocent man, whether Greek or barbarian, to travel within Cyrus' domain wherever he liked without fear and carrying whatever he wanted.

It was universally acknowledged, however, that he especially used to honour people for bravery in warfare. A prime example of this occurred during his war against the Pisidians and the Mysians, when he personally took to the field to invade their territories. He gave those whom he saw readily facing danger responsibility for the territory he was in the process of subduing, and also rewarded them subsequently in other ways as well. This meant that brave men were also seen to prosper the most, while cowards were expected to be their slaves. This is why he always had plenty of men who were prepared to face danger in any situation where they thought that it might come to Cyrus' attention.

Then again, he regarded it as essential to make those who wanted to stand out for their justice wealthier than those who sought to profit from injustice. This meant not only that his affairs in general were handled in an equitable fashion, but in particular that he gained the services of an army which truly deserved the name. For both the generals and the company commanders who crossed the sea to join his army as mercenaries came to realize that honourable support† for Cyrus was worth more to them than their monthly wages. Furthermore, he never let the wholehearted performance of any of his orders go unrewarded, and this was generally held to be the reason why in all his undertakings he always gained the best subordinates.

He never took land away from people who managed their estates with sufficient expertise and justice to improve the land and generate an income from it, but he always added to what they had. This meant that they gladly undertook hard work and went about the business of acquisition with confidence. They also had not the slightest inclination to conceal what they owned from Cyrus, because he made it plain that he did not mind people who made no secret of their wealth, while he made efforts to appropriate the property of those who tried to conceal it.

As for friendship, it is universally acknowledged that there was no one better than Cyrus at looking after all his friends, as long as he found them to be loyal and reckoned them capable of helping him achieve whatever goal he had set his sights on. For just as it was precisely his desire to gain help in some task or other which made him feel that he needed friends, so he himself tried his best to help his friends whenever he saw that there was something one of them wanted. No single individual, in my opinion, ever received more gifts than he did, and there were many reasons why people gave them to him, but he gave them away again, chiefly to his friends, taking into consideration each individual's character and the particular need he perceived anyone as having. For instance, he was sent plenty of finery to wear during times of war or just to look good, and one of his recorded sayings concerns these gifts: he said that while he could not have himself adorned in all this finery, he thought that there was nothing finer for a man than finely turned out friends.

Since he had greater resources, it is hardly surprising that he outdid his friends in the generosity of the favours he did them, but what seems more admirable to me is that he surpassed them in thoughtfulness and in his determination to do favours. For example, when Cyrus came across a particularly pleasant wine, he often sent his friends the jar, still half full of wine, with the message: 'Cyrus has not come across a nicer wine than this for a long time, so he has sent it to you with the request that you drink it up today along with your best friends.' Likewise, he would also send something like a half-eaten goose or half a loaf, and tell the slave who took it to add: 'Cyrus enjoyed this, and he would like you to have a taste of it too.' When fodder was in short supply, but he was able to take care of his own needs thanks to the large numbers of slaves he had, and thanks to his prudent management, he used to distribute it among his friends with the request that they use it to feed the horses they rode themselves, so that the horses his friends rode might not go hungry. And whenever he was likely to be seen by large numbers of people while he was out and about, he would gather his friends around him and engage them in close conversation, so as to let people know whom he valued.

In conclusion, then, it is my personal view that no Greek or barbarian—or none that I have heard of—was loved by more people. There is evidence for this in the fact that, although Cyrus was a slave,* no one deserted him for the king. Only Orontas tried to do so, and he soon found out that the man he thought he could rely on was in fact more loyal to Cyrus than him. On the other hand, once there was open warfare between the king and Cyrus, there were plenty of deserters the other way round, and they were men of whom the king was particularly fond.† They deserted because they thought that, as brave men, they would be more likely to get the respect they deserved from Cyrus than from the king.

Even what happened at his death shows clearly that he was a good man himself and that he was capable of accurately assessing fidelity, loyalty, and dependability in others. For as Cyrus lay dying, his entire entourage of friends and table-companions fought and died over his body. The only exception was Ariaeus, who had been put in charge of the cavalry on the left wing. When he found out that Cyrus had fallen, he fled with all the troops under his command.

[10] So Cyrus' head and his right hand were hacked from his corpse. The king set out in pursuit and burst into Cyrus' camp, where Ariaeus and his men ceased any attempt at resistance and fled through their own camp to the staging area from where they had set out that day—a distance, it was said, of four parasangs. The king and his men seized a great deal of booty, including Cyrus' Phocaean concubine,* who was said to be both clever and pretty. The younger of his concubines, the Milesian woman, was also captured by the king's men, but escaped from their clutches and found her way, naked, to some Greeks who happened to have weapons and formed a last line of defence in the baggage train. These Greeks killed many of the looters and did not run away even though they took casualties. And so they saved this Milesian woman and everything and everyone else which was behind them.

At this point the king and the main body of the Greeks were about thirty stades apart. The Greeks were pursuing the troops they had been ranged against, in the belief that overall victory was theirs, while the king's men had turned to looting, in the belief that their whole army had by then won the day; but eventually the Greeks found out that the king and his men were in the baggage train, and the king was told by Tissaphernes that the Greeks had defeated their immediate opponents and were racing ahead in pursuit. Then the king collected his troops and formed them up for battle, and Clearchus called over Proxenus (who was nearest to him) and they discussed whether they should send a detachment to help the camp or go in full force. But in the meantime it became plain that the king was advancing again—from their rear, as they thought—so the Greeks did an about-face and got ready to meet his attack, expecting him to come from that direction.

The king, however, did not advance straight towards the Greeks, but retraced the same path he had come by, past the outside of Cyrus' left wing. On the way he recovered those of his men who had deserted to the Greeks during the battle, and also Tissaphernes and his troops. Tissaphernes had not retreated during the initial clash, but had ridden along the river and against the Greek peltasts. But his charge failed to inflict any casualties, because the Greeks opened up a gap and then struck Tissaphernes' men with their weapons and hurled javelins at them as they went through. The commander of the peltasts was Episthenes of Amphipolis and he was generally held to have proved himself a sound tactician. At any rate, having come off worst in the encounter, Tissaphernes did not wheel his troops around again, but went on to the Greek camp, where he met the king. Once these two units had formed up together in battle order, they set out.

Before long, they were facing the Greek left wing.* The Greeks were concerned that an attack against their wing would allow the enemy to outflank it on both sides and massacre them. They decided to fold back the wing until they had the river behind them, but before they had finished discussing this manoeuvre the king bypassed them and deployed his men opposite them in the same battle formation he had adopted during the first engagement. When the Greeks saw the enemy troops near by, in battle order, they once again struck up the paean and advanced with far more determination even than before. The barbarians again failed to stand their ground; in fact, they turned to flight when the Greeks were even further off than the first time.

The Greeks chased them as far as a village,* but stopped there because the king and his men had rallied on the hill which over-looked the village. The king no longer had any infantry troops, but the hill was so covered with horsemen that the Greeks could not tell what was going on, though they said they could see the royal standard —a golden spread eagle on a shield.* Even under these circum-stances, however, the Greeks set out against the enemy—and the cavalry immediately began to abandon even the hill. Men rode off in all directions, without staying together as a unit at all, until they had all withdrawn and the hill was empty of horsemen. Clearchus did not take his troops up the hill, but halted them at the foot and sent a couple of men (one of them was Lycius of Syracuse) up the hill with instructions to see what was on the other side and report back. Lycius rode up and had a look, and brought back the news that the enemy was in full flight. The sun was just beginning to set when this was happening.

The Greeks then halted, grounded their weapons, and rested. At the same time they were surprised that Cyrus was nowhere to be seen and that no one else turned up from him either. They had no idea that he was dead; their best guess was that either he was chasing the enemy or he had ridden on ahead in order to occupy some strategic point. There was some discussion about whether they should stay where they were and bring the baggage there, or should return to the camp. They decided on the latter course and got back to their tents around the time of the evening meal.*

So this day ended. The Greeks found that most of their things had been stolen, including their food and drink. As for the carts filled with wheat flour and wine, which Cyrus had provided so that in the event of an emergency he would have something to give the Greeks—and there were generally held to have been 400 of these carts—these too had been stolen by the king's men. As a result, most of the Greeks went without food, and they had gone without a midday meal as well, because the king had turned up before they had stopped to eat. This, then, is how they spent that night.

BOOK TWO

[1] Early the following day the generals met. They were surprised at Cyrus' failure either to send someone to tell them what to do or to appear in person, so they decided to pack up their remaining belongings and carry on under arms until they met him. They were just about ready to set off and the sun was just rising when Procles, the ruler of Teuthrania and a descendant of Damaratus of Sparta,* arrived with Glous the son of Tamos. They brought the news of Cyrus' death and told them that Ariaeus had retreated and was now, along with all the rest of the barbarians, at the staging area from where they had set out the previous day. They also passed on a message from Ariaeus, to the effect that he would wait one day to see whether they were planning to join him, but that on the following day he would set out on the return journey to Ionia, where he had come from.

This news deeply disheartened the generals and, when they heard it, the rest of the Greeks. 'I wish that Cyrus were alive,' Clearchus said, 'but he's dead. So tell Ariaeus that we, at any rate, have defeated the king. Tell him that, as you can see, the enemy has stopped trying to fight us, and that if you hadn't come we would now be marching against the king. And assure him that if he comes here to us, we will seat him on the royal throne. For the right of rulership goes to those who are victorious in battle.' With these words he dismissed the messengers and gave Chirisophus of Sparta and Meno of Thessaly the job of escorting them back. Meno specifically wanted the job, since he was on good terms with Ariaeus, who was his guest-friend.

They set off, and Clearchus waited for them to return. The men did what they could to supply themselves with food, which meant slaughtering the oxen and asses they were using as yoke-animals. For fuel they went to the battlefield (which involved leaving the main body of the army only a little way behind) and used not only large numbers of arrows, which they had forced the deserters from the king's army* to discard, but also wicker shields and Egyptian wooden shields. There were a great many light shields and abandoned carts for them to collect too. They used all these things to boil meat so that they had food for that day.

Late in the morning, heralds arrived from the king and Tissaphernes. They were all barbarians, except for a single Greek* named Phalinus; he was attached to Tissaphernes and had gained his respect because he claimed to be an expert on tactics and hoplite warfare. The heralds approached and called the Greek leaders to a meeting. They said that the king's instructions to the Greeks were as follows: since he was the victor, having killed Cyrus, they were to surrender their weapons and go to the king's court to see if they might meet with good fortune there. These words angered the Greeks, but Clearchus managed at least to say that it was not usual for victors to surrender their weapons. 'However,' he went on, 'it is up to you, my fellow generals, to make the best and most honourable reply you can to these heralds, and I'll be straight back.' For one of his attendants had come to fetch him to examine the entrails which had been taken out of the victim he had been in the middle of sacrificing.

Then Cleanor of Arcadia, the oldest man present, replied that they would die rather than surrender their weapons. And Proxenus of Thebes said: 'What puzzles me, Phalinus, is whether the king is demanding our weapons in the belief that he has defeated us, or as gifts freely given as tokens of our friendship. If he believes that he has defeated us, why should he demand them from us, rather than come and take them? But if he wants to persuade us to give them to him, let him tell our men what they will gain if they do him this favour.'

'It is the view of the king', Phalinus replied, 'that he is the victor, since he has killed Cyrus. After all, is there anyone who is now challenging him for the throne? And he thinks that you too are his vassals, since he has you in the middle of his territory, caught between uncrossable rivers, and is in a position to bring so many men up against you that you wouldn't be able to kill them all even if he made it easy for you.'

Theopompus†* of Athens was the next to speak. 'Phalinus,' he said, 'as you can see, at the moment we have nothing going for us except our weapons and our courage. If we keep our weapons, we think we can make use of our courage, but if we surrender them, we will probably lose our lives as well. So please don't imagine that we're going to hand our only advantage over to you. No, we shall use our weapons to fight you and try to take *your* things from *you*.'

Phalinus laughed at this and said: 'You sound like a philosopher, boy, with your elegant words. But you're being stupid, you know, if you imagine that your courage could defeat the king with all his power.'

Others, it was said, took a softer line and suggested that, just as they had been loyal to Cyrus, so they could prove of immense value to the king too, if he was willing to be their friend. Whatever else he might want to use them for, they said, they could help him subdue Egypt, if he wanted to use them for a campaign there.*

Just then Clearchus came back and asked whether they had already given their reply. Before anyone else could speak, Phalinus said: 'They're all saying different things, Clearchus. Why don't you tell us what you think?'

'Phalinus,' Clearchus replied, 'I was glad to see you and so, I imagine, was everyone else. You are, after all, a Greek and so are all those you see here. As things are, we would like to hear what *you* think we should do in response to your message. So please, in the name of the gods, tell us what you think would be the best and most honourable course of action for us. If you do, the story people will tell in the future will greatly enhance your reputation. "Phalinus", they'll say, "was once sent by the king to tell the Greeks to surrender their weapons, but when asked for his advice he gave it to them and this is what he said." You know that the advice you give is bound to be reported in Greece.'

Clearchus' intention, in offering this bait, was to see whether even the king's representative would advise them not to surrender their weapons, which would raise the Greeks' hopes for the future. But contrary to Clearchus' expectations, Phalinus refused to take the bait. 'My advice,' he said, 'is that you should not surrender your weapons, if you have the slightest chance of saving your lives by fighting the king; but if you have no chance of survival as long as the king remains uncooperative, I advise you to do what you must to save your lives.'

'That may be your advice,' Clearchus retorted, 'but here's our message for the king. It is our opinion that if we're to be the king's friends, we'd be worth more as friends with our weapons in *our* hands rather than in someone else's, and if we're to be his enemies, we'd be more effective enemies with our weapons in *our* hands rather than in someone else's.'

'All right,' said Phalinus, 'we shall take this message back to the king. But he also told us to tell you that there will be a truce if you remain here, but war if you advance or retreat. So please respond to this too. What message shall I deliver to the king? That you will stay where you are and let there be a truce, or is it to be war?'

'On this matter', Clearchus said, 'you can tell him that we agree with him.'

'What do you mean?' asked Phalinus.

'That if we stay there will be a truce, but if we advance or retreat, there will be war,' said Clearchus.

Phalinus repeated his question: 'Am I to report truce or war?' And Clearchus repeated his answer: 'Truce if we stay, war if we advance or retreat.' But he gave no hint of what he was going to do.

[2] Phalinus and his companions went away, and Procles and Chirisophus arrived from Ariaeus—without Meno, who had stayed with Ariaeus. The message they brought from Ariaeus was that there were many Persians more noble than himself who would not tolerate his being king. 'But if you want to join him for the journey home', the messengers said, 'he asks you to come tonight. Otherwise, he says, he'll set off early tomorrow morning.'

'Here's the situation,' said Clearchus. 'If we come, it will be as you say; if we don't come, do whatever you think will be best for you.' But he did not tell them either what he was going to do.

By then the sun was setting. Clearchus summoned the generals and company commanders to a meeting and spoke to them more or less as follows: 'My friends, when I was sacrificing to see whether we should attack the king, the omens were not good. And, as it turns out, it makes good sense that they were not favourable, because I have now discovered that between us and the king there lies the Tigris. This is a navigable river: we would need boats to cross it, but we don't have any boats. However, we can't stay where we are either, because we have no way of getting provisions here. But the omens strongly supported the idea of going to join Cyrus' friends. What you must do, then, is go back to your quarters and make the best meal you can out of what you have. When the horn gives the signal for rest,* pack up your belongings. When it gives the second signal, load up the yoke-animals. At the third signal, follow the group in front of you, with your yoke-animals by the river and your hoplites on the outside.'

The meeting then broke up and the generals and company commanders went and carried out their orders. From then on, Clearchus took command and the rest obeyed—not because they had elected him to this position, but because he was plainly the only one with the mentality of a leader, while the rest were untried.

During the night, Miltocythes of Thrace deserted to the king and took with him about 40 cavalrymen and about 300 Thracian foot soldiers, but the rest carried out Clearchus' instructions and followed his lead. They reached the first staging area around midnight and found Ariaeus and his army there. With the men halted under arms, the Greek generals and company commanders met with Ariaeus. The Greeks and Ariaeus, joined by his senior officers, swore an oath that neither side would betray the other and that they would remain allies; the barbarians also swore that they would act as guides, without treachery. After swearing this oath, they sacrificed a bull, a wolf, a boar, and a ram, letting the blood flow into a shield, where the Greeks dipped a sword and the barbarians a spear.

After this exchange of pledges, Clearchus said: 'Ariaeus, do please tell us, since we're all going to make the same journey, what you think about the route. Do you think we should take the same route back that we came by, or do you have an alternative route in mind which you feel would be better?'

'If we were to return by the same route,' Ariaeus replied, 'we'd starve to death. We're out of provisions already, and even on our way here the land offered us nothing for the last seventeen stages—or we used up what little there was as we passed through. So our plan is to take a route which is longer but will keep us in provisions. But we have to make the first stages of the march as long as we can, so as to put as much distance as possible between us and the king's army. I mean, once we've got two or three days' march ahead of him, it will be impossible for him to catch us up, because he won't dare to follow us with a small force, and a large force will slow him down. And he too may well be short of provisions. Anyway,' he concluded, 'this is my view.'

This plan allowed for only two possibilities: they could either slip away unseen or they could outdistance the enemy. But Fortune had a better plan in mind. They set out at daybreak with the sun on their right, and calculated that they would reach some Babylonian villages as the sun was setting. These calculations proved correct, but late in the afternoon they thought they saw some enemy horsemen. Those of the Greeks who happened to be out of formation ran to rejoin their lines, Ariaeus (who was travelling on a cart because he was wounded) got down and buckled on his breastplate, and the members of his retinue did likewise. But while they were arming themselves, the scouts who had been sent on ahead returned and reported that they were not enemy horsemen, but grazing yoke-animals. Everyone immediately realized that the king had made his camp somewhere near by, and in fact smoke was visible from villages in the middle distance.

Clearchus refused to advance against the enemy because, even apart from the lateness of the hour, he knew that his men were tired and short of food. But he also refused to change direction, because he was taking care to avoid any impression of flight. So he carried straight on and just as the sun was setting he and the vanguard reached the nearest villages, from which the king's army had stolen even the timbers from the houses, and set up camp. The later arrivals, however, came after dark and bivouacked however and wherever they could. In the process they made so much noise, calling out to one another, that even the enemy heard them. The upshot was that the nearest of the enemy troops actually ran away from where they had pitched their tents. This became clear the next day, when there was no longer a single yoke-animal to be seen, nor a camp, nor any trace of smoke anywhere near by. Even the king was apparently terrified at the approach of the army, as his actions the following day clearly showed.

During the night, however, fear gripped the Greeks too, and along with fear there arose, of course, a din and commotion. Now, Tolmides of Elis, the best herald of the time, happened to be there with Clearchus, so Clearchus told him to call for silence and then make the following announcement: 'Your commanding officers proclaim that whoever gives us the name of the man who let the ass loose among the weapons will receive as a reward a talent of silver.'* This announcement made the men realize that their fear was groundless and that their leaders were safe. At dawn the following day Clearchus ordered the Greeks to arm themselves and take up the same positions they had held during the battle.

[3] Although on the previous day the king had ordered the Greeks, by messenger, to surrender their weapons, he now sent heralds at

sunrise to negotiate a truce—and so revealed, as I mentioned above, that he was terrified by the approach of the Greeks. The heralds came up to the sentries and asked to see the Greek leaders. The sentries conveyed their request and Clearchus—who happened at that moment to be inspecting the ranks—told the sentries to tell the heralds to wait until he had time to see them. Once he had arranged the troops so that they would make a fine display as a closely packed phalanx from whichever direction one looked, with none of the men who lacked arms or armour visible from the outside, he summoned the messengers. He went up to meet them with a retinue of his best-looking and best-armed soldiers, and he told the other generals to do the same.

He approached the messengers and asked what they wanted. They replied that they had come to discuss a truce, and that they would be qualified to deliver the king's message to the Greeks and the Greeks' response to the king. 'Tell the king, then,' Clearchus said, 'that we must first fight. For there is no food for our morning meal and it would be a bold man indeed who would negotiate with Greeks about a truce without having supplied them with their morning meal.' The messengers then rode away, but they returned so quickly that the king, or at any rate someone who had been made responsible for these negotiations, must have been near by. They said that the king considered their demand reasonable and that they had brought guides with them who would show them where they could get provisions, provided that a truce had been concluded. Clearchus asked whether the truce would apply only to the men who were coming and going, or to everyone else as well. 'To everyone,' they replied, 'as long as the king has received your answer.'

On hearing this, Clearchus asked them to retire and talked things over with his advisers. They decided to conclude the truce quickly,† so that they could go and get supplies without being harassed. But Clearchus said, 'I agree, but I'm not in a hurry to deliver the news. I shall delay until the messengers start to worry that we might refuse the offer of a truce. Mind you,' he said, 'I suppose our men will feel the same fear.' When he felt that the right time had come, he told the messengers that he accepted the truce and asked to be taken straight away to the provisions.

Despite the truce, Clearchus still had the men march in battle order, following their guides, and he personally took charge of the rear. They kept coming across water-filled trenches and canals which were uncrossable without bridges, but they used fallen palm trees to make causeways, and cut others down themselves. This situation gave one the opportunity to observe Clearchus at work as a leader. He carried a spear in his left hand and a stick in his right, and if he had occasion to think that there was some shirking going on among the crews assigned to construct a causeway, he would single out the appropriate person and beat him.* At the same time, he would step into the mud himself and lend a hand, which shamed everyone into working just as hard as him. The construction work had been assigned to men under the age of thirty, but the sight of Clearchus hard at work made the older men join in too. Clearchus was in a particular hurry because he suspected that the trenches were not always this full of water; after all, it was not the season for irrigating the plain. He suspected that the king had released the water over the plain as a way of making the Greeks think that their way was riddled with obstacles.*

So they made their way to some villages where their guides indicated that they could get provisions. These villages had plenty of grain, and palm wine, and a vinegary drink made by boiling palm sap. As for the actual dates, those of the quality one can find in Greece were kept for slaves, while special ones were reserved for the masters: they were astonishingly beautiful and large, and looked just like amber. Then there were others which they dried and put aside for later use as sweets. These sweets made a tasty accompaniment to wine too, but gave one a headache. This was also the occasion when the men first ate the cabbage of the palm.* Most of them were astonished not only at its appearance but also by its peculiar taste; but it too was very likely to give one a headache. Once the cabbage had been removed from a palm, the whole tree tended to wither.

During their three days there, Tissaphernes came from the Great King, along with the king's wife's brother,* three other Persians, and a large number of slaves as their attendants. Tissaphernes, speaking through a translator, was the first to address the meeting they held with the Greek generals. 'Men of Greece,' he said, 'I myself live close to your homeland. When I saw all the troubles you had run into, I thought it would be wonderful if I could somehow get permission from the king to take you safely home to Greece. For I imagine that I would earn not only your thanks but the gratitude of the whole of Greece as well. Bearing this in mind, I kept asking the king for permission. I reminded him that he owed me a favour, because I was the first to tell him that Cyrus was mounting an expedition against him, because I brought reinforcements along with the message, and because I was the only one of the commanders deployed against the Greeks who did not turn and flee. In fact, I reminded him, I actually broke through your lines and joined forces with him in your camp,* where he found himself after killing Cyrus, and I pursued Cyrus' barbarian corps with the help of these men whom you now see here with me, who are his most faithful servants. He promised me that he would think about it, and he told me to come and ask you why you had joined a campaign against him. I would advise you to give him a prudent answer, because that will make it easier for me to get for you whatever benefits I can from him.'

The Greeks retired to think about their response and then, with Clearchus as their spokesman, they gave the following reply: 'We did not assemble with the intention of making war on the king, nor were we marching against the king. As you know as well as anyone, Cyrus kept coming up with various pretexts, because he wanted to find you unprepared and he wanted us to accompany him all the way here. Eventually, we could see that his situation was desperate, and then we felt that both gods and men would despise us if we let him down, because earlier we had let him be our benefactor. But now that Cyrus is dead, we are not challenging the king for his throne, nor do we have any reason to want to harm the king's territory or kill him. We would rather make our way home without any harassment, but if anyone initiates hostilities against us we will defend ourselves, with the help of the gods, to the best of our ability. However, we will also do our best to surpass the generosity of anyone who takes the lead in helping us.'

After this speech by Clearchus, Tissaphernes said: 'I shall take this message of yours to the king, and I shall bring back his for you. Let the truce remain in force until I return, and in the meantime we shall sell you your provisions.'

Tissaphernes did not return the next day, which worried the Greeks, but he turned up the day after that with the news that he had got permission from the king to keep the Greeks safe, even though the idea had met with vociferous disagreement from those who thought the king was demeaning himself in letting people who had marched against him go free. And at the end of his speech he said: 'And now please accept our assurances: we will make sure that you are unmolested as you travel through our territory; we will guide you back to Greece without treachery; we will sell you your provisions, and wherever we don't we will let you take what you need from the countryside. But for your part you must swear that you will march as though you were passing through friendly territory, without damaging it in any way; that you will take food and drink from it only when we fail to supply you with goods for sale; and that when we do provide a market you will buy your provisions rather than getting them in any other way.'

These terms were agreed upon, oaths were exchanged, and Tissaphernes and the king's wife's brother shook hands on the deal with the Greek generals and company commanders. Then Tissaphernes said: 'I'm going to go back to the king now, but I shall return when I've got what I want. I will be all equipped and ready to guide you back to Greece and, for my part, to return to my own province.'

[4] After this the Greeks and Ariaeus, who had made their camps near one another, waited more than twenty days for Tissaphernes to return. While they were waiting, Ariaeus was joined by his brothers and all the rest of his family, and some of his men were visited by their Persian friends and relatives. These Persians tried to raise their friends' morale, and some brought hand-tokens* from the king, to assure them that he would not hold any of their past actions against them, including joining Cyrus' campaign. With all this going on, it became clear that Ariaeus and his men were less committed to the Greeks, and this was one of the reasons why most of the Greeks were becoming unhappy about their allies. They kept coming up to Clearchus and his fellow generals and saying: 'What are we waiting for? Isn't it clear that the king's highest priority is to destroy us, to deter any other Greeks from campaigning against the Great King? At the moment he's tempting us to stay because his army is scattered, but once it has been reassembled, he's bound to attack us. Perhaps he's digging a trench somewhere, or building a wall, to make our route impassable. He's not just going to sit back happily and let us return to Greece with the news that, for all our small numbers, we defeated the king's army close to his headquarters, made him a laughing stock, and then left.'

Book Two

'I'm aware of all this,' Clearchus would say in response to these remarks, 'but it's my view that if we leave now our departure will be taken as an act of war and a violation of the truce. Moreover, and most importantly, no one will sell us supplies or let us stock up on provisions anywhere. Then again, we shall have no one to guide us, and as soon as we adopt this plan Ariaeus will abandon us. The upshot will be that we'll have no friends left; even those who were our friends before will be our enemies. Then there may be other rivers we need to cross—I don't know about that, but we do know that the Euphrates cannot be crossed in the face of hostile resistance. Also, suppose we have to fight: we have no cavalry on our side, but the enemy has a great many horsemen of outstanding ability. This means that if we win we won't be able to kill anyone, and if we lose we won't be able to save anyone.* Anyway, for my part, and bearing in mind all the support the king has, I fail to see why he would need to swear an oath, shake hands on it, perjure himself before the gods, and destroy the trust both Greeks and barbarians might have in his assurances, if he really wanted to kill us.' This is the kind of response Clearchus gave over and over again.

Meanwhile Tissaphernes returned at the head of his own troops, as if he were intending to go back home, and Orontas arrived with his forces too. Orontas was also taking the king's daughter with him, to be his wife.* Then at last they set off, with Tissaphernes taking the lead and making sure there were provisions for sale. Ariaeus, with Cyrus' barbarian corps, marched along with Tissaphernes and Orontas, and made camp with them too. The Greeks viewed the Persians with suspicion and marched by themselves, with their own guides. The Greeks and the Persians also made their camps each day a parasang or more apart from one another, and both sides took the kind of precautions against each other that they would against hostile forces—which of course increased their mutual mistrust. Sometimes, in fact, when they were collecting wood and fodder and so on from the same place, blows were exchanged, which did nothing to heal the rift between them.

Three days of travel brought them to and then past the so-called Median Wall.* The wall, which is not far from Babylon, was built out of baked bricks bedded in asphalt; it was twenty feet wide and a hundred feet high, and was said to be twenty parasangs long. During the next two stages they covered eight parasangs and crossed two canals, one by bridge and the other by a pontoon made from seven boats. The canals started at the Tigris and in their turn fed trenches which had been excavated all over the land. These trenches started large and then got smaller, until finally there were little irrigation channels, such as one finds in millet fields in Greece.

So they reached the Tigris. Near the river—fifteen stades away— was a large, populous city called Sittace.* The Greeks set up camp next to the city, close to a park which was large, beautiful, and thickly wooded with a variety of trees; the barbarians crossed the river and could not be seen. That evening, after they had eaten, Proxenus and Xenophon happened to be strolling in front of the place where the weapons were stacked, when a man came up to the sentries and asked them where he could find Proxenus or Clearchus. He did not ask for Meno,* despite the fact that he had come from Ariaeus, Meno's guest-friend. Proxenus identified himself as the person he was look- ing for and the man said: 'I was sent here by Ariaeus and Artaozus, who were trusted advisers of Cyrus and are on your side. They suggest that you take precautions against a possible night attack by the barbarians. There's a sizeable force in the nearby park. And they recommend that you post guards on the bridge across the Tigris, because Tissaphernes intends to destroy it during the night, if he can, to prevent you crossing it and to leave you trapped between the river and the canal.'

After hearing the man's message, they took him to Clearchus and told him what he had said. Clearchus was deeply disturbed and became very frightened, but a young man who was there thought it over and pointed out that it did not make sense to launch an attack *and* to destroy the bridge. 'After all,' he said, 'the attackers are bound either to win or to lose. If they win, why would they have to destroy the bridge? Even if there were lots of bridges, we still wouldn't be able to escape and save ourselves. On the other hand, if we win, they won't be able to escape if the bridge has been destroyed. Also, if the bridge has been destroyed, none of all their men on the far side of the river will be able to come to their assistance.'

Clearchus then asked the messenger how much land there was between the Tigris and the canal, and the man replied that there was a lot of land, with villages and even a number of sizeable towns. Then everyone realized that the barbarians had underhand motives in sending the man: they were worried about the Greeks destroying the bridge and staying on the island with the Tigris and the canal to either side as their defences, and with supplies available from the extensive, fertile land (which even had people already living there who could cultivate it). Moreover, the region could also become a place of refuge for rebels against the king.

The Greeks then began to settle down for the night, but they did post guards on the bridge. No one attacked them from any quarter, however, and the guards reported that not one enemy soldier approached the bridge. At daybreak they crossed the bridge (which was made of thirty-seven boats) with extreme caution, because some of the Greeks with Tissaphernes had told them that they would be attacked during the crossing. But this turned out not to be true. What did happen while they were crossing, however, was that Glous appeared, accompanied by some other men, to check that they were crossing the river. After seeing that they were, he rode off.

The next leg was a four-day march of twenty parasangs that took them from the Tigris to the Physcus river,* which was a plethron wide and had a bridge over it. There was a large city there called Opis, and near this city the Greeks were met by the illegitimate brother of Cyrus and Artaxerxes, who had come from Susa and Ecbatana at the head of a large army of reinforcements, apparently for the king. He halted his army and watched the Greeks as they passed by. Clearchus led the troops two abreast, and also had them halt from time to time. While the front sections of the army were halted, the pause inevitably ran back through the entire army, and the upshot was that even the Greeks themselves got the impression of an enormous army, and the watching Persian was astounded.

The next leg was a six-day march of thirty parasangs through the Median desert that brought them to the villages belonging to Parysatis,* the mother of Cyrus and the king. In order to mock the memory of Cyrus, Tissaphernes allowed the Greeks to take whatever they wanted from these villages, except slaves. But there was plenty of grain there, and sheep and goats, and other goods. The next leg was a four-day march of twenty parasangs, keeping the Tigris on their left. During the first stage there was on the far side of the river a large and prosperous city called Caenae, from which the barbarians brought over bread, cheese, and wine on rafts made from animal hides.

[5] They next reached the Zapatas river, which was four plethra wide. During their three days there they had the feeling that the

Persians had designs against them, but nothing actually happened. Clearchus therefore decided to meet Tissaphernes, to see if he could dissolve the tension before it led to open warfare between them. He sent a messenger to ask for a meeting and Tissaphernes promptly invited him to come.

At the meeting, Clearchus said: 'Tissaphernes, I am well aware that we have sworn under oath and pledged that neither of us will initiate hostilities against the other, but I can see that you are taking the kinds of precautions against us that you would against enemies and this has made us take equivalent counter-measures. However, my investigations have produced no evidence that you are trying to injure us and I know for sure that we have no such scheme in mind either. So I wanted to talk things over with you, to see whether we could banish this mutual mistrust. For I know that in the past on various occasions lies and mistrust have made people so frightened of one another that, wanting to act before the others did, they have done irreparable harm to people who had no harmful intentions or desires. Discussion is, I think, the best cure for such misunderstandings, and that's why I've come here. I want to prove to you that your suspicions about us are unfounded.

'The critical first point is that enmity between us is ruled out by the oaths we have sworn before the gods. In my opinion, anyone who knows that he has violated such oaths is bound to suffer. After all, I don't see how anyone could run fast enough to escape the hostility of the gods, or could find anywhere dark enough to hide or strong enough to keep him safe. Everything everywhere is subject to the gods and no matter where or what one is, the gods are in control. Anyway, this is what I think about our oaths and the gods, into whose hands we entrusted our contract of friendship. As for us humans, I believe that at the moment we have no greater benefactor than you. With you, we easily travel every road, cross every river, and keep ourselves supplied with provisions. Without you, every road is shrouded in the darkness of our ignorance, every river is hard to cross, and every crowd is frightening—and yet there is nothing more frightening than solitude, which teems with uncertainties. And what would happen if, in a fit of madness, we were to kill you? Our dead benefactor would be replaced by the most dangerous opponent of all, the king, who would be waiting to take us on.*

'Then again, let me tell you that if I tried to do you the slightest harm, I would be robbing myself of so many high hopes for the future. I wanted to be close to Cyrus because I thought there was no one alive who was better placed to help those he wanted to help. But I can now see that, in addition to preserving your own province, you have also gained Cyrus' resources and his territory, and that all the might of the king, which Cyrus found deployed against him, is backing you up. Under these circumstances, is there anyone mad enough not to want to be your friend?

'But let me also tell you why I hope that you too will want to be on good terms with us. I know that the Mysians are causing you trouble, but I think that with my present army I could make them your subjects. I also know that the Pisidians are troublesome, and I hear that the same goes for a number of other peoples and tribes, but I think that I could stop them constantly bothering you and spoiling your contentment. As for the Egyptians, who I understand make you particularly furious, I can't imagine what army could help you punish them more effectively than the one I now have under my command. Then there are all your neighbours: it's true that you could choose to be on the best possible terms with them, but if any of them caused you trouble, you could behave like their master, with us working for you. We wouldn't serve you just for pay, but also because we would be properly grateful to you for having kept us alive.

'When I bear all this in mind, I find your mistrust of us extraordinary. In fact, there's nothing I'd like more than to be given the name of the man who's such a clever talker that he can persuade you by mere words that we are planning to do you harm.'

Once Clearchus had finished, Tissaphernes replied as follows: 'I'm delighted to hear you making such good sense, Clearchus. After all, as long as you hold these views, you'd be working against your own interests too, I think, if you were to intrigue against me. But now listen to my response, because I want you to appreciate that you too have no good reason to mistrust either the king or me. If we wanted to do away with you, do we strike you as being short of cavalry or foot soldiers or military equipment? Don't you think we have enough of them to harm you without being in any danger of suffering the same in return? Do you perhaps think that we are short of suitable places from which to launch an attack against you? Can't you see how vast these plains are and how arduous your journey across them is even under favourable conditions? Can't you see the huge mountain ranges you're going to have to cross, where we could occupy the passes before you got there and stop you getting through? Look at the size of the rivers, where we could regulate how many of you we wanted to fight. You wouldn't even be able to get across some of these rivers at all, without us to ferry you. Even if we were defeated at all these places, fire of course still defeats crops. We could burn up the crops and use starvation as a weapon of war against you, and you could not fight against that, however brave you were.

'You can see all the resources we can wield against you as instruments of war, without the slightest risk to ourselves. Why, then, given all these possibilities, would we choose the only one which is immoral in the eyes of the gods and contemptible in the eyes of men? It is those who are in dire straits, utterly without resources and stratagems—and even then they must be degenerates—who are willing to achieve their goals by taking the name of the gods in vain and by breaking their promises to men. We are not so obtuse, Clearchus; we are not so stupid.

'Why, then, if it was possible for us to destroy you, did we not go ahead and do it? The reason for this, I can tell you, was my desire to win the Greeks' trust. When Cyrus marched up country with your mercenaries, he put his faith in the fact that he was your paymaster; I want to make the journey back with the same corps of mercenaries, but with the security of knowing that I have done you good. As for all the ways in which you can be useful to me, you have mentioned some, but only I know the most important point. Only the king may wear the royal crown upright on his head, but perhaps, with your support, someone else too might easily so wear the crown that is in his heart.'*

Clearchus thought Tissaphernes was telling the truth, so he said: 'And what about those who are trying by their lies to make us enemies, despite all the good reasons we have for friendship? Don't they deserve to suffer the ultimate penalty?'

'Yes,' Tissaphernes said, 'and if you and your generals and company commanders would like to come and see me, I will disclose the names of those who have been warning me of your "plots" against me and my army.'

'I'll bring all my officers,' Clearchus replied, 'and I'll tell you too the sources of the reports I've been hearing about you.'

After this conversation Tissaphernes, as a gesture of friendship,

invited Clearchus to stay with him for a while. He had Clearchus join
him for the evening meal, and the next day Clearchus returned to the
Greek camp. He made it clear that he had, in his opinion, got on very
well with Tissaphernes, and he repeated what Tissaphernes had
been saying. He went on to say that the officers Tissaphernes had
invited should go, and that any Greeks who were convicted of trying
to set Tissaphernes and him against each other ought to be punished
as traitors who were working against the Greeks' best interests. He
suspected that it was Meno who was trying to stir up trouble,
because he knew that while Meno had been with Ariaeus he had met
Tissaphernes, and he was aware that Meno was trying to arouse
opposition against him and was looking for a way to win Tissaphernes'
friendship by gaining control over the entire army. Clearchus, however, really wanted to have the whole army loyal to him, and to get
rid of the troublemakers. Some of the soldiers began to argue that
the company commanders and generals should not all go, and that
Tissaphernes was not to be trusted; but Clearchus was strongly
insistent* and eventually got them to agree that five generals and
twenty company commanders could go. About 200 soldiers from the
rest of the army also went along, with the intention of buying
provisions.

When they reached the entrance to Tissaphernes' tent, the
generals—Proxenus of Boeotia, Meno of Thessaly, Agias of Arcadia,
Clearchus of Sparta, and Socrates of Achaea—were invited inside,
while the company commanders waited by the entrance. A short
while later, at a single signal, those who were inside were seized and
those who were outside were murdered.* Then some of the barbarian
horsemen rode across the plain, killing every Greek they came
across, whether free man or slave. The Greeks in their camp were
surprised to see all this riding about, but they did not know what the
Persians were doing, until Nicarchus of Arcadia managed to escape.
He reached the Greek camp, holding his entrails in his hands from a
wound to the guts, and told them all that had happened. The Greeks
were terrified, and they ran to get their weapons, thinking that an
attack on the camp was imminent.

Not all the Persians came, however—only Ariaeus, Artaozus, and
Mithradates, who had been Cyrus' most trusted friends. The
Greeks' translator said that he also saw with them a man whom he
recognized as Tissaphernes' brother. They were accompanied by

about three hundred other Persians as well, wearing breastplates. After approaching the Greek camp, they said they had a message from the king and they called on any surviving Greek officers to come up and receive it. Before long two Greek generals—Cleanor of Orchomenus and Sophaenetus of Stymphalus—rode out from the camp with a bodyguard; they were joined by Xenophon of Athens, who wanted to find out what had happened to Proxenus. Chirisophus was not there: he and some others had gone to a village to stock up on supplies.

When they had halted within hearing distance, Ariaeus spoke as follows: 'Men of Greece, Clearchus was found to be perjuring himself and breaking the truce: he has paid for these crimes with his death. Proxenus and Meno,* however, are high in the king's favour, because they denounced Clearchus' intrigues. As for you, the king demands the surrender of your weapons, on the grounds that they are rightly his, because they belonged to Cyrus, who was his slave.'

Cleanor of Orchomenus said: 'Ariaeus, you are an unspeakable villain—you and all the rest of you who used to be Cyrus' friends. Do you not feel shame, before either gods or men, for having joined Tissaphernes, the most godless evildoer imaginable, in betraying us, after swearing that our friends would be your friends and our enemies your enemies? Do you not feel shame for having killed the very men with whom you swore these oaths and for treacherously marching with the enemy against the rest of us?'

'No, I don't,' Ariaeus replied, 'because it has been known for a while now that Clearchus was scheming against Tissaphernes and Orontas, and against all of us who are on their side.'

At this point Xenophon said: 'Well, if Clearchus really was trying to break the truce in violation of his oaths, he has paid for it. Death, after all, is the appropriate penalty for perjurers. But Proxenus and Meno are your benefactors and generals of ours, so please have them come here. It stands to reason that as friends both to you and to us they will endeavour to come up with a plan which is in the best interests of both sides.' At this, the barbarians talked among themselves for a long time and then left without giving any kind of reply.

[6] The Greek generals who were captured as described were taken to the king and beheaded.* One of them, Clearchus, was universally held by those who knew him to have been not just good at warfare, but absolutely devoted to it. For example, he stayed around while the

Spartans were at war with the Athenians,* but after the peace treaty he persuaded his fellow citizens that Greeks were suffering at Thracian hands, and once he had managed to get his way with the ephors,* he set sail to make war on the Thracians who live beyond the Chersonese and Perinthus. For some reason the ephors changed their mind after he had already left, but when they tried to recall him from the Isthmus, he stopped obeying their orders and sailed off to the Hellespont.* For this disobedience, he was then condemned to death by the Spartan authorities. An exile by this time from his native land, he approached Cyrus and won him over with arguments which have been recorded elsewhere.* Cyrus gave him 10,000 darics, but Clearchus did not change and spend the money on a life of ease: he used it to raise an army and make war on the Thracians. Once he had defeated the Thracians in a pitched battle, he plundered their land and carried on fighting them until Cyrus needed his army; then he left Thrace to go to war again, this time with Cyrus.

This strikes me as the behaviour of a man who was devoted to warfare. He could have lived in peace without compromising either his dignity or his safety, but he chose war; he could have lived a life of ease, but he preferred hard work, as long as it involved fighting; he could have lived a risk-free, moneyed life, but he preferred to whittle away his fortune on warfare. Just as other men are happy to spend money on their boyfriend or on some other pleasure, so he spent his on warfare. That is how devoted he was to it. At the same time he also gave the impression of being good at warfare, in the sense that he never hesitated to face danger, he was ready to march against the enemy at any hour of the day or night, and he was level-headed even in the most dangerous conditions, as everyone who served with him on any of his campaigns tended to agree.

He was also generally regarded as a good commander, in so far as that is possible for someone with his temperament. At any rate, he was as good as anyone at making sure that his men could get provisions and at procuring them, and he was also good at impressing upon his companions that Clearchus was to be obeyed. His severity helped him in this: he looked stern, had a harsh voice, and used to hand out brutal punishments—sometimes in anger, which meant that he occasionally regretted what he had done. But he also used to punish on principle, because he believed that an army without discipline was useless. In fact, one of his recorded sayings was that a soldier had to be more frightened of his commanding officer than of the enemy if he was to do guard duty, refrain from disputes with his friends, or attack the enemy without finding reasons not to.

At times of danger, then, his men were prepared to obey him unhesitatingly and never elected anyone else to lead them. They said that at such times his sternness manifested itself as joy† and his severity seemed to be self-assurance in the face of the enemy, so that it did not come across as harsh, but gave them a feeling of security. However, when they were out of danger and could go and serve under other commanders, many of his men deserted him, because he was not an agreeable person; his severity and savagery made his men feel the same about him as schoolboys do about their teacher. In other words, men never followed him out of affection or loyalty: he was surrounded by people who had been assigned to him by their cities or had been compelled to join him by poverty or some other pressing need, and he demanded absolute obedience from them. But once they began with his help to defeat their enemies, the factors that made his men efficient soldiers turned out to be important. For it was possible for them to be confident in the face of the enemy and their fear of being punished by him engendered discipline in them. These were his qualities as a leader, but it was widely held that he was not very good at being led by others. He was about fifty years old at the time of his death.

As for Proxenus of Boeotia, even as a boy he wanted to be capable of achieving great things, and he paid Gorgias of Leontini* to help him fulfil this desire. After he had spent time with him, he considered himself capable not only of leadership, but of helping any powerful friends he might acquire as much as they could help him. And so he joined Cyrus on this enterprise because he expected to gain from it fame, power, and wealth. But although he longed for these things, it was also perfectly clear that he was not prepared to compromise his integrity to get them; in his view, he should get them fairly and honourably, or not at all. He was a good leader of men of the better sort, but he failed to inspire rank-and-file soldiers with respect or fear; in fact, he was more in awe of his men than they, his subordinates, were of him. Also, he was obviously more afraid of being disliked by his men than his men were of disobeying him. He thought that, in order to be and to be acknowledged as a good leader, it was enough for him to praise his men when they did well and to deny praise to those who did wrong. This is why he earned the loyalty of those of his companions who were men of the better sort, while unscrupulous men worked against him and regarded him as easy to manipulate. He was about thirty years old at the time of his death.

As for Meno of Thessaly,* it was obvious that he longed to be rich; he wanted military command because it would bring him a greater share of the spoils, he wanted prestige because it would help him increase his wealth, and he wanted to be on good terms with the most powerful men because then he could avoid being punished for his crimes. He thought that the quickest way for him to achieve his goals was to use perjury, lies, and deceit; in his opinion, openness and truthfulness were synonyms for stupidity. He evidently felt no affection for anyone, and if he claimed to be somebody's friend it soon became clear that he was trying to sabotage him. He never laughed at his enemies, and in conversation he always seemed to be mocking his acquaintances. He never tried to find ways to appropriate his enemies' property, because he thought it hard to get things from people who were on their guard, and he thought he was the only one who knew that it is easiest to take things from friends because they are unguarded. He was frightened of people he found breaking promises and committing crimes, because he regarded them as well protected, and he tried to exploit people who were moral and honest because he regarded them as weak. A man might be proud of being god-fearing, truthful, and just, but Meno was no less proud of his ability to deceive, to invent lies, and to make his friends appear ridiculous; and he always thought of upright people as unsophisticated. If he wanted to get particularly close to someone, he thought that slandering those who were already intimate with that person was the way to achieve his objective. His technique for making his men compliant was to join in their wrongdoing; in fact, he expected to win respect and admiration by showing that he had the ability and the will to do more wrong than anyone else. When someone split up with him, he considered that he had done him a favour if he had not ruined him while they were still intimate.

It is possible to be mistaken about the inner workings of the man's mind, but there are aspects of his life which are public knowledge. While he was still in the bloom of youth,* he managed to secure an appointment as one of the generals of the mercenary corps from

Aristippus, and although Ariaeus was a barbarian, Meno became very close to him, because Ariaeus had a fondness for beautiful young men.† Also, Meno himself, though still a beardless youth, had Tharypas as his boyfriend, although Tharypas was mature enough to have a beard.* Although Meno had done exactly the same as his fellow generals, he was not executed when they were killed for having helped Cyrus on his expedition against the king: he was put to death by the king later than the others and was not beheaded as Clearchus and the rest of the generals were (which is considered to be the swiftest form of execution). As a man with no redeeming features, he was kept alive in constant torment for a year, it is said, before being killed.

Agias of Arcadia and Socrates of Achaea were also put to death. No one ever scorned these men as cowards in war or found fault with them in matters of friendship. They were both about thirty-five years old.

BOOK THREE

[1] After the capture of the generals and deaths of the company commanders and the soldiers who had gone with them, the Greeks reflected on their desperate predicament. They were close to the king's headquarters; they were surrounded on all sides by countless hostile tribes and cities; there was no longer anyone who would sell them provisions; they were at least 10,000 stades from Greece; there was no guide to show them the way; there were uncrossable rivers blocking their route home; even the barbarians who had made the journey up country with Cyrus had betrayed them; and they had been left all alone, without a single horseman in their army, which, they were sure, meant that even if they won a battle they would not kill any of the enemy, while if they lost, not one of them would survive. Weighed down by these depressing thoughts, few of them managed to eat anything that evening and few lit fires; a lot of them spent the night not in their quarters, close to where the weapons were stacked, but wherever they happened to find themselves. But sleep was banished by distress and by longing for homes, parents, wives, and children, whom they no longer expected ever to see again. And so they all passed a restless night.

There was in the army a man called Xenophon, from Athens. He had come along not as a general, nor as a company commander, nor as a soldier, but because Proxenus, a long-standing guest-friend, had invited him to leave home and join him, and had held out the promise of friendship with Cyrus, who was, Proxenus said, more important to him than his homeland. After reading Proxenus' letter, however, Xenophon consulted the famous Socrates of Athens* about whether or not he should go. Socrates thought that friendship with Cyrus might well be actionable in the eyes of the Athenian authorities, because Cyrus was widely believed to have wholeheartedly supported the Spartans in their military operations against the Athenians,* and he advised Xenophon to go to Delphi and consult the god about whether or not he should go.* Xenophon went and asked Apollo which of the gods should receive his sacrifices and prayers to ensure that the journey he had in mind would go honourably and well and to guarantee a safe return after a successfully completed endeavour, and in his response Apollo named the gods to whom he should sacrifice.

Back in Athens, Xenophon reported the oracle's response to Socrates, who told him off for having failed to ask the preliminary question whether it would be better for him to go or to stay—for having already decided that he was going to go, and then asking Apollo how to ensure a successful journey. 'However,' Socrates said, 'since that was the question you put to the god, you had better carry out all his instructions.' So once Xenophon had sacrificed as instructed to the gods named by Apollo he set sail and caught up with Proxenus and Cyrus in Sardis just as they were about to set off up country. Proxenus was very insistent that Xenophon should stay with them, and Cyrus, to whom Xenophon had been introduced, backed Proxenus up with equal enthusiasm and promised to see that Xenophon got home as soon as the campaign was over. An attack on the Pisidians was mentioned as the objective of the expedition.

Xenophon joined the expedition, then, because he had been thoroughly misled as to its purpose—though not by Proxenus, because he was as unaware as the rest of the Greeks, except Clearchus,* that the purpose of the expedition was to attack the king. By the time they reached Cilicia, however, everyone was sure that they were going against the king. Despite their fears about the journey and their lack of enthusiasm, most of the Greeks carried on because they did not want to earn the contempt of one another and of Cyrus. Xenophon was one of those who chose to carry on.

At the time when their situation seemed hopeless, Xenophon was as agitated as everyone else and found sleep impossible. When at last he did fall briefly asleep, he had a dream, in which thunder rumbled and lightning struck his family home and brilliantly illuminated it all. He woke up terrified. From one point of view, he was inclined to put a positive interpretation on the dream, since a great light from Zeus had appeared in the midst of trouble and danger; but from another point of view, he found it alarming, because he assumed that the dream had been sent by Zeus the King,* and the fact that in the dream the fire had cast its light all around suggested that he might not be able to escape from the king's territory, but might be hemmed in on all sides by various difficulties.

But the true meaning of a vision such as this can be judged by the events which followed the dream. What happened was, first, that as soon as he woke up he fell to thinking: 'Why am I lying here? The night is passing and at dawn the enemy will probably arrive. If we fall into the king's hands, we'll inevitably die inglorious deaths, after witnessing all the most ghastly scenes one could possibly imagine and suffering the full range of the most gruesome tortures. Yet no one is showing the slightest interest in defence or doing anything practical about it; we're just lying here as if we were in a position to take it easy. From what other city do I expect a general to come and organize things? Why am I waiting? How old do I have to be?* I won't get any older at all if I just surrender to the enemy today.'

Next, he got up and immediately called together Proxenus' company commanders. When they were all there, he said: 'My friends, I'm finding it as impossible to sleep as I imagine you are; I'm too aware of our situation even to stay lying down any more. After all, it goes without saying that our enemies have made open war on us only because they now think they're good and ready, and none of us has responded by giving the slightest thought to how we might resist them. And yet, if we give in and fall into the king's hands, what can we expect to happen to us? This is the man who mutilated the corpse of his full brother* by cutting off his head and his hand, and who then impaled them on a stake. We have no one to protect us, and we launched this expedition against him with the intention of toppling him from his throne and making him a slave instead, and of killing him if we could—so what can we expect to happen to us? Don't you think he'll stop at nothing in his efforts to make us suffer in agony, so as to deter everyone in the world from marching against him ever again? So we must do all we can to avoid falling into his hands.

'Speaking for myself, whilst the truce was in force, the sight of all their land and its fertility, their plentiful provisions, and all their slaves, livestock, gold, and clothing, constantly made me feel sorry for us and think how lucky the king and his men were. Then, when I considered the situation of our troops and the fact that we couldn't get any of these goods without paying for them—and I was aware that there were only a few of us who had the wherewithal to pay for these things, and I knew that our oaths restricted us from getting our provisions other than by paying for them—when I took all this into account I occasionally found the truce more alarming than the hostilities are now. But it seems to me that when they dissolved the truce they also dissolved their advantage and our helplessness. I mean, now these goods of theirs are there to be won by whichever side proves itself braver, and the judges of the contest are the gods, who, in all likelihood, will be on our side. Why? Because although we've been able to see all these good things, we have resolutely kept our hands off them in accordance with the oaths we made before the gods, while our opponents have broken their oaths. So I think we can enter the contest with far greater confidence than they can. Also, our bodies are better than theirs at putting up with cold and heat and hard work, and our spirits are, thanks to the gods, more courageous. And finally, if the gods grant us victory as they did before, our opponents are easier to wound and kill.*

'Now, the same ideas may well have occurred to others among the Greeks, but, by the gods, let's not wait for others to come and summon us to perform glorious deeds. Let us be the ones who first arouse others to demonstrate their valour. Prove yourselves the best possible officers! Prove yourselves more worthy of command than your commanders! As for me, if you are willing to set out on this course of action, I will gladly follow, but if you make me your leader, I will not refuse on account of my age. No, I think I am at the peak of my ability to defend myself against adversity.'

After this speech by Xenophon, all the officers asked him to take command except for a man called Apollonides, who had a Boeotian accent. He said that the only way they could save themselves was to talk to the king and win him over, if they could, and that it was nonsense to suggest that they had any other options. He had just begun to talk about their helplessness when Xenophon interrupted him and said: 'I can't believe what you're saying, man! Don't you recognize what's right before your eyes? Don't you take in a word you hear? You were there with the rest of us when the king, full of confidence after Cyrus' death, ordered us by messenger to surrender our weapons. When we refused, and instead came and camped fully armed close to him, he sent his representatives, he begged us for a truce, he supplied us with provisions—he bent over backwards to obtain a truce. Then the generals and company commanders did what you're suggesting, and went unarmed to meet him, relying on the truce—and look what happened to them. Are they not at this very moment being beaten, tortured, brutalized, and denied the death their suffering surely makes them long for? Why, if you're aware of all this, do you call it nonsense to suggest that we defend ourselves? Why do you urge us to go to the king again and try to win him over? My friends, I think we should not only banish this oaf from our company, but strip him of his commission, load him up, and use him as a baggage-handler. The fact that he's such a fool, despite being Greek, makes him an embarrassment not just to his homeland but to the whole of Greece.'

At that point Agasias of Stymphalus broke in and said: 'Actually, he doesn't belong in Boeotia or anywhere in Greece: he has both ears pierced, Lydian-style*—I've seen them.' This was true, and they evicted the man from their company. The others went around the various divisions and invited the general (if he was still alive) to a meeting, or the second-in-command (if the general was missing), or any company commanders who had survived. When they had all assembled—by which time it was almost midnight—they sat down in front of the place where the weapons were stacked. There were about a hundred generals and company commanders at the meeting.

Hieronymus of Elis, the oldest of Proxenus' company commanders, was the first to speak. 'Fellow officers,' he said, 'in view of our present circumstances, we decided to meet and to invite you along as well, to see if we can come up with a good plan. Xenophon, why don't you repeat the gist of the speech you made to us?'

So Xenophon said: 'We're all aware, of course, that the king and Tissaphernes have taken as many of us as they could, and they're obviously planning to kill the rest of us if they can. I think we should do everything possible to avoid falling into the hands of the barbarians and to gain the upper hand for ourselves instead. And I want you to understand that this is an absolutely critical moment for all of you, all of those assembled here. Your men are all watching you. If they see you disheartened, you won't have a single brave soldier left; but if you are visibly getting ready to attack the enemy, and you call on the men to do likewise, you can rest assured that they will follow you and will do as you do to the best of their ability—though in truth you should really do better than them, because *you* are generals and *you* are the commanders of divisions and companies. In peacetime you had more money and standing than them; in a time of war like this you should insist on being better than the rank and file, to plan for them, and, if the need arises, to work for them.

'But I think you should start by giving some thought to electing generals and company commanders, as quickly as possible, to replace those who have died. I'm sure this would help the army enormously, because without leaders—if I may be permitted the generalization— nothing ever comes out right or good in any sphere, and certainly not in warfare, where, as is generally acknowledged, discipline makes for survival and lack of discipline has often in the past been responsible for loss of life.

'Once you've appointed as many leaders as you need, I think you'd be doing exactly what the situation demanded if you were to assemble the men and try to inspire them with confidence. You probably noticed as well as I did how miserable they were just now as they were standing down for the night and going off for guard duty, and while they're like this I'm not sure what use they'd be if we should need them at any hour of the day or night. But if their mood is changed, so that they're not thinking just of what's going to happen to them, but also of what they can do to others, they'll be much more confident. I mean, you are aware, of course, that wars are not won by numbers or strength; no, when one side, thanks to the gods, attacks with more confidence, their foes invariably give way before them. And there's something else that I've observed, my friends: in warfare those who seek to stay alive, no matter what it takes, are usually those who die cowardly and ignominious deaths, while those who have realized that death is the common lot of all men, and therefore strive for noble deaths, are those who, in my experience, are somehow more likely to reach old age and to enjoy the time they have while they are alive. This is what we too need to understand at the moment, in the critical situation in which we find ourselves, if we're to be brave men ourselves and if we're to instil courage in the men.'

After Xenophon had finished speaking, Chirisophus said: 'Up until now, Xenophon, I knew nothing about you, except that people had told me you were from Athens; but now I commend your words and your conduct, and I wish we had a lot more men like you, because we'd all benefit from it. But now,' he said, turning to the others, 'let's not waste time. Those of you who need to must go and choose leaders, and afterwards bring the men you've chosen into the middle of the camp. Then we'll assemble all the rest of the troops. Tolmides, the herald, had better be there too.'

With these words Chirisophus, who wanted to get straight on with what needed to be done, rose to his feet, and then commanders were chosen: Timasion of Dardanus instead of Clearchus, Xanthicles of

Achaea instead of Socrates, Cleanor of Arcadia instead of Agias, Philesius of Achaea instead of Meno, and Xenophon of Athens instead of Proxenus.

[2] By the time the election was over it was almost daybreak. At their meeting in the middle of the camp, the officers decided to post sentries and assemble the troops. Once they were all there, Chirisophus of Sparta was the first to get to his feet and address them. 'Men,' he said, 'our situation is difficult. We have lost fine generals, company commanders, and comrades in arms; in addition, Ariaeus and his men, our former allies, have betrayed us. Nevertheless, the situation demands that we prove ourselves men of valour. We must not give in, but we must endeavour to win a glorious victory and save ourselves, if we can; if we cannot, let us at least meet death with honour, and as long as we're alive, let us never fall into the hands of the enemy. For if we do, we will surely meet the kind of suffering I pray the gods may inflict on our enemies.'

Next Cleanor of Orchomenus got up and said: 'Men, the perjury and impiety of the king are plain for you all to see, as is the treachery of Tissaphernes. It was Tissaphernes who said that since he lived on the borders of Greece he would make it his primary objective to save us, and he backed up these words with solemn promises to us. It was he who shook hands to seal his oaths, and it was he who treacherously made prisoners of our generals. And so far from having respect for Zeus, the god of hospitality, he used the very fact that Clearchus had eaten at his table as a way of setting the trap by which he killed our men. And what about Ariaeus? We wanted to make him king, we exchanged assurances that we wouldn't betray one another, and now he too has shown how little he fears the gods. Even though there was no one Cyrus valued more while he was alive, Ariaeus has shown complete contempt for him, after his death, by going over to Cyrus' worst enemies and by trying to harm us, who were Cyrus' friends. These men will, I pray, be punished by the gods, but it's up to us, now that we've seen what they've done, never again to be taken in by them. No, we must fight as effectively as we can and endure whatever fate the gods decide for us.'

Xenophon was the next to stand up. He had put on his most splendid war-gear, because he thought that if the gods gave them victory, victory deserved the finest display, and that if he was to die, it was right for him, since he had demanded the best gear, to be dressed in it when he met his death. 'Cleanor has reminded you', he began, 'of the barbarians' lies and treachery, of which you are, I'm sure, well aware. Now, if we choose to renew our friendship with the barbarians, we can only feel deep pessimism, given what happened before our very eyes to our generals when they entrusted themselves to them. However, if we intend to use our weapons to punish them for what they've done and in the future to wage all-out war against them, then, with the help of the gods, we have plenty of reasons to be optimistic about our survival.'

Just as he was saying this, someone sneezed.* Hearing the sneeze, all the soldiers simultaneously did homage to the god,* and Xenophon said: 'Men, just as we were discussing our safety we were vouchsafed a portent from Zeus the Saviour. I move that we should make a vow that as soon as we reach friendly territory we will sacrifice to Zeus the Saviour in gratitude for our salvation, and should also undertake to sacrifice to all the other gods to the best of our ability. If you agree with this motion, raise your hand.' Everyone raised their hands. They made their vows and chanted a paean, and once the gods' business had been duly settled, Xenophon resumed his speech.

'I was saying', he went on, 'that we have plenty of reasons to be optimistic about our survival. Above all, this is because we have stayed true to the oaths we swore before the gods, while our enemies have lied and have broken the truce, in violation of their oaths. Under these circumstances, the gods are likely to line up against our enemies and to fight on our side—and the gods are capable of humbling the strong in an instant and, should they choose to do so, of effortlessly delivering the weak even from terrible danger.

'Second, I'm going to remind you of the danger faced by our ancestors, because I want you to understand not only that you have to be brave, but also that, thanks to the gods, brave men survive even extreme peril. When the Persians and their allies invaded in enormous numbers with the intention of obliterating Athens, the Athenians heroically stood up to them all by themselves and beat them.* They had made a vow to Artemis that they would offer her in sacrifice a goat for every enemy soldier they killed, but they couldn't find enough goats and so they decided to sacrifice five hundred a year, and they are still carrying out this annual sacrifice.* Later, Xerxes raised an incalculably huge army and attacked Greece, but on that occasion too, on land and sea,* our ancestors defeated the ancestors of the men we face. The trophies* still stand, as visible proof of their prowess, but the most important evidence is the freedom of the cities where you were born and raised. For you pay homage to no mortal master, but only to the gods.

'This is what your ancestors were like. I don't of course mean to imply that you are lesser men than they were: after all, not many days have passed since you took the field against the descendants of those same Persians and, with the help of the gods, defeated them despite being heavily outnumbered. You proved your courage on that occasion, when the issue was Cyrus' throne, but now you are fighting for your own survival, so it would be reasonable to expect a far higher degree of bravery and determination. You should also be more confident when facing the enemy, because before the previous battle you didn't know anything about them; nevertheless—and even though you could see that their numbers were beyond counting—you summoned up your ancestral courage and heroically attacked them. By now, however, you know what they're like, and you know that even if they vastly outnumber you they aren't prepared to stand their ground against you; so what possible reason can you still have to fear them?

'There's also no need for you to consider yourselves worse off because you've lost your former allies, Ariaeus' troops, to the other side. Ariaeus' men abandoned us and fled at the approach of troops we defeated, which proves that they are even more cowardly than troops we can defeat. It's far better to have troops who are habitually the first to flee on the side of one's opponents than on our side.

'If any of you are at all concerned about our lack and the enemy's abundance of cavalry, you should bear in mind that 10,000 horsemen are no different from 10,000 men. No one ever got bitten or kicked to death in a battle by a horse; men are responsible for everything that happens in a battle. And we are supported far more securely than their horsemen: they are precariously balanced on their horses, frightened of falling off as well as of us, while we stand on the ground, which means that we can deliver more power when we strike anyone coming at us and are far more likely to hit our targets. Men on horseback have only one advantage: they are more likely to save their lives when they flee than we are.

'You may not find the prospect of battle disheartening, but still be worried because Tissaphernes is not going to guide you and the king is not going to sell you provisions. If so, you should consider whether it's better to have as our guide Tissaphernes, a man known to be plotting against us, or any prisoners we happen to capture, who we can order to act as our guides and who will know that any mistakes they make which affect us will also affect their lives and limbs. And as for provisions, is it better for us to buy them from the market provided by the barbarians, where only small quantities are available at a high price (when we don't have money anyway), or is it better to defeat the barbarians and then take provisions ourselves, in whatever quantity each of us wants?

'Suppose you recognize that in these respects we're better off, but you think that the rivers will prove problematic and that in crossing them you were led into a trap. If so, you should consider whether in fact this was not an act of sheer stupidity on the part of the barbarians, in the sense that all rivers—even those which are impossible to cross far from their sources—become crossable, without even wetting one's knees, as one gets close to their sources.

'Even if the rivers prove to be uncrossable and even if we never find a guide, we still don't need to lose heart. We know the Mysians, and we wouldn't count them braver men than we are, and yet they have a number of prosperous and large towns inside the king's territory. We know that the same goes for the Pisidians, and we've seen with our own eyes how the Lycaonians* have seized fortresses in the plains and cultivate land which belongs to the Persians. Personally, I'd suggest that we shouldn't yet make it obvious that we're setting off home, but should make our arrangements as if we were going to settle here. I'm sure the king would offer the Mysians plenty of guides to escort them out of the country, and plenty of hostages to guarantee his sincerity; if they wanted to leave on four-horse chariots he'd even build a road for them. And I'm sure he'd be three times as pleased to do all this for us, if he saw that we were planning to stay.

'In actual fact, though, I'm afraid that once we've become accustomed to a life of idleness and luxury, and to the company of Median and Persian women and girls, who are tall and beautiful, we'll become as oblivious of our homeward journey as the lotus-eaters were.* So I think it right and proper that our main efforts should be put towards getting back to Greece and our families, so that we can prove to the Greeks that their poverty is self-inflicted. They could bring here those who are now living a hard life there and watch them prosper.

'Men, to the victors belong all the advantages of this land—that goes without saying. But I also need to explain how we can reduce the risks of our journey as much as possible and how, if we have to fight, we can try to make sure that we win. In the first place, I think we should set fire to all our carts, to stop the yoke-animals dictating our strategy and to ensure that we take whatever route best suits the army. In the second place, I think we should also burn our tents, since they're awkward to transport and make no contribution towards either fighting or getting hold of provisions. In the third place, we should get rid of all excess baggage, keeping only what we need for fighting, for food, or for drink. Then we will have as many men as possible under arms and as few as possible carrying baggage. And the basic point is that, as you know, everything that belongs to the losers in a war becomes someone else's property, while if we win we can regard our enemies as our baggage-handlers.

'I turn finally to the issue which I consider to be the most important. You can see that our enemies didn't dare to open hostilities against us until they had made prisoners of our generals. This is because they believed that while we had our leaders, and did what they told us to do, we were capable of getting the better of them, but that, with our leaders in their hands, lack of order and discipline would prove to be our undoing. So our present commanders must be far more vigilant than the previous ones were, and those under their command must be far less unruly and far more obedient to their superiors than they were before. We need to pass a regulation to the effect that whichever of you happens to be near by should help the relevant commander punish any cases of insubordination. This will make a mockery of the enemy's plans, because from today they will see not one but ten thousand Clearchuses, who will prevent the slightest infringement.

'But now it's time to put these ideas into practice, because the enemy may appear at any moment. Those of you who think these ideas are sound should ratify them as soon as possible, so that they can become a practical reality. But if anyone, even an ordinary soldier, can think of a better way to go about things than this, let him explain it to us without fear. For our survival is the common concern of all.'

Once Xenophon had finished, Chirisophus said: 'If there's anything we need to add to Xenophon's proposals, we can do so shortly.
But I think it best if we put the measures he has just proposed to the
vote as quickly as possible. So raise your hand if you are in favour of
his proposals.' Everyone's hand went up.

Then Xenophon got to his feet again and said: 'Men, I'll tell you
what else I think we need to do. We obviously have to go and get
provisions from somewhere, and I hear there are some fine villages
no more than twenty stades from here. You know how cowardly dogs
chase and try to bite passers-by, but run away from anyone who
chases them; I wouldn't be surprised if the enemy behaved in the
same way, and pursued us as we retreated. To make our journey as
safe as possible, then, I suppose we should have the hoplites form a
square to protect the baggage carts and the camp followers. If we
were now to appoint someone to lead the square and organize the
front of it, and others to look after each of the sides and to protect
the back, we wouldn't have to make these arrangements after the
enemy had come, but without wasting any time we could rely on
those already assigned the jobs. If anyone has a better plan in mind,
let's adopt it, but otherwise I would suggest that Chirisophus takes
the lead, especially since he's a Spartan,* that the two oldest generals
take charge of the two sides, and that for the time being the youngest
of the generals—Timasion and I—guard the rear. Later, after we've
tried out this formation, we can discuss what course of action seems
best in any given situation. Anyway, if anyone has a better plan in
mind, let's hear it.'

No one had any counter-proposals to make and so Xenophon said:
'All those in agreement, raise your hands.' The proposals were
carried. 'All right, then,' Xenophon continued, 'now is the time for
us to leave and put our plans into action. If you want to see your
families again, summon up your courage. There's no other way to
get what you want. If you want to survive, do your best to win,
because it is the winners who kill and the losers who die; and if you
want to get rich, do your best to conquer, because victors not only
keep their own belongings, but also take what belongs to the losers.'

[3] After these speeches, the meeting broke up, and they went back
to their quarters and burnt the carts and tents. They threw all their
superfluous belongings onto the flames, unless one of their comrades
needed something, in which case they gave it away. Then they

turned to their midday meal, in the middle of which Mithradates arrived, along with about thirty horsemen. He asked the generals to come close enough to hear him and then he said: 'Men of Greece, I was, as you know, one of Cyrus' trusted advisers. Even now, I'm still on your side—in fact, it's extremely risky for me to be spending time here. So if I knew that you were thinking of saving yourselves, I'd come to you and bring all my retainers with me. Do please tell me your plans, then, with the assurance that I am your loyal friend and that I would like to join you for your journey.'

The Greek generals talked things over, and Chirisophus delivered the response they decided on. 'As long as we're allowed to go back home without being molested,' he said, 'our plan is to make our way through the land as peacefully as possible; but we will resist anyone who gets in our way with all the power at our command.'

Mithradates then tried to make them believe that there was no way for them to save themselves as long as the king was hostile towards them, and at this point the Greeks realized that his mission was not all it seemed. In fact, one of Tissaphernes' relatives had come with him to ensure his reliability. The generals therefore decided that it would be better to make a regulation to the effect that whilst they were in enemy territory they would receive no delegations from the enemy, since the men the enemy sent kept trying to corrupt their troops. In fact, they did succeed in corrupting one of the company commanders, Nicarchus of Arcadia, who left during the night with about twenty men.

Next, after they had finished their morning meal, they crossed the Zapatas river* and made their way in formation, with the yoke-animals and the camp followers in the middle of the square. They had gone only a short distance when Mithradates appeared again, with about 200 horsemen and almost 400 bowmen and slingers—very flexible and mobile troops. He approached the Greeks as if he had friendly intentions, but, once he was close, his archers, both mounted and on foot, suddenly fired their bows and his slingers hurled their stones. Some Greeks were wounded, and the rearguard suffered badly without being able to retaliate, because the Cretan archers did not have the range of the Persians and, being unprotected by armour, were also shut up inside the hoplite square. Moreover, the javelin-men could not throw their javelins far enough to reach the slingers. Xenophon therefore decided that they ought to set out after the enemy, but the hoplites and peltasts under his command in the rear who set out in pursuit failed to catch up with a single enemy soldier. For the Greeks had no cavalry and their foot soldiers could not catch up with the enemy foot soldiers, who had a good head-start in their flight, within the short distance allowed them by the fact that they could not afford to chase their opponents so far that they became separated from the rest of the army. Also, even in flight the barbarian horsemen were inflicting wounds, by turning and shooting arrows from the backs of their horses, and every foot the Greeks covered in pursuit had to be fought for as they fell back again. The upshot of all this was that they took the whole day to cover no more than twenty-five stades, but they did reach the villages late in the afternoon.

Despondency was once again widespread, of course, and Chirisophus and the oldest generals reprimanded Xenophon for breaking formation and setting out in pursuit of the enemy; he had put himself in danger, they said, without increasing his ability to harm the enemy. After listening to what they had to say, Xenophon admitted that they were right to criticize him and pointed out that events supported their case. 'However,' he said, 'pursuit was forced upon me because, staying put, we were suffering badly and had no ability to retaliate at all. As a matter of fact, though,' he went on, 'when we did set out in pursuit, it was just as you said: we didn't increase our ability to injure the enemy, and it was extremely hard for us to withdraw back to our own lines. We should thank the gods that they came with only a small force, rather than a sizeable army, because they didn't hurt us too badly and they've shown us where our deficiencies lie. At the moment, you see, the enemy can fire arrows and sling stones further than our Cretans can respond with their own arrows or our hand-thrown missiles can reach. And when we chase them, we can't leave the main body of the army far behind, and in a short distance no foot soldier, however fast, can catch up with another foot soldier who's already a bow-shot away.

'So, if we're to put paid to their ability to hurt us in the course of our journey, we urgently need slingers and horsemen. Now, I hear that we have some men from Rhodes* in our army, and people say that most Rhodians know how to use a sling and that their missiles carry twice as far as those of the Persian slingers, because whereas the Persians use fist-sized stones in their slings, which can't travel very far, the Rhodians know how to use lead shot as well as stones. So I suggest that we first discover if any of them own slings, and then buy their slings off them and also pay for more slings to be made, if anyone is prepared to do so; and if we then find some exemption that we can offer anyone who voluntarily accepts slinging duties, I expect that people with the ability to help us will turn up. And I can see that there are horses in the army, either belonging to my men or left behind by Clearchus' men,* and plenty of others which have been captured from the enemy and are being used to carry baggage. So if we round them up, replace them with pack-animals, and equip the horses for use by cavalrymen, I expect that they too will cause trouble for our opponents as they run away.'

This proposal was carried also. That night a unit of about 200 slingers was created, and on the following day about fifty horses and horsemen passed muster.* The riders were issued leather jerkins and breastplates, and Lycius of Athens, the son of Polystratus, was appointed cavalry commander.

[4] That day they stayed put, but the next day they set off. They got up earlier than usual, because they had a gully to cross and they were afraid that the enemy would attack them as they were trying to cross it. But it was only after they had crossed it that Mithradates appeared again, this time with 1,000 horsemen and about 4,000 archers and slingers. Tissaphernes had granted his request for a force of this size because Mithradates had promised that, with this many men, he would hand the Greeks over to him as his captives. By this time he had no respect for the Greeks, because despite the small size of his force in the earlier attack, he had, as he thought, injured the Greeks badly, while remaining unscathed himself.

By the time Mithradates and his men crossed the gully after them, the Greeks were about eight stades beyond it. Those peltasts and hoplites who were to pursue the enemy had received their instructions, and the horsemen had been told to press their pursuit confidently, on the grounds that a large enough force would be close behind them. Once Mithradates had caught up with the Greeks, and his sling-stones and arrows were beginning to reach them, the trumpet sounded the signal and immediately the troops who had been detailed for the job ran to engage the enemy and the horsemen rode out. The barbarians gave way and fled towards the gully. In the course of this rout a lot of barbarian infantry lost their lives and as many as eighteen cavalrymen were captured alive in the gully. Acting on their own initiative, the Greek soldiers mutilated the corpses of the dead,* to make the sight of them as terrifying as possible for the enemy.

After this defeat the enemy withdrew, and the Greeks carried on safely for the rest of the day, until they reached the Tigris. Here they found a large, deserted city called Larisa, which in the old days had been inhabited by Medes.* Its wall (which was made from clay bricks on a stone foundation twenty feet tall) was twenty-five feet thick and a hundred feet high, and had a perimeter of two parasangs. The Persian king* had besieged this city during the Persian annexation of the Median empire, but nothing he tried enabled him to take it. But then a cloud hid the sun from sight* until the inhabitants left, and so the city fell. Near by there was a pyramid made of stone, which was one plethron wide and two plethra high, and was being used as a place of refuge by a lot of barbarians from the neighbouring villages.

The next leg was a one-day march of six parasangs that brought them to a large, deserted fortress, close to a city called Mespila, which had once been inhabited by the Medes.* The foundation of the fortress was made from polished, shell-bearing stone, and was fifty feet thick and fifty feet tall. On this foundation there was built a brick wall, fifty feet thick and a hundred feet tall and with a perimeter of six parasangs. This is supposed to be the place where Medea, the king's wife,* took refuge after the Persian conquest of the Median empire. The Persian king besieged the city, but neither attrition nor direct assault enabled him to take it—but then Zeus stupefied the inhabitants with thunder, and the king succeeded in taking it.

The next leg was a one-day march of four parasangs. In the course of this stage Tissaphernes appeared with an army consisting of the cavalry unit he had brought with him, the forces under the command of Orontas (the husband of the king's daughter), the barbarian troops Cyrus had brought on his march up country, and the troops which the king's brother had brought as reinforcements for the king—not to mention all the troops the king had given him. In other words, the army looked enormous.

When they got close to the Greeks, Tissaphernes stationed some of his units behind them and moved others into position along either side of the square, but he did not dare to launch an attack. Rather than risking a decisive battle, he ordered his men to use their slings and bows. But then the Rhodians discharged their sling-shot from the various positions where they had been deployed, and the archers† fired their arrows. Every single shot hit a mark (in fact, it would have been hard to miss even if they had really wanted to), Tissaphernes hastily pulled his men back out of range, and all the other contingents withdrew as well.

For the rest of the day the Greeks kept moving and the barbarians followed them. The long-range tactics the barbarians had been using until then were now ineffective, because the Rhodians could hurl their sling-shot further than the Persians, and the Cretan archers could shoot further than their Persian counterparts.† Persian bows are large, and this meant that the Cretans were able to use all the arrows they could collect. In fact, they were constantly using enemy arrows, and they practised by shooting arrows far up into the sky. A number of bow-strings were also found in the villages, and some lead, which could be used as sling-shot. At the end of the day, when the Greeks found some villages and made camp, the babarians pulled back, having come off worst in the long-range skirmishing. The next day the Greeks stayed where they were and stocked up on provisions, because there was a lot of grain in the villages. The day after that they continued on their way across the plain, while Tissaphernes followed them and kept harassing them from a distance.

At this point the Greeks realized that an equal-sided square was a bad formation to adopt with the enemy on their heels. For whenever the sides of the square converged, either because the road narrowed or because mountains or a bridge left them no choice, some hoplites were inevitably squeezed out and all the jostling and confusion impaired their progress, until, of course, they became more or less useless, since they were out of formation. Moreover, when the sides diverged again, the hoplites who had previously been squeezed out were necessarily out of position, the centres of the sides were bound to be unmanned, and the men affected by these accidents inevitably felt threatened, with the enemy on their heels. Then again, when they had to cross a bridge or something, everyone speeded up because he wanted to be the first across, and this made them vulnerable to an attack from the enemy.

Once the generals had come to recognize these problems, they created six companies of 100 men each, under company commanders, and then troop commanders and section commanders

under them.* With this structure, whenever the sides of the square
converged in the course of their march, the company commanders at
the rear would drop back so as not to get in the way of the sides and
for a while would lead their men behind the sides; and when the
sides of the square diverged, they would fill up the space in the
middle. If the gap they were passing through was rather narrow, they
filled up the centre company by company; if it was a bit wider, they
did so troop by troop; and if it was particularly wide, they did so
section by section.* As a result, the centre was always filled. And if
they had to cross a bridge or something, there was no confusion,
because the companies took turns to make the crossing, and if any
part of the main body of the army needed them for anything, they
went over to help. And so they marched on for four days with this
system in place.

During the fifth stage of this leg of their journey, they caught
sight of a palace of some kind with a number of villages grouped
around it. The road to this spot passed through high hills, which
were the foothills of the mountain under which the villages were
situated. It goes without saying, given that the enemy had cavalry,
that the Greeks were delighted to see the hills; but after leaving the
plain and marching up the first hill, they were marching down the
other side before climbing the next one when the barbarians, urged
on by whips,* attacked them with javelins, sling-shot, and arrows
fired down the slope from the top of the hill. A number of Greeks
were wounded and their light-armed troops were overpowered and
boxed up within the lines of hoplites so that both the slingers and the
archers were caught up among the non-combatants and were completely ineffective the whole day long. Despite being hard pressed,
the Greeks tried to go after the barbarians, but since they were
heavy-armed hoplites it took time for them to reach the top of the
hill, while the enemy troops sprinted away, and each time the hoplites made their way back to the rest of the army they came under the
same hail of fire.

The same thing happened again on the second hill, and so, before
moving off the third hill, they decided to send a detachment of
peltasts from the right side of the square up the side of the mountain
to a position above the enemy troops who were following them. The
enemy then stopped attacking the Greeks on the downhill stretches,
because they were afraid of being cut off and finding themselves with

hostile forces to either side of them. So this is how the Greeks
carried on for the rest of the day, with some of them taking the road
over the hills and the rest on a parallel course on the mountainside.
Finally they came to the villages, where they appointed eight doctors*
to look after all the wounded men.

They stayed in these villages for three days, partly for the sake of
the wounded, but also because they found a lot of provisions there,
which had been stockpiled by the satrap responsible for the region.
There was wheat flour, wine, and plenty of barley which had been
stored as fodder for horses. On the fourth day they marched down to
the plain, where Tissaphernes and his army caught up with them.
But the Greeks had learnt the hard way that they should make camp
at the first village they found, rather than marching and fighting at
the same time; and in any case a lot of the men were *hors de combat*—
some because they were wounded, but others because they were
carrying the wounded or the arms and armour of those who were
carrying the wounded. After they had made camp, the barbarians
approached the village and tried to make use of their long-range
missiles, but the Greeks came off much better in this engagement;
there was a big difference between repelling the enemy by making a
sortie from a stable position and fighting off an attack while on the
march.

The afternoon drew on and the time came for the barbarians to
leave. They never made their camp within sixty stades of the Greek
encampment, because they were frightened of a night attack by the
Greeks. And with good reason: at night a Persian army is worthless.
They not only tether their horses, but usually hobble them too, to
stop them running off if the tether comes undone, and in the event
of an alarm a Persian horseman cannot mount until the saddlecloth
and bridle have been put on his horse, and he has donned his breastplate—none of which is easy at night when an alarm has sounded.
That is why they used to make their camp a long way from the
Greeks.

Once it was clear that the barbarians intended to leave and that the
order to do so was passing through their ranks, the Greeks received
the command, shouted out within hearing of the enemy, that they
were to pack up their baggage. The barbarians delayed their departure for a while, but left when it got late, because they did not relish
the idea of marching and reaching their camp after dark. When the

Greeks saw that the enemy were now definitely withdrawing, they
too broke camp and set out. They went about sixty stades, which
meant that the two armies were so far apart that they saw no sign of
the enemy the next day or the day after that. The next day, however,
as a result of having pushed on through the night, the barbarians
occupied a position above the Greeks' intended route, on a spur of
the mountain overlooking the way down to the plain.

When Chirisophus saw that the spur was already occupied, he
ordered Xenophon up from the rear and told him to bring the
peltasts with him up to the front. But Xenophon could see clear
indications that Tissaphernes was approaching with his whole army,
so he did not take the peltasts, but rode up and asked Chirisophus
why he had asked for him. 'Just use your eyes,' Chirisophus said.
'The high ground overlooking our way down has already been occupied. We can't get past unless we clear them off it. But why didn't
you bring the peltasts?'

Xenophon replied that he did not want to leave the rear
undefended with the enemy already coming into sight. 'Fine,' said
Chirisophus, 'but now we've got to come up with a plan for driving
those men off the hill.'

Just then Xenophon noticed that the peak of the mountain was
right above their own army, and that there was a way to approach the
enemy's position from the peak. 'Chirisophus,' he said, 'the best plan
would be for us to make our way as quickly as possible to the top of
the mountain. If we occupy that, it will be impossible for the men
overlooking the road to stay where they are. I'd be glad to undertake
the mission, if you like, while you stay with the army—or if you
prefer you can go to the mountain while I stay here.'

'It's up to you,' said Chirisophus. 'You choose.'

Xenophon said that, as the youngest, he chose the mission, and he
asked Chirisophus to let him have some men from the front, since it
would take too long to get them from the rear. Chirisophus let him
take the peltasts who had been posted in the front, and replaced
them with some from the middle of the square. He also detailed the
300 elite troops whom he had under his personal command at the
front of the square to go with Xenophon.

Xenophon and his men set out as rapidly as they could, but as
soon as the enemy troops stationed on the hill noticed them making
their way towards the top of the mountain, they set off too, in a race

to see who could reach the top first. Shouts filled the air, as the Greeks urged their men on and Tissaphernes' men did the same. Xenophon rode alongside his men and called out encouragement: 'Men, think of this as a race with Greece, with your children and wives, as the prize! A little effort now will be rewarded with no more fighting for the rest of the journey!' But Soteridas of Sicyon said: 'It's not fair, Xenophon. You're on horseback, while the weight of my shield has totally worn me out.' At this, Xenophon jumped off his horse, pushed Soteridas out of the column, took his shield from him, and marched on as quickly as he could with the shield—and since he was wearing his cavalryman's breastplate, it was hard going for him. He kept urging the men in front of him to lead the way and the men behind to overtake him, because he was struggling to keep up. But the other men punched Soteridas, threw stones at him, and called him names, until they forced him to take his shield back and march on with it. Xenophon remounted and led the way on horseback, as long as the terrain made that possible, and then he abandoned his horse and hurried forward on foot. And they did reach the top before the enemy.

[5] With the Greeks occupying the top of the mountain, the barbarians turned and fled, each man looking out for himself, while Tissaphernes' and Ariaeus' troops turned aside and left by another route. Chirisophus led his men down to the plain and camped in a village, which was just one among the many villages in this plain by the Tigris that were well stocked with provisions. In the late afternoon, the enemy suddenly appeared on the plain and slaughtered any of the Greeks they found scattered over the plain in search of plunder; in fact, several herds of cattle had already been captured while they were being driven across to the far side of the river. At this point Tissaphernes and his men tried to set fire to the villages, and the prospect of not having anywhere to get provisions from, if the villages were burnt, deeply worried some of the Greeks.

Chirisophus had taken some men to go and help the raiders on the plain and had just got back, and Xenophon, then down from the mountain, fell in with the rescue party. He rode alongside them and said: 'Men of Greece, do you see how they admit that the land is now ours? I mean, they stipulated, as one of the terms of the truce between us, that we should not set fire to the king's territory, but now they are burning it themselves, as if it belonged to someone else.

Well, if they leave any provisions behind anywhere for their own use, they'll see us making our way there, but, Chirisophus, I think we should defend the villages against the men who are trying to burn them, as if the villages really were ours.'

'I disagree,' Chirisophus replied. 'Let's set fire to them ourselves as well, and then they'll stop soon enough.'

Back in the camp, while the men were busy with their provisions, the generals and company commanders had a meeting. They were quite uncertain what to do next, given that on one side of them were towering mountains, and on the other was a river which was so deep that the spears men used to probe for the bottom vanished below the surface. While they were still in this state of uncertainty, a Rhodian came forward and said: 'My friends, I can get you across the river in blocks of 4,000 hoplites. You have only to let me have what I need and pay me a talent.' When he was asked what he needed, he said: 'Two thousand skins.* I can see all the sheep, goats, oxen, and asses we've got. Once they've been skinned, and their skins have been inflated, the crossing will be easy. I'll also need the ropes you use for your yoke-animals, which I'll use to tie the skins together, and also to stabilize the skins: I'll fix stones to every skin with these ropes and let the stones down into the water to act as anchors. Next I'll make a bridge of the skins across the river and secure them at both ends, and finally I'll lay branches on them and cover the branches with earth. You don't need to worry for a moment about drowning, because every skin will support two men and stop them from drowning, and the branches and earth will make a non-slippery surface.' The generals thought this idea was clever but unrealistic, given the presence of large numbers of horsemen on the other side of the river, who would immediately prevent even the first part of the plan from being carried out.

So the next day they burnt to the ground the villages where they had spent the night, and then retraced their route back to the villages which remained undamaged by fire. This meant that the enemy did not advance on them, but just watched, as if they were wondering where the Greeks would go and what they had in mind. While the men were busy foraging, the generals held another meeting. They had the prisoners brought before them and questioned them about what lay in every direction around them. The prisoners said that Babylon and Media lay to the south, past the land through which

they had already come; that to the east lay the route to Susa and
Ecbatana, where the king was said to have his spring and summer
residences;* that to the west, across the river, lay the way to Lydia and
Ionia; and that the way north, through the mountains, would take
them to the Carduchians.* They described the Carduchians as a
belligerent, mountain-dwelling people who had never submitted to
the king; in fact, they said, the mountains were so harsh that the king
had once sent an invading force of 120,000 men against the Carduchians and not one of these men came back. Still, they added, there
were some dealings between them and the Carduchians, because the
Carduchians occasionally needed to negotiate a truce with the satrap
responsible for the low country.

After listening to the prisoners' accounts, the generals had those
who claimed familiarity with any of the surrounding districts sit
apart from the rest, though they did not let them know which direction they were planning to take. But they were inclining towards the
view that they had to cross the mountains into Carduchian territory,
because the prisoners had told them that on the other side of the
mountains they would come to Armenia, a large and prosperous land
governed by Orontas. From there, the prisoners assured them, they
could easily go wherever they wanted. At this, the generals performed sacrifices, so that they could set out exactly when it seemed
right to do so,* because they were worried that the pass into the
mountains might fall into enemy hands before they got there. After
the evening meal they passed the word around that the men were to
pack up their baggage, rest, and wait for the order to move out.

BOOK FOUR

[1] The order to move out came at about the time of the final watch,* when there was still enough of the night left for them to cross the plain under cover of darkness. They got up and set out. At daybreak, they reached the mountain, where Chirisophus took the lead, with his own men and all the light-armed troops as well, while Xenophon followed behind with the hoplites of the rearguard, but with no light-armed troops, because there seemed to be no danger of their being attacked from the rear while they were marching uphill. Chirisophus reached the top of the mountain before being noticed by any of the enemy, and then he led the way cautiously, and each successive section of the army as it crested the peak followed his lead into the villages which lay in the vales and hollows of the mountains.

The Carduchians immediately took their wives and children, abandoned their houses, and ran away to the mountains. There were plenty of provisions available, and the houses were also fitted out with large numbers of bronze utensils, but the Greeks took none of these utensils and did not go after the inhabitants—though, since they had no choice, they did take any provisions they found. They went easy on the Carduchians because they wanted to see whether, given their hostility to the king, they might be willing to let them pass through their land as if it were friendly territory, but the Carduchians did not respond when the Greeks called out to them and did not make any other friendly gesture either. But when the last of the Greeks were coming down from the peak into the villages—by which time it was dark, because the road was so narrow that the march up the mountain and then down the other side to the villages had taken all day—some of the Carduchians banded together and attacked the tail-enders. Even though the attackers were few, they killed some men and wounded others with their stones and arrows. The Greek army had come upon them unexpectedly, but if the Carduchian band had been larger, a substantial number of men would probably have been killed. So the Greeks camped for the night in the villages, while the Carduchians lit a large number of fires on the mountains all around them and kept one another in sight.

At dawn the Greek generals and company commanders met and

decided to carry on with only the essential and strongest yoke-animals, having abandoned the rest, and without all the recently captured slaves held in the army. Their thinking was, first, that their progress was slowed by all the yoke-animals and slaves; second, that a lot of men were unable to fight because they were looking after the captives and animals; and, third, that they needed to find and carry double the amount of provisions for all those people. The order was given to carry out this decision of theirs, and when they set out after their morning meal, the generals discreetly stood by a narrow stretch of the road and removed any of the proscribed things they found that had not been left behind. The men complied with the generals' wishes, apart from a few cases where someone smuggled something past them—the sort of thing that might help him if a good-looking boy or woman caught his fancy.

They marched on like this for the rest of the day, except for occasions when they were fighting or resting. The next day, there was a strong wintry storm, but they had to carry on because they were low on provisions. Chirisophus led the way, while Xenophon held the rear. The enemy launched a series of fierce assaults, and in the narrow passes they came close enough to fire their bows and slings at the Greeks from no great distance. This meant that the Greeks were forced to chase them off and then withdraw, which slowed their progress. Xenophon often called for a halt during the worst of the enemy assaults, and though Chirisophus invariably halted when he received Xenophon's request, on one occasion he did not, but kept the men pushing forward at a rapid pace and passed the word back to Xenophon that he should keep up with them. There was obviously some kind of trouble, but there was no time to go up to the front and discover the reason for Chirisophus' haste, and the upshot was that the rearguard was not so much marching as running away. This was the occasion when a brave man, a Spartan called Cleonymus, lost his life, shot in the side by an arrow that passed through his shield and his jerkin. Basias of Arcadia also died from a deep head wound.

As soon as they reached a staging area, Xenophon went straight to Chirisophus and remonstrated with him for not waiting, which left them no choice but to fight and retreat at the same time. 'As a result,' he said, 'two good, brave men have lost their lives, and we couldn't recover their bodies or bury them.'

'Just look at the mountains,' said Chirisophus in reply, 'and observe how impassable they all are. There's only the one road—a steep one, as you can see—and you'll notice that there's a horde of people on it. They've occupied the pass and are guarding it against us. I pushed on ahead and didn't wait for you because I wanted to try to seize the pass before they did. The guides we have with us say there's no other road.'

'Well, I've got two prisoners,' said Xenophon. 'The enemy were giving us a hard time, so we set an ambush for them. This gave us a chance to catch our breaths and to kill some of them, but we were also determined to take some prisoners precisely so that we would have guides who know the region.'

They lost no time in having the prisoners brought before them, and they questioned them one at a time, to see if they knew of any road other than the obvious one. However often and however fiercely they tried to intimidate the first man, he denied knowing of any other road, so since he had no useful information for them they cut his throat in front of the second man. The remaining man then said that the first man had denied knowledge of an alternative route because he had a married daughter living there, but that he would show them a route which even the yoke-animals could manage. When he was asked whether there was any part of the route that would present them with problems, he said that there was a peak they would have to take, otherwise they would be unable to get by it.

They decided, therefore, to call a meeting of the officers in command of both the peltast and the hoplite companies, to explain the situation to them, and to ask if any of them were willing to demonstrate his courage by volunteering for this mission. From among the hoplites, the volunteers were three Arcadians—Aristonymus of Methydrium, Agasias of Stymphalus, and Callimachus of Parrhasia. Callimachus tried to go one better than the others by saying that he was prepared to take volunteers from the whole army with him on the mission, 'because I'm sure that a lot of the young men will follow if I am their leader'. Then the generals asked if any of the officers in command of peltast units were prepared to join the mission, and Aristeas of Chios volunteered—and this was not the only time he proved his value to the army in this kind of situation.

[2] By then it was after noon, and the generals ordered the volunteers to set out as soon as they had eaten. They gave them the

guide, with his hands tied, and arranged that the volunteers would guard the peak that night, if they took it, and at daybreak would sound a trumpet. Those on the peak were then to attack the Carduchians who were occupying the obvious road through the mountains, while the generals would come to their assistance as quickly as they could. With these arrangements in place, the volunteer force of about two thousand set out in pouring rain, while Xenophon led the rearguard towards the obvious road, to keep the enemy's attention focused there and to make it more likely that the volunteers would go unnoticed as they went around the other way.

The rearguard had just reached a gully which had to be crossed before carrying on up the steep road when the barbarians began to roll spherical boulders of various sizes, but each big enough to make a cart-load, down the slope. The boulders crashed down onto the rocks and bounced off in all directions, making it completely impossible even to approach the entrance to the pass. Some of the company commanders gave up on that route and kept trying alternatives until nightfall, when they thought they could make their way back without being seen. Then they went back to eat, since those of them who had been in the rearguard had missed out on the midday meal too. But the whole night long the enemy kept rolling boulders down the hillside, as the Greeks could tell from the noise.

The detachment with the guide took the long way round and came upon the expected enemy guards sitting around a campfire. Those they did not kill they chased off, and then they stayed there themselves, under the impression that they were occupying the peak. In fact, though, they were not occupying the peak; there was a hill above them and the narrow road where the guards had been posted ran alongside this hill. Nevertheless, there proved to be a way for them to get from where they were to the enemy who were occupying the obvious road.

At daybreak, after a night spent there, they formed up for battle and set off silently against the enemy. It was misty, so they got close without being seen. When the two sides caught sight of each other, the trumpet sounded and the Greeks raised the battle-cry and charged the enemy. The Carduchians gave way, abandoned the road, and ran off, but their agility kept their casualties low. When Chirisophus and his men heard the trumpet, they immediately charged up the obvious road. Some of the other generals, however, set off without taking any proper paths, but just by whatever route happened to present itself to them. They scrambled up as best they could, using their spears to haul one another up, and they were the first to link up with the Greeks who had already occupied the place.

Meanwhile, Xenophon and half the rearguard set out along the route taken by the detachment with the guide, because this was the route that best suited the yoke-animals, and he ordered the other half of the rearguard to follow the baggage train. As Xenophon and his detachment were marching along, they found that the enemy had occupied a hill overlooking the road, which would have to be cleared if they were to be able to link up with the rest of the Greeks. The men could have taken the same route as the others, but this was the only way the baggage train could go, and so with cries of encouragement to one another they advanced towards the hill with their companies formed into columns. They did not completely surround the hill, but left a way off in case the enemy chose to run away. For a while, as each man picked his own way up the hillside, the barbarians fired arrows and other missiles at them, but then they turned and fled, preferring to abandon the place rather than fight at close quarters.

So the Greeks got past this hill, but then they saw another one in front of them, which was also occupied by the enemy. They decided to advance on this second hill too, but Xenophon was worried about leaving the hill they had already taken unoccupied, in case the enemy might take it again and attack the baggage train as it came past—and the baggage train was strung out because of the narrowness of the road. So he left three companies on the hill under the command of two Athenians—Cephisodorus the son of Cephison and Amphicrates the son of Amphidemus—and an Argive exile called Archagoras, while he personally took the rest of the troops, marched against the second hill, and took it by using the same tactics as before.

There remained a third hill, by far the steepest, which overlooked the spot captured by the detachment of volunteers during the night, where the enemy guards had built a campfire. But as the Greeks were approaching, the barbarians abandoned the hill without a fight. Everyone was surprised at this and assumed that they had left from fear of being surrounded and trapped on the hill, but in fact their position on the peak allowed them to see what was happening further back along the route, and they had gone to attack the men who had been left behind as guards. Xenophon set off up to the peak with the youngest men under his command, having ordered the rest to march slowly on along the road, so that the tail-enders could link up with them, until they reached the level ground ahead, where they were to halt with their weapons at the ready.

Just then Archagoras of Argos ran up with the news that they had been driven off the first hill, and that everyone who had not jumped off the cliff and reached the rearguard had been killed, including Cephisodorus and Amphicrates. After this success, the barbarians went and occupied a hill on the other side of the road from the third hill, and Xenophon sent over a translator to negotiate a truce with them and to ask for time to recover the bodies of the dead. The barbarians said that they would let them have the bodies back as long as they undertook not to burn their houses—a condition to which Xenophon agreed. While these negotiations were going on, however, and the rest of the Greek army was passing by, all the local inhabitants had flocked together and the enemy began to make a stand there. And when Xenophon and his men started to climb down the hill with the intention of going to where the others were waiting under arms, a hostile horde charged at them, making a terrible din. As soon as the enemy reached the peak of the hill which Xenophon was descending, they began to roll rocks down the slope. They broke one man's leg, and Xenophon's shield-bearer* deserted him, with the shield he was carrying. But a hoplite called Eurylochus, an Arcadian from Lusi, ran over to him and held his shield in front of them both while they retreated. Everyone else also managed to withdraw to the ranks of the main army.

Afterwards, with the whole Greek army reunited, they made camp there, surrounded by beautiful houses. There was no shortage of supplies, and there was plenty of wine too, which the Carduchians kept in plaster-lined cisterns. Xenophon and Chirisophus succeeded in persuading the enemy to let them have the corpses of the dead in exchange for the guide and they did everything they could under the circumstances that is usually done when burying brave men.

The next day they carried on without a guide, while the enemy tried to hinder their progress by engaging them in battle and by occupying any narrow stretches before they got there. Whenever it was the van whose progress was impeded, Xenophon would take his men up towards the mountains from the rear and set about opening the road again for the vanguard by trying to get higher than the enemy fighters who were causing the problem; and whenever the rear was under attack, Chirisophus took his men, tried to get higher than the enemy fighters who were causing the problem, and set about clearing the road for the rearguard. In this way they constantly helped each other and assiduously looked out for each other. But sometimes, when the Greeks who had gone up into the mountains were on their way down again, the barbarians made things extremely difficult for them.

The barbarians were light enough on their feet to make good their escape even if they started running when they were quite close, because they carried nothing except bows and slings. They were also outstanding bowmen. Their bows were almost three cubits from tip to tip and when they shot they stepped on the bottom of the bows with their left feet as they drew back the string. Their arrows, which were more than two cubits long, could pass through shields and breastplates, and when the Greeks got hold of them, they fitted them with loops* and used them as javelins. The Cretan troops, led by Stratocles of Crete, were immensely useful in these regions.

[3] At the end of this day too they bivouacked among the villages overlooking the plain of the Centrites river, which is two plethra wide and forms the border between Armenia and Carduchian territory. The Greeks rested here, glad to be able to see the plain and the river, which was six or seven stades away from the Carduchians' mountains. So on this occasion they bivouacked in good spirits: they had provisions, and they could cast their minds back over all the hardship they had endured. They spent seven days* marching through Carduchian territory, there were battles every single day, and they suffered more losses than on all the occasions they had clashed with the king and Tissaphernes put together. So they slept that night in a good frame of mind, imagining that the worst was behind them. At daybreak, however, they saw armed horsemen on the far side of the river to stop them crossing, and foot soldiers lined up on the banks above the horsemen to stop them entering Armenia. These troops were Armenians, Mardians, and Chaldean* mercenaries, under the command of Orontas and Artuchas. People said that the Chaldeans were a free and courageous people; they carried large wicker shields and spears.

The banks on which these troops were arrayed were three or four

plethra beyond the river, and there was only one visible road heading inland, which seemed to be man-made. This, then, was the
point where the Greeks attempted a river crossing, but the water
turned out to be more than chest deep and the bed was rough, with
large, slippery stones. Also, they could not wear their armour and
wield their weapons and shields in the water without the river
sweeping things away, and if they carried them on their heads they
were vulnerable to arrows and other missiles. So they pulled back
and camped where they were, by the river, but then, when they
looked back to where they themselves had spent the previous night
on the mountainside, they saw a horde of armed Carduchians. The
Greeks' spirits sank very low at this point. Fording the river was
obviously going to be tricky, in front of them they could see troops
whose purpose was to stop them crossing, and behind them they
could see the Carduchians who would attack them as they were
crossing.

They stayed where they were for a whole day and night, without
having the slightest idea what they should do next. Then Xenophon
had a dream: he was bound with fetters, but the fetters fell off of
their own accord, so that he was free and could take whatever length
of stride he wanted.* In the morning he went to Chirisophus, told
him that he felt hopeful, and described the dream to him. This
cheered Chirisophus up and as the first rays of the sun began to
shine all the generals who were there performed a sacrifice. The
omens were good straight away, with the first victim, and after leaving the place of sacrifice the generals and company commanders told
the men to prepare their morning meal.

While Xenophon was eating, two young men ran up to him.
Everyone knew that, if they had a military matter to discuss, they
could approach him during mealtimes and could wake him up if he
was asleep. These young men told him that they had been out collecting kindling for a fire, when they had seen on the far side of the
river, among some rocks that came down to the water's edge, an old
man, a woman, and some young girls putting what looked like bags
of clothing inside a hollowed-out rock. They took a look and decided
that it was safe to cross, because at that point the terrain was unsuit-
able for the enemy cavalry. They undressed, they said, and took only
their swords, because they supposed that they would have to swim
across, but in fact they waded across without getting their genitals

wet. When they reached the other side, they took the clothes and crossed back over again.

Xenophon's first reaction was to pour a libation* himself and to tell his attendants to fill a cup for the young men and to beseech the gods who had shown the dream and the ford for good fortune in the future too. After the libation, he took them straight over to Chirisophus. They repeated their story, and on hearing the news Chirisophus, too, performed a libation. Afterwards he and Xenophon gave the troops the order to break camp and convened a meeting of the generals, to come up with the best possible plan for crossing the river, defeating the enemy force in front of them, and avoiding being hurt by those behind them. They decided that Chirisophus should take half the men across while the other half waited for a while with Xenophon, and that the yoke-animals and the camp followers should cross between Chirisophus and Xenophon.

When everything was in place, they set out with the two young men showing them the way, keeping the river on their left. It was about four stades to the ford and, as they marched along, the cavalry squadrons on the other side took a parallel course. When they reached the crossing and the river bank, they halted with their weapons at the ready. Chirisophus was the first to act: he put a wreath on his head,* took off his cloak, and was handed his weapons. He ordered everyone else to do the same, and told the company commanders to form their companies into columns to the right and left of him. The diviners let the blood from the throats of their victims pour into the river. The enemy kept shooting arrows and hurling sling-shot at them, but they were still out of range. When the omens were favourable, all the soldiers struck up the paean and raised the war-cry, while the women (there were a lot of kept women* in the army) all joined in with the ritual cry.*

Then Chirisophus and his men entered the river, while Xenophon took the fastest men from the rearguard and sprinted back to the ford opposite the road up to the Armenian mountains, in a feint designed to make the horsemen by the river think that he was going to cross there and trap them. When the enemy troops saw Chirisophus and his men easily wading through the water, and Xenophon and his men running back, they were terrified of being cut off; they galloped back towards the road which led up into the mountains from the river and once they they reached it, they raced for the mountains.

When Lycius, the cavalry commander, and Aeschines, the officer in charge of the peltasts who were attached to Chirisophus, saw that the enemy troops were in full flight, they set out after them, with their troops calling to the others in an attempt to get them to keep up and join them as they made for the mountain. And as soon as Chirisophus had crossed, rather than pursuing the horsemen, he made his way over to the banks that abutted the river to attack the enemy soldiers who were up there. At the sight of their own cavalry in flight, and of hoplites advancing on them, the barbarians abandoned the ridges overlooking the river.

Once Xenophon saw that everything was going well on the far side of the river, he retraced his steps as quickly as possible back to where the army was crossing, because by then the Carduchians could be seen coming down to the plain to attack the tail-enders. The high ground was in Chirisophus' hands, and the attempt of Lycius and his small cavalry squadron to hunt down the fugitives had resulted in their capturing the remnants of the baggage train, including some beautiful clothing and goblets. The Greek baggage train and camp followers were just in the process of crossing, when Xenophon wheeled his men around to face the Carduchians and halted them with their weapons at the ready. He ordered the company commanders to divide their companies into sections and to form up for battle section by section, starting on the left, until the company and the section commanders faced the Carduchians and the last man in each line stood with his back to the river.

Without the camp followers, the rearguard looked very thin and low on numbers, and the Carduchians picked up speed and struck up their martial songs. But once Chirisophus was sure that everything was secure on his side of the river, he detailed the peltasts, slingers, and archers to go to Xenophon and put themselves entirely under his command. When Xenophon saw them starting across, he sent a man with their instructions: they were to stay put by the river, without crossing, but when his men started to cross, they—the men on the other side—were then to enter the water to either side of his men, as though they were going to cross, the javelin-men with their fingers already through the loops of their javelins and the bowmen with arrows notched; but they were not to advance far into the river.

The instructions he gave his own men were that as soon as they were within range of the enemy slingers and could hear the sling-shot hitting shields, they were to strike up the paean and then charge at the enemy; when the enemy turned, the trumpeter by the river would give the signal for battle—but that would be the signal for them to turn right and about-face, so that the last man in each line was at the front, and then everyone was to race across the river as fast as he could while maintaining his place in the formation, so that they would not obstruct one another; and whoever got to the other side first would be considered the best man among them.

By now, there were only a few men remaining, because quite a lot even of those who had been ordered to stay had already left, to look after the yoke-animals or the baggage or the women, so the Carduchians approached full of confidence and began to fire sling-shot and arrows. The Greeks struck up their paean and charged at them. The Carduchians did not stand their ground, because although their equipment was perfect for swift strikes and hasty retreats in the mountains, it was inadequate for hand-to-hand combat. At that point the trumpeter gave the signal, and while the Carduchians hugely increased the speed of their flight, the Greeks turned around and started to cross the river as fast as they could. Some of the enemy noticed what was going on, rushed back towards the river, and managed to wound a few men with their arrows, but most of them could be seen to be still running even when the Greeks were on the other side of the river. As for the reinforcements, their courage got the better of them and they advanced further into the river than they were supposed to, which meant that they crossed back again after Xenophon's men, and a few of them too were wounded.

[4] It was midday by the time they were all across. They formed up and marched through Armenia over a plain which was interrupted only by gentle hills. They marched at least five parasangs, because the frequency of warfare between the Armenians and the Carduchians meant that there were no villages close to the river. The village they eventually reached was large: it contained a residence for the satrap and most of the houses were fortified. There were plenty of provisions. The next leg was a two-day march of ten parasangs which took them past the sources of the Tigris. The next leg was a three-day march of fifteen parasangs that brought them to the Teleboas river, which made up in beauty for what it lacked in size. There were a lot of villages in the region of this river, and the area as a whole was called Western Armenia.

The governor* of Western Armenia, a man called Tiribazus (who was on such good terms with the king that, if he was available, no one else was allowed to help the king mount his horse), then rode up with a cavalry squadron. He sent a translator ahead to convey his request for a conference with the Greek leaders. The generals decided to hear what he had to say, and when they came within hearing distance they asked what he wanted. He replied that he wanted to enter into a truce with them, the terms being that he would not initiate hostilities against the Greeks and they would not burn any houses in his territory, though they could take all the provisions they needed. The generals agreed and the two sides concluded a truce on these terms.

The next leg was a three-day march of fifteen parasangs across the plain, with Tiribazus and his men following about ten stades behind them, until they came to a palace with a number of villages clustered around it, all of which were well stocked with provisions. While they were camped there for the night, there was a heavy snowfall, and the next morning they decided that the various divisions of the army, along with their generals, might as well be quartered in different villages, because there was no sign of hostile activity and the depth of the snow seemed to guarantee their safety. The provisions they found in these villages were all of a high quality—cattle, grain, aged and fragrant wines, raisins, and all kinds of legumes. However, some of the men who had drifted away from the main camp reported seeing many fires gleaming in the night, so the generals changed their minds, thinking that it might not be safe to disperse the men in different quarters, and decided to bring them together again. So they all regrouped—and in any case the weather seemed to be clearing up.

That night, however, snow fell in amazing quantities, until it buried the weapons, covered the men as they were lying on the ground, and even made movement difficult for the yoke-animals. No one really wanted to get up, because the snow that had fallen was a source of warmth for everyone on the ground, except in cases where it had slipped off. Xenophon finally braced himself and got up without his cloak to chop wood, but someone else soon got up too and took over the wood-chopping. Then everyone else got up as well and set about lighting fires and greasing their bodies;* they had found plenty of ointment there, made out of lard, sesame oil, almond oil (made from bitter almonds), and turpentine, and they used this as a substitute for olive oil. They also found a perfumed ointment made from the same ingredients. After this they decided once again to take up separate quarters in houses throughout the various villages. The men were delighted to be back under cover and surrounded by provisions, and they cheered out loud. But those who had been irresponsible enough to have burnt houses down when they left them before paid the penalty of uncomfortable quarters.

That night they assigned some troops to Democrates of Temnus and sent him to the mountains, where the men who had drifted away from the main camp had reported seeing fires. Democrates had a reputation, based on many earlier instances, for delivering accurate information in such situations; if he said something was the case, it was the case, and if he said it was not, it was not. He returned from his mission without having seen any fires, but with a prisoner who had a Persian bow and quiver, and a battleaxe similar to the kind used by the Amazons.* When the prisoner was asked where he was from, he said he was Persian and that he had come from Tiribazus' camp to get provisions; when he was asked how big a force Tiribazus had and why it had been assembled, he said that Tiribazus had Chalybian and Taochian mercenaries in addition to his own men, and that the intention underlying all his preparations was to attack the Greeks in the mountain pass where there was a narrow ravine and no alternative route.

The generals decided to recombine the army in response to this information. As soon as this had been done, they detailed a garrison to stay behind, with Sophaenetus of Stymphalus in charge, and set out with the prisoner as their guide. As they were marching through the mountain pass, the peltasts, who had gone on ahead, caught sight of the enemy camp and, without waiting for the hoplites, they shouted out loud and charged towards the camp. The noise was enough to make the barbarians turn and flee, but some of them still lost their lives; the Greeks also captured about twenty horses and took possession of Tiribazus' tent, along with its silver-footed couches and its goblets, and some men who claimed to be the governor's bakers and cup-bearers. When the hoplite generals found out what had happened, they decided to return to camp as quickly as possible, in case the men they had left behind were attacked. They recalled the men with a blast of the trumpet, set off back, and reached the camp later that same day.

[5] The next day they decided that they had better cover as much ground as possible before Tiribazus reassembled his forces and occupied the ravine. They packed up and set off straight away through thick snow with a number of guides, and that same day they passed the peak where Tiribazus had been planning to attack them, before making camp. The next leg was a three-day march of fifteen parasangs through uninhabited countryside to the Euphrates, which they waded across with the water reaching only up to their midriffs, since they were not far, according to their informants, from the sources of the river.

The next leg was a three-day march of thirteen parasangs across a plain that was blanketed in thick snow. The third of these stages was difficult: the north wind was blowing straight into their faces, the cold was searing, and the men were freezing. One of the diviners suggested that they should sacrifice to the wind, and once they had done so everyone got the distinct impression that the wind became less bitter. But the snow was lying a fathom deep on the ground, and the cold caused the deaths not only of many of the yoke-animals and the slaves, but also of about thirty soldiers. They got through that night by keeping fires alight—there was plenty of wood at their staging area—but there was no wood left for the late-comers, and those who had been there for some time and had fires going refused to let the late arrivals near their fires unless they gave them some of their wheat or whatever else they had to eat. So each group shared with the other what they had. Wherever there were fires, the snow melted all the way down to the ground, forming huge pits. This, of course, was what made it possible to measure the depth of the snow.

The whole of the following day was spent marching through snow, and a lot of the men suffered from hunger faintness.* Xenophon, who was bringing up the rear, kept coming across men who had fallen by the wayside and did not know what was wrong with them, until someone who had met it before told him that the men were obviously suffering from hunger faintness and would be able to get to their feet if they had something to eat. So Xenophon searched through the baggage train and handed out anything edible he found or sent those who were capable of running to give the food to those who were ill—and after they had eaten something they got to their feet and carried on.

As evening was drawing in, Chirisophus came to a village where he found women and girls from the village outside the fortifications, fetching water from the well. The women asked who they were and the translator replied in Persian that they were on their way from the king to the satrap. The women then said that the satrap was not there, but was about a parasang away. Since it was late, they accompanied the water-carriers inside the fortifications to visit the village headman. So Chirisophus camped there, along with everyone else who made it that far, but some of the other soldiers were unable to complete the stage and spent the night without food or fire, and this caused the death of several more soldiers.

Some of the enemy had formed themselves into bands and were following the Greeks; they would seize any yoke-animals which had collapsed and fight one another for them. At the same time, the soldiers who were suffering from snow-blindness were finding it hard to keep up, as were those whose toes had rotted off from the freezing cold. Wearing a protective covering of something dark-coloured over the eyes as one marched stopped a man losing his sight, and keeping one's feet constantly in motion, never still, and taking one's footwear off at night helped prevent frostbite; but whenever men slept with their shoes on, the straps sank into their flesh and their shoes froze onto their feet, especially because those whose old shoes had worn out were wearing no more than pieces of leather made from the hides of recently skinned oxen.

Emergencies such as these, then, caused some men to fall behind. In one case, a few men saw a dark patch of ground free of snow and guessed that it had melted—as indeed it had, because of a spring which was steaming in a glen close by. They turned aside there, sat down, and refused to carry on. When Xenophon came by with the rearguard and saw them, he begged and implored them, using every device and resource at his disposal, not to fall behind. He pointed out that there were large bands of hostile soldiers on their trail, and in the end he lost his temper. But they told him to cut their throats, since they could not carry on. Under these circumstances, the best course of action seemed to be to frighten the enemy off, if possible, because otherwise the exhausted men would certainly become their victims. It was already dark, and the enemy troops were making a lot of noise as they advanced, quarrelling about their booty. The men of the rearguard, who were in good health, leapt forward and charged the enemy, while the sick men shouted as loudly as they could and clashed their shields and spears together. The terrified enemy soldiers threw themselves down through the snow into the glen, and not the slightest sound was heard from them afterwards.

Xenophon and his men told the invalids that people would come back for them the next day and carried on. But before they had gone four stades they came upon some more soldiers lying down on the road in the snow wrapped up in their cloaks, without even a single sentry on duty. They tried to get them on their feet, but the men said that those in front would not let them through. Xenophon left them there and ordered the fittest of the peltasts forward to see what the hold-up was. The report came back that the whole army was doing the same: they had all stopped for the night. So Xenophon and his men bivouacked without fire or food, and posted sentries as effectively as they could. When the night was nearly over, Xenophon sent the youngest of his troops back to the sick men with instructions to make sure that they got up and carried on.

Meanwhile, Chirisophus sent some of the men from the village to find out what the tail-enders were up to. The rearguard were glad to see them, gave them the invalids to take to the camp,* and then carried on themselves. Within twenty stades they reached the village where Chirisophus had spent the night. Now that they were all together again, it seemed safe for the divisions of the army to be quartered in separate villages; Chirisophus stayed where he was, while the other generals drew lots for the villages they had seen and then set off separately, each with his own men. At this point Polycrates, a company commander from Athens, asked to be released from the column. He took the fastest runners and dashed ahead to the village which the lottery had assigned to Xenophon, where he caught all the inhabitants, including the headman, inside the village, along with seventeen colts, which were being kept as tribute for the king,* and the headman's daughter. She had been married eight days earlier, but her husband had gone out hunting hares and so avoided falling into Polycrates' hands in the village.

The village houses were built underground. The entrance was like the mouth of a well, and then the houses opened up lower down. The entrance passages were excavated for their animals, while men went down by ladder. Their livestock—goats, sheep, cattle, and poultry—lived with their young inside the houses and were fed indoors. Large jars contained wheat, barley, lentils, and barley wine.

The jars of wine had barleycorns floating level with the lips of the jar, and unjointed reeds of various lengths had been placed on the jars; one drank by picking up a reed, putting it in one's mouth, and sucking. The wine was very strong, unless it was diluted with water,* but it made a very pleasant drink when one got used to it.

Xenophon had the headman of this village join him for the evening meal and told him not to worry: he would not lose his children, he said, and before leaving they would fill his house with provisions if he served the army well as their guide until they reached another tribe. He promised to act as their guide and, as a gesture of friendship, told him where there was a buried cache of wine. So that night all Xenophon's men lay down to sleep, surrounded by plenty of everything they needed, in this village where they were quartered, but they made the headman and his children stay together where they could keep a watchful eye on them.

The next day Xenophon took the headman with him when he went to see Chirisophus. Whenever he passed a village, he turned aside to visit the men who were quartered there and in every case he found them eating well and in good spirits—and he was never allowed to leave before he had been served a meal, which always consisted of lamb, kid, pork, veal, and poultry, served up all at once along with plenty of loaves of wheat and barley. And whenever, as a gesture of friendship, someone wanted to offer someone else the cup, he would drag him over to the jar, where he had to bend over and slurp the wine down as if he were an ox. They gave the headman permission to take anything he wanted, but he refused all offers, except that he had every one of his relatives that he met join him. When they reached Chirisophus, they found his men, too, dining in their quarters, wearing garlands of hay and attended by Armenian boys in their native clothes. The men used gestures to show the boys what to do, as if they were deaf and dumb.

Once Chirisophus and Xenophon had greeted each other, they questioned the village headman together, with the help of the Persian-speaking translator. They asked him what country they were in, and he said 'Armenia'. Next, they asked him who the horses were being kept for, and he said they were tribute for the king. He also informed them that across the border lived the Chalybians, and he told them how to get to the road that would take them there. When Xenophon left, he took the headman back for the time being to his family and,

because he had been told that the horse was the animal they sacrificed to the Sun God,* he gave him a horse he had which was rather
old, so that the headman could fatten it up and sacrifice it. Xenophon
had taken the horse as booty, but he was afraid that it would die from
the ill effects of the journey. He took for himself some of the colts,
and he gave one to each of his fellow generals and company commanders. The horses in that part of the world were smaller than the
Persian breed, but much more lively. Also at this time the headman
taught Xenophon to wrap the feet of the horses and the yoke-animals
in small bags for any journeys through snow, because without the
bags they used to sink up to their bellies.

[6] Seven days later Xenophon handed the guide over to
Chirisophus, but left behind all the members of his family except his
son, who was just reaching puberty. He gave the boy to Episthenes of
Amphipolis to look after, on the understanding that the headman
could take the boy with him when he left, if he had done a good job
as their guide. They filled the headman's house to capacity with
provisions, and then they broke camp and set out.

The headman, who was not restrained in any way, guided them
through the snow. But in the course of the third day of this leg,
Chirisophus got angry with him for not having taken them to villages
(the headman said that there were no villages near by), and he hit the
man. He did not tie him up, however, and during the night the
headman ran off, leaving his son behind. Throughout the whole
journey, this was the only occasion when Chirisophus and Xenophon
fell out, over the issue of the maltreatment and careless neglect of the
headman. But Episthenes fell in love with the boy, took him home,
and found him a very loyal companion.

After this they marched for seven days, at the rate of five parasangs a day, until they came to the Phasis river,* which was a plethron
wide. The next leg was a two-day march of ten parasangs. At the
pass from the plain into the mountains, they were met by a force
consisting of Chalybians, Taochians, and Phasians. With the enemy
in sight at the pass, Chirisophus called a halt while there was still a
gap of about thirty stades between the two armies, so that the Greeks
would not get too close to them while still marching in a column. He
ordered the other officers to bring up their troops by companies until
the army was in battle formation. Once the rearguard had arrived, he
summoned the generals and company commanders to a meeting. 'As

you can see,' he said, 'the enemy control the mountain pass. We need to come up with the best plan for engaging them. I think we should tell the men to prepare their midday meal, while we think about whether we want to try to cross the mountains today or tomorrow.'

'In my view,' Cleanor said, 'we should arm ourselves and attack them without delay, as soon as we've eaten. If we do nothing today, the enemy troops who can see us now will grow in confidence and that will probably encourage more men to join them.'

Xenophon was the next to speak. 'I'll tell you what I think,' he said. 'If we have to fight, we had better go about it so that we fight as effectively as we can. We presumably want to get across the mountains with as little trouble as possible, and that means, I suppose, that we need to consider how to make sure that we sustain as few wounds as possible and lose as few men as possible. Now, the mountain range is, as far as we can tell from here, more than sixty stades long, but we can see that the only place they are guarding against us is the actual road. So it would be much better for us to try surreptitiously to steal a part of the mountain that is unoccupied and to see if we can seize it before they do, rather than advancing on strongly held positions and fighting men who have had time to prepare. After all, it's far easier to march unmolested uphill than it is to march across level ground with hostile forces all around, and even at night a man who's not involved in a fight can see what's right before his feet better than he can in daylight if he's fighting, and a rough road is kinder to the feet of those who are marching without fighting than a level surface is to those who have missiles raining down on their heads. I don't think it would be impossible for us to steal a position anyway, since we can march at night, to avoid being seen, and we can leave enough of a gap between us and the enemy to stop them noticing us in any other way. But I do think that if we led them to believe we were going to attack here, we would find the rest of the mountain even more deserted, since the enemy would be more likely to stay bunched together where they are.

'But I'm a fine one to be suggesting that we do some stealing. After all, Chirisophus, I hear that those of you Spartans who are Similars practise stealing from a very early age,* and that it's an admirable rather than a despicable thing for you to steal anything that is not specifically prohibited. Moreover, in order to make you better thieves and to help you try to get away with it, it is your custom to flog anyone who's caught stealing. So it would be particularly appropriate for you now to show us how well brought up you were, and to make sure that we're not caught stealing a bit of the mountain. We don't want to get beaten.'

'Well,' said Chirisophus, 'what *I*'ve heard is that you Athenians are skilled at stealing your public funds, even though the thief runs an enormous risk, and that in fact most of the stealing is done by your best men—that is, if your best men are actually the ones who are chosen for political power. So it's *you* who should show us how well *you* were brought up.'

'All right,' said Xenophon. 'In the evening, after we've eaten, I'll gladly take the rearguard and establish a position on the mountain. I've already got guides, because our light-armed troops set a trap for the thieves who were following us* and took some of them prisoner. I've also found out from them that the mountain is not impassable, but is used for grazing goats and cattle, which means that once we've taken possession of part of the mountain, we'll be able to find a path for our yoke-animals. But in fact I don't expect that the enemy will stay where they are once they see us on high ground, cancelling out their advantage. After all, they're not prepared to come down and face us on level terms even now.'

'Why should you go,' Chirisophus said, 'and abandon your role as rearguard? Detail others to go, if you don't get volunteers.' Then Aristonymus of Methydrium offered himself and his hoplites, as did Aristeas of Chios and Nicomachus of Oeta with their light-armed troops. The arrangement they made was that they would light a lot of fires to show when they were in possession of the high ground. Once they had made their plans, they ate their midday meal, and afterwards Chirisophus had the whole army advance about ten stades closer to the enemy, to make them think that the Greeks were definitely going to take that route against them.

After the evening meal, when it was dark, the men assigned to the task left and seized a ridge of the mountain, while the others spent the night at rest where they were. When the enemy saw that the mountain had been occupied, they stayed awake and kept a lot of fires alight throughout the night. The next day, after he had sacrificed, Chirisophus led the rest of the army along the road, while the men who had seized the ridge advanced over the high ground. Most of the enemy soldiers remained at the mountain pass, but some of

them came out to meet those who were advancing over the high
ground, and a fight took place on the high ground before the two
main armies clashed. The Greeks were victorious and set out in
pursuit of their defeated opponents. Meanwhile, the peltasts from
the Greek forces on the plain had set off at a run towards the enemy
position and Chirisophus was following at a brisk pace with the
hoplites. But when the enemy troops on the road saw the defeat of
their comrades on the high ground, they turned and fled. There
were only a few casualties, but the Greeks captured huge numbers of
wicker shields, which they slashed with their swords until they were
useless. Once they reached the top of the pass, they performed sacrifices and set up a trophy. Then they marched down the other side to
the plain, where they found villages which were well stocked with
everything they needed.

[7] The next leg was a five-day march of thirty parasangs that
brought them into the land of the Taochians, where they began to
get very low on provisions, because the Taochians had removed all
their supplies to the strongholds where they lived. However, one of
the Taochian strongholds they came to was not an established community with houses, but just a place where men and women had
gathered, along with a lot of livestock. Chirisophus therefore
launched an attack on the place as soon as he got there. The stronghold was perched on top of precipitous cliffs, so the Greeks could
not surround the place and attack it all together; companies came up
into the attack one by one, each replacing the one before it when the
men grew tired.

No sooner had Xenophon arrived with the peltasts and hoplites of
his rearguard than Chirisophus said: 'You've come in the nick of
time. We've got to take this place. The men will have nothing to eat
unless we capture it.' They put their heads together to come up with
a plan, and when Xenophon asked what was stopping them entering
the stronghold, Chirisophus said: 'There's only one way in—the one
you can see—and whenever we try to go along it, they roll rocks
down on us from that cliff overlooking the road. And you can see', he
added, pointing to men with crushed legs and ribs, 'what happens to
anyone who's caught there.'

'What about if they use up all their stones?' Xenophon asked.
'Then there'll be nothing stopping us, surely, because there are
plainly only a few people over there and only two or three of them

are armed. Also, as you can see as well as I, although the distance we have to cross while under attack is almost one and a half plethra, about a plethron of the ground has pine trees growing on it, with wide spaces between the trees. If the men stood behind the trees, how could they be hurt by thrown stones or rolled rocks? Then there would be only about half a plethron left, which they'd have to cover at a run when the stones and rocks stop.'

'But the stones and rocks rain down on us as soon as we start to approach the trees,' Chirisophus said.

'That would be perfect for us,' Xenophon replied, 'because they'll use up their stones all the more quickly. But let's move up to a spot from which we'll have only a short distance to run across, if we can, and from where it will be easy to retreat, if we want to.'

So Chirisophus and Xenophon set out, along with Callimachus of Parrhasia, one of the company commanders, whose turn it was that day to hold the position of senior company commander of the rear-guard. The company commanders of other divisions of the army stayed out of danger. Then about seventy men set out for the shelter of the trees, taking the utmost care and leaving one by one, not all at once. But some men, including Agasias of Stymphalus and Aristonymus of Methydrium (who were also commanders of rear-guard companies), took up positions before the shelter of the trees, because there was room for only one company of men to stand among the trees.

Callimachus suddenly had a clever idea: he repeatedly ran two or three paces forward from the shelter of his tree, and ran back again when the stones started to fly. Each time he ran forward, more than ten cart-loads of stones and rocks were used up. But when Agasias saw what Callimachus was up to, and realized that the whole army was watching, he became anxious in case someone else beat him into the stronghold, and so he set off by himself, without calling on anyone at all to join him, not even Aristonymus or Eurylochus of Lusi,* though they were near by and were his friends. He overtook everyone else, but when Callimachus saw him going past, he grabbed hold of the rim of his shield—but just then Aristonymus of Methydrium ran past them both, with Eurylochus of Lusi right behind him. All four of these men were constantly involved in a keenly contested rivalry to see which of them was the bravest, and on this occasion their rivalry enabled them to take the stronghold,

because once they had made it inside, the stones altogether stopped
flying from above.

What followed was terrible to behold. Women threw their children
off the cliff and then hurled themselves off afterwards, and the men
did the same. At one point Aeneas of Stymphalus, one of the company commanders, saw a well-dressed man running as if to throw
himself over the edge, and he grabbed hold of him to stop him, but
the Taochian dragged Aeneas with him, and they both fell to their
deaths on the rocks below. So very few prisoners were taken, but
they got plenty of oxen, asses, sheep, and goats.

The next leg was a seven-day march of fifty parasangs through
Chalybian territory.* Of all the peoples through whose lands they
travelled, the Chalybians were the most valiant, and the Greeks
were constantly involved in hand-to-hand fighting with them. The
Chalybians wore linen cuirasses which reached down to their lower
abdomen and had a thick fringe of twisted cords instead of flaps.*
They also wore greaves and helmets, and tucked into their belts they
carried a dagger about the size of a Laconian dirk,* which they used
to slit the throats of anyone they managed to overpower. Then they
would cut off their victim's head and take it with them, and whenever their adversaries were going to see them, they would break into
song and dance. They also carried a spear which was about fifteen
cubits long* and had a point at only one end. They stayed inside their
towns until the Greeks had passed, and then followed them and
harassed them all the way. They lived in strongholds, inside which
they also stored all their provisions, which meant that there was
nothing for the Greeks to take from their territory and they survived
on the animals they had taken from the Taochians.

The Greeks then came to the Harpasus river, which was four
plethra wide. The next leg was a four-day march of twenty parasangs
through Scythenian territory, across a plain to some villages where
they stayed for three days and replenished their provisions. The next
leg was a four-day journey of twenty parasangs that brought them to
a large and prosperous inhabited city called Gymnias. The local ruler
sent the Greeks a guide from this city to take them through the land
of his enemies. The guide came and told them that within five days,
under his guidance, they would reach a place from where they could
see the sea, and that if he failed they had his permission to kill him.
When he took them into the land of his people's enemies, he kept

insisting that they burn and devastate the countryside, until it was clear that he had come not out of any goodwill towards the Greeks, but to make sure that this happened.

On the fifth day they did in fact reach the mountain, which was called Theches. When the first men got there,†* a huge cry went up. This made Xenophon and the rearguard think that the van too was under attack from another enemy force, as in the rear they were being followed by men from the land they were burning. The rearguard had killed some of them and, as a result of a successful ambush, had taken some prisoners and gained about twenty wicker shields which were covered in untreated oxhide with the hair still on it. But the cry kept getting louder and nearer, as each successive rank that came up began to sprint towards the ever-increasing numbers of those who were shouting out. The more men who reached the front, the louder the cry became, until it was apparent to Xenophon that something of special significance was happening. He mounted a horse, took Lycius and the cavalry, and rode up to lend assistance; and before long they could make out that the soldiers were shouting 'The sea! The sea!' and this was the word they were passing along. Then all the men in the rear began running too, and the yoke-animals and the horses broke into a gallop. When everyone reached the top of the mountain, they immediately fell into one another's arms, even the generals and the company commanders, with tears in their eyes.

Suddenly, at someone's suggestion, the soldiers began to bring stones and to make a great cairn, on which they placed, as dedications, a number of untreated oxhides, some sticks they had used for walking, and the shields they had captured. The guide not only slashed the shields himself, but encouraged the others to do so. Then the Greeks sent the guide back home with gifts from the common pool—a horse, a silver cup, Persian clothing, and ten darics. But he asked above all for some of their rings, and he was given a lot of them by the men. He showed them a village where they could set up camp, pointed out the road that would take them to the Macronians, and late in the day set off home through the darkness.

[8] The Greeks then marched for three days through the land of the Macronians, and covered ten parasangs. On the first day they reached the river which divided the land of the Macronians from that of the Scythenians, and found themselves between extremely forbidding ground on their right and on their left another river, into

which flowed the river-border which they were going to have to cross. The river to their left was thickly wooded with trees of no great girth, and when they got there the Greeks began to cut the trees down, because they were eager to leave the place as quickly as they could. But the Macronians, with their wicker shields, spears, and hair tunics, were lined up on the other side of the crossing-place, cheering one another on and hurling stones which failed to reach the Greeks and only fell harmlessly into the river.

At that point, one of the peltasts, who said he had been a slave in Athens, approached Xenophon and said that he recognized the language the men were speaking. 'I think', he said, 'that this is my native land. If you have no objection, I'd like to speak to them.'

'No, I've got no problem with that,' said Xenophon. 'Do talk to them and try to find out first of all who they are.' And 'Macronians' was the answer they gave to the question.

'Now,' Xenophon went on, 'ask them why they have taken the field against us—why they want to be our enemies.'

'Because you are attacking our land,' they said.

The Greek generals then told the man to say that they meant no harm, but were on their way back to Greece after having fought the king, and wanted only to get to the sea. The Macronians asked whether the Greeks would confirm the truth of what they were saying with the usual pledges, and the generals replied that they would be happy to give and receive pledges of good faith. So the Macronians gave one of their native spears to the Greeks, the Greeks gave the Macronians a Greek one (since the Macronians said that spears were pledges), and both sides called on the gods to witness their agreement.

With this assurance in place, teams of mingled Macronians and Greeks worked together to cut down the trees and build a causeway on which the Greeks could cross the river. The Macronians also supplied them with as many goods for sale as they could, acted as their guides, and two days later left them at the border between their land and that of the Colchians. On the mountain range they found there (which was massive, but not impassable), the Colchians were lined up in battle order. At first the Greeks formed up themselves into an opposing phalanx, with the intention of advancing in that formation towards the mountain, but then the generals decided to meet and confer about how best to conduct the battle.

Xenophon's view was that they should break up the phalanx and form the companies into columns, and he said as much. 'It will take hardly any time', he explained, 'for the phalanx to fall apart, because in some parts of the mountain we'll find rough terrain, even if in other places the going is easy, and as soon as the men see this phalanx fall apart, their confidence will be sapped. Also, if we advance on the enemy in lines that are short but deep,† they'll outflank us and the men who outflank us will have a free hand; and if we advance in lines that are long but shallow, it's highly likely that our lines will be broken open by the solid hail of men and missiles that will fall upon us—and that has to happen only in one place for the whole phalanx to be in trouble. No, I think we should form the companies into columns and space them out so that we cover enough ground for the outermost companies to extend beyond the wings of the enemy lines. If we adopt this formation, not only will we be beyond the enemy phalanx,† but the column formation will ensure that our best men take the lead, so that each company commander will pick the easiest route for his men. It's true that the companies will be spaced out, but it won't be easy for our adversaries to penetrate these gaps with companies to either side of them, and breaking through a company which is advancing as a column will be no easy matter either. Anyway, if one of the companies does get into trouble, the company next to it will come to its assistance; and as soon as just one of our companies has made it up to the crest, the enemy troops will all flee.'

This plan was approved and they formed the companies into columns. As Xenophon made his way over to the left wing from the right wing,* he repeatedly addressed the troops. 'Men,' he said, 'the enemy troops you can see are all that stand between us and the place we have for so long been determined to reach. We must find a way to eat them alive.'

So the companies took their places and formed up as columns; there were about eighty hoplite companies, with each company containing almost 100 men. The peltasts and the bowmen were formed into three units—one beyond the left wing, one beyond the right, and one in the centre—with each unit containing almost 600 men. The generals then gave the order to make a vow, and once the men had done so and had chanted a paean they began to advance. Chirisophus and Xenophon, along with the peltasts assigned to them, were beyond the enemy lines as they advanced, and when the enemy noticed this they ran to face them, some to the right and some to the left; but this manoeuvre pulled their phalanx apart and left a large gap in their centre. Seeing them splitting off to either side, the peltasts of the Arcadian unit, under the command of Aeschines of Acarnania, thought they were running away, and with a shout they broke into a run. They were the first to get to the top of the mountain, with the Arcadian hoplites, under Cleanor of Orchomenus, close behind them. As soon as the Greeks broke into a run, the enemy lines crumbled and men scattered here and there in flight.

Having scaled the mountain, the Greeks encamped in a number of villages, which were well stocked with provisions. Generally speaking, there was nothing out of the ordinary there, but there were a lot of swarms of bees, and all the men who ate honeycomb became deranged, suffered from vomiting and diarrhoea, and were too weak to stand up. Those who had eaten a little behaved as though they were drunk, while those who had eaten a lot behaved like madmen, or even like people on the point of death.* The ground was so thickly covered with supine men that it looked like the aftermath of a defeat, and morale plummeted. On the next day, however, no one died, and they began to recover their senses at about the same time of day that they had eaten the honeycomb. Two or three days later, they were back on their feet, as if they had been treated with medicine.

The next leg, a two-day march of seven parasangs, brought them to the sea at Trapezus, an inhabited Greek city on the Euxine Sea which was originally founded in Colchian territory by emigrants from Sinope. They stayed there for about thirty days in Colchian villages, which they used as a base for raids on Colchis. The Trapezuntians sold the Greeks their supplies, made them welcome, and gave them oxen, barley, and wine as tokens of friendship. They also helped the nearby Colchians, most of whom lived on the plain, in their negotiations with the Greeks, and the Greeks were given oxen as tokens of friendship by these Colchians too.

Next they made all the arrangements necessary for the sacrifice they had vowed to make,* and by then they had gained enough oxen to offer in gratitude for their guidance to Zeus the Saviour and to Heracles, and to fulfil their vows to the other gods as well. They also held an athletic competition on the mountain where they were encamped, and they chose Dracontius the Spartiate* (who had been banished from his home while still a boy for having accidentally stabbed another boy with his dagger and killed him) to be responsible for the racetrack and to supervise the contest. After the sacrifice, the generals gave the animal skins* to Dracontius and told him to show them where he had laid out the track. He pointed to the place where they happened to be standing and said: 'This hill is perfect for running in any direction.' 'But how', they asked, 'will they be able to wrestle on hard, shrub-covered ground like this?' And Dracontius replied: 'It'll be a bit more painful for the one who is thrown.'*

The events were a stade race for boys (most of their captives were boys), a long-distance race* in which more than sixty Cretans took part, and wrestling, boxing, and pancratium.* It was a wonderful spectacle. There were a great many entrants for each event and, with their friends watching,* there was enormous rivalry. There were also horse races, in which the riders had to ride downhill, turn their horses on the seashore, and make their way back up the hill again towards the altar. On the way down, most of the horses lurched around, and on the way back up they could hardly walk on the steepest stretches, and so the air was filled with shouts, laughter, and cheers.

BOOK FIVE

[1] After the games, there was a meeting to plan the rest of their journey. The first to get to his feet was Leon of Thurii. 'Speaking for myself, my friends,' he said, 'by now I'm fed up with packing my baggage, walking and running, carrying my arms and armour, marching in formation, standing guard, and fighting. Now that we've reached the sea, I want to put all this hard work behind me and sail the rest of the way. I'd like to arrive in Greece flat on my back, like Odysseus.'*

The soldiers liked the sound of this and cheered loudly, and then someone else expressed the same view—and so did everyone else who was there. Then Chirisophus got to his feet and said: 'Men, I'm on friendly terms with Anaxibius, the naval commander of Sparta.* If you send me to him, I'm sure I'll return with triremes and merchant ships to transport us. If you really want to travel by sea, wait for my return. I won't be long.'

The men were delighted to hear Chirisophus' suggestion and voted that he should set sail as soon as possible. Then Xenophon stood up and said: 'So Chirisophus is to go and fetch ships, while we wait for him. I want to tell you what I think we should do while we're waiting. First, we had better get provisions—and we have to get them from enemy territory, because there aren't enough goods for sale here and only a few of us have the wherewithal to buy food. But the surrounding territory is hostile, so the chances are that casualties will be heavy if you set out after provisions in a careless and unguarded fashion. I think your safety lies in organizing foraging patrols to get provisions, instead of wandering around at random, and I think you should let us generals take charge of them.' This proposal was carried.

'Here's another idea,' Xenophon went on. 'Some of you are going to go out looting. It would be best, I think, for anyone who is planning such a raid to inform us generals and to tell us where he's going, so that we know how many people have left and how many people have stayed behind. Then we can help you with the arrangements, if you want us to, and if you ever need armed assistance, we know where to send it. Also, if less experienced men are involved in some such enterprise, we can try to find out the strength of those against whom they are going and offer advice accordingly.' This proposal too was carried.

'Here's a third point for you to consider,' Xenophon said. 'Our enemies have the opportunity to make plundering raids on us and they are devising schemes for doing so, which is only fair, since their property is in our hands. Moreover, they are occupying the hills above us. So I think we should post guards around the camp. If we each do our bit as guards and scouts, our enemies will have less chance to harass us.

'Then again, what about this? If we were absolutely certain that Chirisophus would return with enough ships, there'd be no need for me to say what I'm going to say. But we can't actually be certain of that, so I think we should, for our part, try to get ships for ourselves from here too. Then, if Chirisophus does make it back, we shall have more than enough ships, with those we have here, to sail home in, and if he doesn't bring enough ships, we can use the ones we have here. I've often seen merchant ships sailing past this place. If we ask the people of Trapezus to lend us warships, we can use the warships to bring the merchantmen back to harbour here. Then we can disable them by removing their rudders and put them under guard, until we have enough to carry us. In this way, we might well resolve the problem of getting the kind of transport we need.' This proposal was carried too.

'You should also consider', Xenophon continued, 'whether it would be fair for us to draw on our common fund to maintain any sailors we bring back here—after all, it will be thanks to us that they'll be waiting here—and to agree to pay them for our passage, so that in doing us a favour they'll be doing themselves one too.' This proposal was carried too.

'But what if it turns out that even these efforts of ours fail to secure enough ships?' he went on. 'Then, I think, we should order the inhabitants of the coastal cities to repair the roads, because at the moment our information is that they're unfit for travel. I'm sure they'll obey us, partly out of fear and partly out of the desire to get rid of us.'

The men cried out that there was no need for an overland journey. Xenophon realized that they were being short-sighted, but did not put the matter to the vote. Instead, he persuaded the cities to repair the roads of their own accord, arguing that serviceable roads would accelerate the army's departure. The Greeks were given a fifty-oared warship by the people of Trapezus, and they put Dexippus, a free Laconian,* in charge of it, but he ignored the job of collecting merchant ships, took the ship, and sneaked out of the Euxine. But he got what he deserved later: he became involved in some intrigue or other at the court of Seuthes in Thrace and was killed by Nicander of Sparta.

They were, however, also given a thirty-oared warship. Polycrates of Athens was put in command of it and he brought back to the camp all the merchant ships he captured. They unloaded any cargo the ships had and posted guards to keep it safe, while they reserved the ships themselves for their own transport. While this was going on, Greek raiding parties went out foraging, but only a few of them were successful. In the course of one of these raids, when Cleaenetus took out two companies—his own and another one—to attack a well-defended place, quite a few Greeks were killed, including Cleaenetus himself.

[2] The time came when it was no longer possible to get hold of provisions and make it back to camp on the same day. Xenophon therefore took as guides some men from Trapezus and led half the army into the territory of the Drilae. The other half he left to protect the camp, because the Colchians, who had been evicted from their houses, had gathered in large numbers and had occupied the high ground above the camp. The Trapezuntians refused to take the Greeks to places where provisions were easily available, because they were on friendly terms with the people there, but they were glad to take them into the territory of the Drilae, at whose hands they were constantly suffering. But the terrain was mountainous and rough going, and there was no more warlike people on the Euxine.

When the Greeks reached the mountains, the Drilae set fire to those of their villages which struck them as being vulnerable to attack, and withdrew. There was nothing for the Greeks to take except for the occasional pig or ox, or some other animal that had escaped the flames. One stronghold, however, was their mother city and this was where they had all congregated. There was an extremely deep gully around the place and all the approaches to it were difficult to negotiate. The peltasts, who had run five or six stades ahead of the hoplites, crossed the gully and attacked the place, because they had spotted plenty of livestock, including sheep and goats. Over two thousand men crossed the gully, because the peltasts were joined by large numbers of spearmen,* who had come out after provisions. They were unable to take the place by force of arms, however, because a wide trench had been excavated around it, and the embankment made from the excavated earth had been fitted with a palisade and wooden towers set at close intervals. So the Greeks tried to withdraw, but the Drilae kept attacking and making it impossible for them to run away, since descent from the stronghold into the gully was possible only in single file. The Greek troops sent word to Xenophon, who was commanding the hoplites, and when the messenger arrived he said, 'There's a stronghold filled with plenty of livestock, but the place is too well defended for us to take and we can't retreat either, because they come out and fight, and the way back is awkward.'

When Xenophon heard this he brought his men up to the gully and ordered the hoplites to wait there under arms, while he himself crossed the gully along with his company commanders to investigate whether it would be better to bring back those who had already crossed or to have the hoplites cross over, if the place looked as though it could be taken. The impression they gained was that bringing the men back over the gully would cost them many lives, but the company commanders thought that the place could be taken and Xenophon agreed, because he trusted the omens. For the diviners had declared that there would be fighting, but that the expedition would turn out well. So he sent the company commanders back to bring the hoplites across, while he himself stayed there, once he had got all the peltasts to fall back and had ordered them not to discharge their missiles from far away.

When the hoplites arrived, Xenophon bore in mind the fact that the company commanders who had throughout been trying to outdo one another in bravery* were near one another, and he told every company commander to organize his company in the way that he thought would make it the most effective fighting unit. While they were doing this, he gave the order that all the peltasts were to advance with their fingers through their loops, ready to throw their javelins on his signal, that the bowmen were to have their arrows notched, ready to fire their bows on his signal, and that the light-armed troops were to have their bags filled with stones; and he sent the appropriate people to see that these orders were carried out.

After a while everything was ready. The company commanders and their junior officers had all fallen in side by side, along with those who considered themselves just as brave as their officers. Everyone could see everyone else, because the contours of the terrain meant that the line was crescent-shaped. Once they had chanted their paean and the trumpet had sounded, they raised the war-cry to Enyalius and at the same time the hoplites broke into a run. A hail of missiles began to fly from the Greek lines—spears, arrows, sling-shot, and huge numbers of hand-thrown stones—and there were even some who brought fire. The massed missiles forced the enemy to abandon the palisade and the towers, and so Agasias of Stymphalus and Philoxenus of Pellene put down their arms and armour and climbed up wearing only their tunics, with one of them pulling the other up after him. Meanwhile, someone else had climbed up too, and it began to look as though the stronghold had been captured.

The peltasts and the light-armed troops sprinted inside and set about grabbing whatever they could, but Xenophon stood by the gates and kept as many hoplites as he could outside, because further enemy soldiers were beginning to appear on some of the defensible ridges near by. Soon, however, shouting could be heard from inside and men began to run out, some clutching what they had managed to take, and before long there was the occasional wounded man among them. There was a terrific press at the gates, and in response to enquiries those who were being driven out said that there was an acropolis inside, which was strongly held by the enemy, who were making sorties and laying into the Greeks inside the stronghold.

On hearing this, Xenophon told Tolmides, the herald, to announce that anyone who wanted booty should go inside. A lot of men rushed inside, and those who were trying to force their way in overcame those who were dashing out and pinned the enemy troops once more on their acropolis. The Greeks then stole everything that was outside the acropolis and carried it away, while the hoplites took up positions either at the palisade or on the road which led to the acropolis. Xenophon and the company commanders were looking to see if there was any way to take the acropolis, because that would guarantee their safety and survival, and otherwise retreat looked extremely difficult, but they decided that the place was completely unassailable.

So they prepared to withdraw. Each unit tore down the nearest section of the palisade, and they dismissed not only those who were unfit for combat or had loads to carry, but also most of the hoplites, with the company commanders keeping only those men they felt they could rely on. As soon as the retreat began, hordes of men, armed with wicker shields, spears, greaves, and Paphlagonian helmets,* ran out from the acropolis, while others climbed onto the roofs of the houses on either side of the road which led to the acropolis. This made it unsafe even to chase fugitives in the direction of the entrance to the acropolis, because huge bits of timber would be hurled from the rooftops, which made staying put or retreating equally tricky. The approach of night was another cause for fear.

The Greeks were still fighting, and still uncertain quite what to do, when one of the gods offered them a means of safety: one of the houses on the right, which had presumably been set alight by someone or other, suddenly blazed up and when it began to collapse, the people who were occupying the houses on the right fled. When Xenophon heard about this gift from Fortune, he ordered the houses on the left to be set alight too; the wooden houses were soon ablaze and the people who were occupying them abandoned them as well. Then it was only the forces directly in front who were causing them trouble. They were obviously going to attack the Greeks during their evacuation of the stronghold and descent into the gully, so Xenophon ordered everyone who was out of range of the enemy missiles to bring up wood and pile it between themselves and the enemy. When there was enough, they set it on fire, and they also set about torching the houses right beside the palisade, so that the enemy would be occupied with that. The ruse of building a fire between themselves and the enemy enabled them to withdraw from the place, although it was still not easy. The whole town burnt to the ground—the houses, the towers, the palisade, and everything except the acropolis.

Next day the Greeks returned to their camp with their provisions. They were worried about the way down to Trapezus, however, which was steep and narrow, and so they set up a false ambush. A Mysian (who was also called Mysus) took ten Cretans and waited in a thicket. They pretended that they were trying to stay out of sight of the enemy, but from time to time the bronze on their shields caught the light and made the enemy troops frightened, because they assumed that an ambush had been laid for them. Meanwhile, the rest of the Greeks were on their way down, and when Xenophon thought they had crept far enough, he signalled to the Mysian that he was to run away at top speed, and the Mysian and the men he had with him broke cover and ran away. The Cretans, sure that the enemy was gaining on them in the race, hurled themselves off the road and into the undergrowth, and saved themselves by tumbling down the glens, but the Mysian, who was running down the road, kept calling for help. The Greeks sent a rescue party, which recovered him, but he was wounded. Then the rescuers themselves began slowly to back down the road while being shot at by the enemy. Some of the Cretans returned the enemy fire with their bows. By these means they all got back to the camp without any loss of life.

[3] Since Chirisophus had not yet come back, and since they did not have enough ships and there were no longer any provisions for the taking, they came to realize that they had to leave. They put on board the ships those who were unwell, those who were over forty years old, the children and the women, and any equipment that they did not absolutely need to keep. They also had Philesius and Sophaenetus, the oldest of the generals,* go on board, with instructions to take care of all the passengers and cargo, while the rest set out overland on a newly repaired road. On the third day of their march they came to Cerasus, a Greek city on the coast which was a colony of Sinope in Colchian territory, and they stayed there for ten days. While they were there, they conducted a review of the men under arms and found, on counting them, that there were 8,600 in total. These were the men left alive, while the rest had been killed by their enemies, by the snow, and in a few cases by illness.

At Cerasus they also distributed the money that had been raised by selling the prisoners of war.* They reserved a tenth of the amount for Apollo and Artemis of Ephesus,* and the generals divided this portion of the total among themselves (Neon of Asine* was given Chirisophus' share), with each man looking after his share for the gods. Xenophon had Apollo's portion made into a dedication which he set up in the Athenian treasury in Delphi,* and he inscribed on it, in addition to his own name, that of Proxenus, the guest-friend of his who had been killed along with Clearchus. And when he left Asia with Agesilaus for the expedition against Boeotia,* he deposited the portion that was due to Artemis of Ephesus with Megabyzus,* the warden of the temple of Artemis, because it looked as though his journey would be dangerous. He left instructions that, if he survived, Megabyzus was to return the money to him and, if anything happened to him, Megabyzus was to have it made into a dedication to Artemis, using his own judgement as to what would please the goddess.

After Xenophon became an exile,* when he was living near Olympia in Scillus, where he had been settled by the Spartans, Megabyzus came to Olympia as a spectator* and returned the deposit. Xenophon used it to buy land for the goddess, after consulting the god* about where precisely this land should be. It so happened that there was a river Selinus running through the land he bought, and there is also a river Selinus in Ephesus, which flows past the temple of Artemis. Both rivers contain fish and shellfish, but the land at Scillus is also good for hunting every species of wild animal that is normally hunted. Xenophon also built an altar and a temple from the sacred money, and afterwards he always set aside a tenth of the produce of the estate and performed a sacrifice to the goddess; and all his fellow citizens and neighbours, men and women, joined in the feast.* The goddess would supply the diners with barley meal, loaves, wine, dried fruit, and a portion not only of the sacrificial victims from the sacred herd, but also of any animals which had been hunted down by Xenophon's sons and the sons of the other townspeople, who used to go out hunting for the festival, along with any other man who wanted to join them. The animals—boars, roe deer, and stags—were caught partly on the actual sacred land and partly on Mount Pholoë.

The spot is about twenty stades from the temple of Zeus at Olympia, on the Olympia–Sparta road. The sacred land also contains meadows and tree-covered hills with good fodder for pigs, goats, oxen, and horses, and so even the yoke-animals belonging to the people who come to the festival eat well. Immediately around the temple there has been planted an orchard containing every kind of tree that produces edible fruit season by season. The temple was constructed as a small version of the one at Ephesus, and the image of the goddess, though made out of cypress wood, resembles the golden one in Ephesus.* Beside the temple stands a stele with the following inscription: THIS PLACE IS SACRED TO ARTEMIS. HE

WHO OWNS IT AND HARVESTS ITS FRUITS MUST EVERY YEAR
OFFER A TENTH OF THE PRODUCE TO THE GODDESS, AND MUST
USE SOME OF THE REMAINDER TO KEEP THE TEMPLE IN GOOD
REPAIR. NEGLECT OF THESE DUTIES WILL NOT GO UNNOTICED
BY THE GODDESS.

[4] After Cerasus, the same people who had travelled by sea before
continued to do so, while the rest continued on foot. When they were
about to cross over into the land of the Mossynoecians,* they sent
Timesitheus, the Trapezuntian who had the job of representing
Mossynoecian interests,* to ask the Mossynoecians whether they
should assume that they would be marching through friendly or
hostile territory. The Mossynoecians, feeling that their strongholds
would keep them safe, replied that they would not let the Greeks
pass. But then Timesitheus said that the Mossynoecians who lived
further west were at war with these Mossynoecians, and he thought
it would be a good idea to invite them to a meeting, to see if they
wanted to enter into an alliance. So Timesitheus was dispatched to
them and returned with their leaders, who then met with the Greek
generals.

At the meeting Xenophon (with Timesitheus as translator) said:
'Mossynoecians, we want to get back to Greece safe and sound, and
we have to travel by land because we don't have ships. But these
people, who we hear are your enemies, are in our way. If you want,
you can have us as your allies, and then you can punish them for any
wrong they have ever done you and in the future they will be your
subjects. If you're inclined to reject our offer, you should consider
whether you will ever again find such a large army anywhere to
support your cause.'

The chief of the Mossynoecians replied that the plan met with
their approval and that they wanted to enter into an alliance with the
Greeks. 'Tell us this, then,' said Xenophon. 'What will you require
of us, should we become your allies, and how will you be able to help
us complete our journey?'

'We can invade the territory of these people who are our common
enemies from the other side,' they said, 'and we can send you here
ships and men to fight alongside you and show you the best route.'

The Mossynoecians vouched for these terms by giving and receiv-
ing pledges, and then they left. The next day they returned with
300 boats made out of the trunks of single trees, each containing

three men. In each case two of the men disembarked and fell in under arms, while the remaining man stayed in the boat. Then the one lot took the boats and sailed away, while the rest stayed behind and marshalled themselves for parade. They stood in lines about 100 men long, facing one another like the two halves of a chorus;* all of them carried wicker shields which were covered with the skins of hairy, white oxen and were shaped like an ivy leaf, and in their right hands they held a spear which was about six cubits long and had a sharp point at its tip, while the butt of the shaft was rounded. They had dressed in short tunics which ended above their knees and were made out of material which was as thick as linen bags for bedclothes, and on their heads they wore leather helmets in the Paphlagonian style, with the leather tufted around the middle so that it looked like nothing so much as a tiara. They also had iron battleaxes.

Then one of them took the lead and all the rest marched off after him, chanting in time with their pace. They passed through the various Greek units and through the ranks of the hoplites, and marched straight towards the enemy, heading for a stronghold which seemed to be particularly vulnerable to assault. This strong-hold had been built in front of the city which they referred to as their mother city and which contained the principal acropolis of the Mossynoecians. This acropolis was in fact the focus of the war between the rival groups, because those who held it at any time were supposed to be the masters of all the Mossynoecians, and the rebels claimed that the present occupants had illegally taken it over for themselves, when it should have been theirs as well, in order to lord it over them.

Some of the Greeks also went with them, not because they had been ordered to do so by the generals, but because they were after booty.* At first, as they approached, the enemy did nothing, but when they were close to the stronghold the enemy charged out and put them to flight. They killed quite a lot of the barbarians and a few of the Greeks who had gone up with them, and set out in pursuit— until the sight of further Greeks coming to the rescue made them fall back. They cut the heads off the corpses and showed them to the Greeks and to their own enemies, while dancing and chanting a kind of song. The Greeks were furious, not just because the action had increased enemy morale, but also because it was quite a sizeable force of Greeks which had gone out with the rebels and they had been routed—the first time this had happened in the course of the expedition.

Xenophon convened a meeting and addressed the Greeks. 'Fellow soldiers,' he said, 'don't let what has happened get you down. Try to see that the outcome is good and bad in equal measure. In the first place, you now know that the men who are going to act as our guides really are the enemies of the people against whom we have to fight. In the second place, even those Greeks who thought they could ignore the military discipline we practise, and supposed that they could achieve in the company of barbarians the same results that they could with us, have been punished and will therefore be less inclined to abandon our battle formation again. No, you must make sure that even those barbarians who are on our side think of you as more effective fighters than themselves, and that you demonstrate to the enemy that they are now going to come up against men who are quite different from the undisciplined mob they fought before.'

They spent the rest of the day waiting as they were, but the next day, once the omens from the sacrifices were favourable, and after they had eaten, they formed the companies into columns, posted the barbarians, who were also formed into columns, on the left, and set out. The archers were deployed between the columns and a little way in front† of the first row of hoplites, because the enemy had mobile troops who kept running down the hill and pelting the Greeks with stones, and the archers and peltasts kept them at bay. The rest of the Greeks advanced at a steady pace.

Their first objective was the stronghold from which the barbarians and those who had joined them had been repulsed the day before, because that was where the enemy troops had been drawn up to meet them. The barbarians stood their ground against the peltasts and engaged them, but turned and fled at the approach of the hoplites, and the peltasts immediately chased after them up towards the city. The hoplites followed in formation, and when they had made the ascent and were close to the residential areas of the mother city, the enemy, who had massed together, began to fight back by throwing their javelins and using their other spears, which were so sturdy and long that a man could hardly carry one, to defend themselves in the hand-to-hand fighting. So far from giving ground, however, the Greeks kept pressing forward to engage them at close quarters, until the barbarians began to run away from there too, as well as from the stronghold, which they had completely abandoned. However, their king, who was inside the wooden tower* built on top of the hill and who was maintained by contributions from the whole population while he was the resident and guard of the tower, refused to leave it, and so did the ruler of the stronghold they had taken earlier. So they were incinerated along with the towers.

When the Greeks looted the strongholds, they found in the houses piles of stored loaves, which according to the Mossynoecians were made from the previous year's flour, while the fresh grain was stored with the straw. Most of the grain was spelt. There were also jars of dried dolphin meat and pots of dolphin blubber, which the Mossynoecians used for the same purposes that the Greeks use olive oil. The attics of the houses contained a great many flat, unsegmented nuts which, when boiled and baked into loaves, were the Mossynoecians' main food. There was also wine, which tasted sharp when undiluted, because it was so rough, but when diluted it had a pleasant scent and flavour.

The Greeks ate there and then carried on, after handing the place over to the Mossynoecians who had fought alongside them. All the other strongholds they passed that were in the hands of people who had sided with their enemies had either been abandoned, if they were vulnerable to attack, or—and this was the most common occurrence—voluntarily surrendered. Towns were located at intervals of more or less eighty stades, but the layout of the land, with its mountains and valleys, was such that the inhabitants of one town could hear people shouting to them from the next one.

The people of the friendly towns to which their journey brought them showed them the sons of the well-off members of their society. These boys, who had been fattened up on a diet of boiled nuts, were soft and extremely pale, and almost as wide as they were tall. They had complex and colourful flower designs tattooed all over their backs and fronts. The Mossynoecians also wanted to have sex in the open with the kept women whom the Greeks had brought, because that was their custom there. All the Mossynoecians, men and women, were pale. The soldiers who took part in this expedition agreed that, of all those whose lands they passed through, the Mossynoecians were the most alien and the most remote from Greeks in their customs. They used to do in public what others did when no one was looking, and when they were alone they did the

kinds of things that others did in company; they used to talk to
themselves and laugh by themselves, and they would start dancing,
wherever they happened to be, just as if they were putting on a
display for others.

[5] It took the Greeks eight days to march through both the
hostile and the friendly parts of this land, and then they came to the
Chalybians, a scant people, who were subjects of the Mossynoecians
and most of whom made a living from working with iron. Next they
came to the Tibarenians, whose land was far more flat and whose
villages by the sea were less well fortified. The generals wanted to
attack the villages, to give the men a little something by way of profit,
so they refused to accept the tokens of friendship which arrived from
the Tibarenians, but told them to wait until they had decided what to
do. They performed sacrifices, and eventually, after many victims
had been sacrificed, the diviners unanimously declared that the gods
were absolutely opposed to war. So they then accepted the tokens of
friendship and marched for two days through their land, which they
could now treat as friendly territory, until they came to the Greek
city of Cotyora, a colony of Sinope, which was situated in the land of
the Tibarenians.

They stayed near Cotyora for forty-five days, during which time
they first sacrificed to the gods and then each ethnic group of Greeks
performed their own religious processions* and held athletic competitions. They took their provisions partly from Paphlagonia and partly
from the villages attached to Cotyora, because the inhabitants of
Cotyora refused to sell them provisions and would not let even those
of them who were sick inside the wall.

After a while, a delegation arrived from Sinope, out of concern
not only for Cotyora, which belonged to them and paid them tribute,
but also for the surrounding land, which they had heard was being
devastated. The members of the delegation came into the Greeks'
camp and, with Hecatonymus (who had a reputation as a formidable
speaker) as their spokesman, they said: 'Soldiers, the citizens of
Sinope sent us to congratulate you on your victory—a victory of
Greeks over barbarians—and to say that they share your joy at
having survived all the appalling dangers we've heard about and at
having got this far. But we think that, as Greeks ourselves, we should
be treated well by you, since you are Greeks, and that you should not
do us harm. After all, we've never taken even the first step towards

injuring you. The people of Cotyora are our colonists and we gave them this land after having taken it from barbarians. That is why they, along with the citizens of Cerasus and those of Trapezus too, pay us a fixed amount of tribute. And it follows that the citizens of Sinope regard any harm you do to any of these people as harm done to them. As far as the present situation is concerned, word has reached us that you—or some of you, at any rate—have forced your way into the city and are using the houses there as your quarters, and that you are taking what you need from the villagers by force, rather than trying to win them over. We don't think this behaviour of yours is right, and if you insist on acting this way, we shall feel compelled to ally ourselves with Corylas and his Paphlagonians, and with any-one else we can.'

In response, Xenophon got to his feet and spoke on behalf of the troops. 'Men of Sinope,' he said, 'there was no way that we could simultaneously forage and fight our enemies, so we're pleased just to have got this far alive and still in possession of our arms and armour. We have at last reached Greek cities, and in Trapezus, where they provided us with a market, we got our supplies by paying for them and we also repaid the people there in kind for the honours they bestowed upon us and the gifts they gave in friendship to the army. Also, we steered clear of any barbarians they were on good terms with, and we did all we could to injure their enemies, against whom they themselves led us. Ask them what sort of people they found us to be. You can do so because, in an act of friendship, the citizens of Trapezus gave us guides to escort us on our journey, and these guides are here now. However, if we found ourselves somewhere where we were not offered provisions for sale—whether the land was occupied by barbarians or by Greeks—we took our supplies, prompted not by arrogance but by sheer necessity. So although the Carduchians, the Taochians, and the Chaldeans were not subjects of the king, we still aroused their hostility, even though they were terrifying opponents, because we had to take what we needed, since they hadn't provided us with a market. On the other hand, although the Macronians were barbarians, we treated them well and took noth-ing from them by force, because they provided us with as good a market as they could.

'As for the people of Cotyora—your subjects, you say—they have only themselves to blame for the loss of anything we've taken, since they did not make us welcome, but shut their gates against us and refused either to let us in or to send provisions for sale out to us. And the person responsible for this attitude towards us was, they said, the man sent by you to govern them. As for your assertion that we've forced our way into the city and taken up quarters there, we asked them to give those of our men who were ill shelter in their homes, and when they refused to open the gates we used an entrance offered us naturally by the place itself. We've done nothing else that involved the use of force, our invalids who have taken up quarters in people's homes are paying their way, and if we have set armed guards over the city gates, that is only so that we have the ability to collect the invalids whenever we want and to prevent them falling into the hands of your governor. All the rest of us, as you can see, have made camp out in the open air, where we've arranged ourselves by units so that we are ready to repay any good treatment we receive and to retaliate if anyone does us harm.

'As for your threat that you might decide to enter into an alliance with Corylas and the Paphlagonians against us, we will fight you both, if we have to. After all, we have already taken on other hostile forces many times the size of yours. But we might decide to get on good terms with the Paphlagonian ourselves—we hear that he desires your city and its coastal villages—and then we will try to prove our friendship by helping him satisfy his desires.'

It was perfectly obvious at this point that Xenophon's words annoyed Hecatonymus and his fellow representatives, but one of them stepped forward and said that they had not come to provoke war, but to demonstrate their friendly intentions. 'If you come to Sinope,' he said, 'we will welcome you there with gifts of friendship, and we're going to urge the people here to give you what they can, because we can see that you've spoken nothing but the truth.' And so the people of Cotyora began to send tokens of friendship and the Greek generals made the Sinopean representatives welcome and held long and cordial talks with them. In particular, both the Greeks and the Sinopeans asked one another what they wanted to know about the journey that lay ahead.

[6] So this day came to an end. The next day the generals convened a general meeting of the troops, and the men decided to invite the Sinopeans to the meeting so that they could hear their advice about the journey that lay ahead. For if they had to march overland, the

Sinopeans, with their knowledge of Paphlagonia, were likely to be useful, and if they went by sea they thought they would still need the Sinopeans, given that they seemed to be the only ones who were in a position to supply them with enough ships for the whole army. So they invited the delegates to join in their deliberations and asked them above all, as Greeks dealing with Greeks, to make them welcome by taking their side and by offering them the best advice.

Hecatonymus got to his feet and began by defending himself for his remark about their allying themselves with the Paphlagonian. He said that he had not meant to sound as though they were intending to fight the Greeks and that, on the contrary, although it was possible for them to be on good terms with the barbarians, they would side with the Greeks. When the Greeks asked him for his advice, he started with a prayer, as follows: 'If I recommend what seems to me to be the best course of action, may profuse good fortune attend me, and if I fail to do so, may the opposite be my lot. For I seem to have the opportunity here to deliver what the saying describes as "sacred counsel".* For if the advice I give you now turns out to be good, my praises will be on many lips, and if it turns out to be bad, there will be many to call down curses on me.

'Although I know that the necessity of supplying you with ships means that we shall be considerably more inconvenienced if you travel by sea, whereas if you go by land it is you who will have to do all the fighting, all the same I had better speak my mind, based on my knowledge of the land and the resources of the Paphlagonians. The land contains both extremes—both wonderfully fertile plains and extremely high mountains. Now, in the first place, you have no choice about where to enter the land, and I know exactly where that is: it is where the spurs of the mountain range rise high on either side of the road. If just a very few men occupied the high ground at this point they could control the route and stop the entire population of the world from negotiating the pass. If you like, you can send someone with me, and I could show him the features I'm talking about. In the second place, I know that as well as plains the barbarians have cavalry which, in their view, could overcome the king's cavalry at full strength. Not long ago, in fact, they failed to turn up in response to a summons from the Persian king: that's how confident their king was.

'Now, suppose you did succeed in taking the mountains by stealth or in seizing them before the enemy got there, and suppose, on the plain, you did succeed in defeating both their horsemen and their foot soldiers, who number more than 120,000, in battle. Then you will come to a series of rivers. First, there is the Thermodon, three plethra wide, which in my opinion is difficult enough to cross anyway, let alone when you have sizeable enemy forces before and behind you. The second river is the Iris, which is also three plethra wide, and the third is the Halys, which is at least two stades wide. You would need boats to cross the Halys, but who is going to supply you with boats? The Parthenius is just as uncrossable, and that's the one you'd come to next, if you succeeded in crossing the Halys.

'In short, then, the overland route is not difficult, in my opinion, so much as downright impossible for you. But if you go by ship, you can sail from here to Sinope and from Sinope to Heraclea, and then from Heraclea you shouldn't have any difficulty by land—or by sea either, because there are plenty of ships at Heraclea too.'

There were various responses to this speech by Hecatonymus. Some suspected that his words were prompted by friendship for Corylas, whose representative at Sinope he was; others thought that he also hoped to be rewarded for this advice; and still others suspected that his words were designed to put the Greeks off going by land and damaging territory belonging to the Sinopeans. But in any case, the Greeks voted to go by sea.

Then Xenophon spoke. 'Men of Sinope,' he said, 'the troops have chosen the route you recommended, but this is how things are: if there turn out to be enough ships to allow us not to leave a single person here, we will set sail; but if it turns out to be a case of some being left behind and others setting sail, we shall not board the ships. For we recognize that as long as we have the upper hand we can stay alive and keep ourselves supplied with provisions, but it goes without saying that if we're ever caught in a weaker position than the enemy, we shall be reduced to slavery.' In reply, the Sinopean delegates urged the Greeks to send a delegation of their own, and they chose Callimachus of Arcadia, Ariston of Athens, and Samolas of Achaea, who left for Sinope.

Meanwhile, Xenophon had been looking at how many Greeks there were there, counting not just the hoplites, but also the peltasts, archers, slingers, and horsemen; their experiences seemed to him to have given them a high degree of proficiency and there they were on the coast of the Euxine, where it would have taken a great deal of money to organize such a large army. As a result of these reflections, it occurred to him that it would be a fine achievement to found a city and acquire extra land and resources for Greece. It would be a size-able city, he thought, when their numbers were added to the local inhabitants of the Euxine coast. Next, before telling anyone in the army about this idea of his,* he set about performing sacrifices, and he called for Silanus of Ambracia, who had been Cyrus' diviner. But Silanus, frightened that the plan might actually come to fruition and that the army might stay somewhere there, spread a rumour among the troops that Xenophon wanted the army to stay and wanted to found a city for his own fame and power. Silanus was personally motivated to get back to Greece as quickly as possible, because he had managed to preserve the 3,000 darics which Cyrus had given him when he sacrificed for him and revealed the truth about the ten days.*

When the troops heard of Xenophon's plan, some of them thought it was an excellent idea for them to stay there, but the majority were against it. And Timasion of Dardanus and Thorax of Boeotia told some Heraclean and Sinopean traders who were there that if they did not pay the troops their wages, so that they could get hold of provisions and sail away, there was a good chance that this enormous force would stay by the Euxine. 'You see,' they said, 'Xenophon is very insistent that when the ships arrive we should suddenly say to the troops: "Men, it's just occurred to us that you lack the means either to get hold of provisions during the voyage home or to help those at home if you do in fact get back there. But if you want, you can pick any place you like on the inhabited coastline around the Euxine and seize it, and then anyone who wants to leave can do so, but those who want to stay can stay. You do of course have the ships to enable you to make sudden raids wherever you want." '

When the traders heard this, they took the news back to their cities, and Eurymachus of Dardanus and Thorax of Boeotia went along with them, on the orders of Timasion of Dardanus, to deliver the same report. In response to the report, the people of Sinope and Heraclea sent a message to Timasion in which they offered to finance him if he arranged for the army to sail away. Timasion was delighted with the suggestion, and during a general assembly of the troops, he said: 'Men, you shouldn't even think about staying. There should be nothing more important to you than Greece. I hear that some people are performing sacrifices with a view to staying, and haven't said a thing to you. But I give you my word that, if you sail away, I shall pay you from the beginning of the month one Cyzicene stater* per man per month, and I will take you to the Troad, the region from which I have been exiled. My native city will look after you, because they'll be glad to have me back. And I personally will guide you to places where you'll find plenty of valuable booty. I know my way around Aeolis, Phrygia, the Troad, and the whole of Pharnabazus' domain,* partly as a result of being from the region, and partly as a result of having served there with Clearchus and Dercylidas.'*

Next, Thorax of Boeotia, a man who was always disputing matters of strategy with Xenophon, got to his feet. He said that if they left the Euxine, the Chersonese, a fertile and prosperous land, would be theirs and anyone who wanted to could live in it, while those who did not want to could sail home. It was ridiculous, he said, to strive for land in barbarian territory when there was plenty of abundantly rich land in Greece.* 'And until you get there,' he concluded, 'I join Timasion in guaranteeing that you'll be paid.' He said this because he knew what the people of Heraclea and Sinope had promised Timasion for getting the army to sail away.

Xenophon kept quiet throughout this speech, but then Philesius and Lycon, both from Achaea, stood up and said that it was monstrous of Xenophon to be trying privately to persuade people to stay and to be sacrificing to this end, but not to have said anything about it in a public meeting. So Xenophon was forced to get up and speak. 'As you know, my friends,' he said, 'I perform as many sacrifices as I can on your behalf, as well as some for myself, to ensure that my words and thoughts and actions are the kind which combine honour and advantage in the highest degree, for both you and me. And the issue about which I have recently been sacrificing was precisely to see whether it would be better for me to start discussing this matter with you, and to start moving on it, or whether I should leave the whole business well alone. On the crucial issue, the diviner Silanus announced that the omens were favourable—after all, he knew that I had some knowledge of reading omens myself, because of my habit of attending all the sacrifices I can. But he said that the sacrificial victims revealed a kind of trap and plot against me, because, as it turned out, he knew that he himself was planning to get me into trouble, by spreading the rumour that I was already intending to take action over this without having won your agreement.

'Now, if I saw that you had no resources, I would have tried to come up with a plan whereby you could capture a city, so that then people could either immediately sail back home or, if they didn't want to do that, could do so once they had acquired enough to do some good to friends and family back home. But since it is clear that the people of Heraclea and Sinope are sending you ships so that you can sail away, and that men are promising you regular, monthly pay, I have no objection to our getting where we want to be, safe and sound, and being paid for it as well. And so I hereby drop that plan of mine, and I suggest that all those who came to me and expressed approval of the idea should also drop it.

'I'll tell you what I think. If you stick together in your present numbers, I think you will win respect, and also—since the strong can take what belongs to the weak—get hold of provisions. But if you split up and divide your strength into little pieces, you won't be able to get hold of food and you also won't get away from here unscathed. So I agree with you: let's leave for Greece. And if anyone stays here or is caught deserting before the whole army has reached a place of safety, he should be brought to trial as a criminal. If you agree with this motion, raise your hand.'

Everyone raised their hands, but in a loud voice Silanus attempted to argue that in all fairness anyone who wanted to leave should do so. The troops, however, would not let him proceed and threatened to punish him if they caught him deserting. Next, when the people of Heraclea found out that the decision had been taken to sail away, and that even Xenophon had voted for the proposal, they sent the ships, but proved to be liars when it came to paying the money they had promised to Timasion and Thorax. The men who had undertaken to pay the troops were dismayed and frightened of what the army would do. They gathered all the generals whom they had told about their earlier actions—and that was all the generals except Neon of Asine, who was standing in for the still-absent Chirisophus—and went to Xenophon. They said that they had changed their minds and now thought that, since they had ships, it would be best to sail to Phasis and seize the land of the Phasians (whose king was a grandson of Aeëtes*). Xenophon replied that he would not breathe a word of their plan to the army. 'But if you want,' he said, 'you can call the men to a meeting and tell them.' But Timasion of Dardanus then explained his idea, which was that, rather than convening an assembly, each of the generals should first try to win his own company commanders over to the plan. And the generals went away and set about doing just that.

[7] So the troops found out what was happening, and Neon claimed that Xenophon had won the rest of the generals round to his point of view and was now intending to deceive the soldiers and take them back to Phasis.* The soldiers were furious when they heard this: meetings were held, cliques formed, and there was the terrifying possibility that they might do something like what they had done to the Colchian heralds and the market regulators, who had all been stoned to death, except for those who managed to escape to the sea.* When the ugly mood of the troops came to Xenophon's attention, he decided to convene an assembly as soon as he could, to put an end to these unauthorized meetings, and he told the herald to summon the men to an assembly. As soon as the men heard the herald, they ran to the meeting-place in a state of eager anticipation, and Xenophon, without implicating the generals by mentioning that they had come to him, spoke as follows:

'Men, I've been informed that a certain individual is trying to get me into trouble, by saying that it looks as though I'm intending to deceive you and take you to Phasis. I beg you, in the name of the gods, to listen to what I have to say. If it turns out that I've done wrong, you shouldn't let me leave here until I've been punished; but if it turns out that it's my accusers who have done wrong, you should deal with them as they deserve.

'You do of course know', he went on, 'where the sun rises and where it sets. You know that a journey to Greece involves going west, whereas if one wants to travel to barbarian lands, one must do the opposite and head east. How could anyone deceive you about this? How could he claim that the sun sets where it rises and rises where it sets? And another thing you know perfectly well is that it's the north wind that takes you out of the Euxine Sea and to Greece, whereas it is the south wind that takes you to Phasis. There's even a saying: "When the north wind blows, the sailing is fair for Greece." So how could anyone deceive you on this matter and get you to set sail on a south wind? But perhaps I shall get you to embark when there is no wind blowing. Well, I shall be on board one ship, and you will have at least a hundred. So how could I force you to sail with me if you didn't want to, or how could I deceive you about where I was taking you? But suppose you've been taken in by me—bewitched by me, rather—and you've come to Phasis, and suppose we actually disembark there. I'm sure you'd realize that you weren't in Greece—and I, the one who misled you, will be a single individual, while you, the ones who were misled, will be getting on for ten thousand, with arms and armour. What better way could there be for a man to offer himself up for punishment than by getting himself and you involved in such a scheme?

'No, these are tales told by stupid men who are envious of the high regard in which you hold me. But their envy is misplaced. Have I ever stopped any of them making a useful contribution to one of your public debates, or fighting on your behalf and his own, if that is what he wants to do, or lying awake at night worrying about your safety? Or again, do I make things difficult for any of you when you are choosing leaders? I give in: let him lead, as long as he can prove that he will act to your advantage. Anyway, I think I've said enough about these lies, but if any of you imagines that he personally could be taken in by such tales, or could use them to deceive someone else, I'd like him to explain why he thinks so. And when you've finished with this, please don't go away until you've heard me tell you the trouble I see just beginning to rear its ugly head in the army. If it assaults us and really is as bad as it threatens to be, we should now be thinking about ourselves and discussing how to avoid appearing to be the worst and most contemptible men in the eyes of both gods and men, whether they are friends or foes.'

These words of Xenophon's astonished the troops. They had no idea what he was getting at, and they asked him to explain. So he began to speak once more, and said: 'You know those barbarian villages in the mountains that were friendly to the Cerasuntians? Men used to come down from them and sell you some of their possessions, such as livestock for sacrifice, and I think that some of you visited the nearest of their villages, bought some goods, and then returned to our camp. Well, when Clearetus, the company commander, found out that the village was small and undefended (after all, it regarded itself as friendly), he went there one night with the intention of sacking it, without telling any of us generals what he was up to. If he succeeded in taking the village, his plan was not to return to the camp, but to board a ship—some of his army comrades happened to have a ship that was making its way along the coast—load it up with his loot, and sail away out of the Euxine. His comrades from the ship, I've recently discovered, had agreed to help him.

'Anyway, he gathered together all those he had persuaded to take part and led them against the village. But day broke while he was still on the march, and the villagers banded together, took up strong positions, and rained missiles and blows down on the raiders. They killed Clearetus and a lot of his men, but a few of them managed to get back to Cerasus. This happened on the day we set out from Cerasus to come here by land, but some of those who were going to travel by sea had not yet set sail and were still in Cerasus.

'The report I have from the Cerasuntians says that next three of the village elders came to the city with a view to addressing one of our public meetings, but since we had already left, they told the people of Cerasus that they couldn't understand why we had decided to attack them. The Cerasuntians, according to their report, told the elders that the attack had not been authorized, and the villagers were glad to hear it. They planned to sail here, to tell us what had happened and to suggest that those who wanted to could collect the bodies of the dead and bury them. Unfortunately, however, some of the Greeks who had escaped were still in Cerasus, and when they found out where the barbarians were going they had the audacity to stone them and to try to enlist the help of others in doing so. All three of the men died, stoned to death, though they were the official representatives of their village.*

'Afterwards, the people of Cerasus came and told us generals what had happened, which we found deeply distressing. We began to discuss with them how we might arrange for the burial of the dead Greeks, but while we were still in session outside the camp we suddenly heard loud cries of "Beat them up! Beat them up! Stone them! Stone them!" The next moment we saw a crowd of men, some of whom were running towards us with stones already in their hands, while others were picking stones up. The Cerasuntians, having already witnessed the incident that had taken place in their city, retreated back to their ships in terror; in truth, there were some of us who were frightened as well. As for me, I went up to the men and asked what the matter was. Some of them had no idea what was going on, despite the fact that they had stones in their hands. I eventually met someone who knew what was up and he told me that the market regulators were treating the army abominably.* Meanwhile, someone spotted Zelarchus, one of the market regulators, retreating towards the sea, and raised the alarm. Hearing the man's shouts, the others charged at Zelarchus as though they had sighted a wild boar or a deer. When the Cerasuntians saw men charging in their direction, they in their turn, convinced that they were the targets, raced off and hurled themselves into the sea. Some of our own men also hurled themselves into the sea along with the Cerasuntians, and if they didn't know how to swim they drowned. Why do you think they did that? They had done no wrong, and yet they were frightened that we had been seized, like dogs, by a fit of madness.

'What do you suppose will happen to us, as an army, if incidents of this sort occur? You, the main body of the army, will lose the right to declare war on an enemy of your own choosing, or to bring it to an end, and anyone who wants to, for his own personal reasons, will lead the army towards his own preferred target. If ambassadors come to you to sue for peace or for some other purpose, men will cut them down, if they feel like it, and will stop you hearing what your visitors have to say. Then again, the leaders chosen by all of you in assembly will be irrelevant, and whoever elects himself general and is prepared to shout "Stone them! Stone them!" will have the ability to cut down any of you he wants without trial, whether officer or ordinary soldier, as long as there are those who will obey him. This is what happened in the recent incident.

'But just look at what these self-appointed generals have done for you. If Zelarchus the market regulator did you wrong, he has sailed off without being punished; if he did no wrong, he has fled from the army in fear of being put to death illegally and without a trial. As for those who stoned the envoys to death, their achievement is to have made you the only Greeks who cannot safely go to Cerasus without substantial military back-up; and they've seen to it that it is now no longer safe even for someone under the protection of a herald's staff to collect the bodies of our dead, when previously the very men who killed them were telling us to come and bury them. After all, who'll be prepared to go to them as a herald when he has killed heralds himself? Instead, we generals have asked the people of Cerasus to bury them.

'If all this is as it should be, give it the seal of your approval. Then, given that this is how things will be in the future, anyone can create his own private body of guards and attempt to seize the defensible high ground and pitch his tent there. But if you think this is the behaviour of wild animals rather than of human beings, try to find a way to end it. Otherwise, how, in the name of Zeus, shall we sacrifice to the gods with joyful hearts when we're committing acts of sacrilege? How shall we fight our enemies if we're cutting one another down? How will any city welcome us as friends when they see anarchy rampant among us? Who will have the courage to make their market available to us when they can see us committing such gross offences? If we conduct ourselves in this fashion, how will we find anyone to praise us in that land where we expected to win praise from everyone?* For I am sure that we ourselves would describe such behaviour as obnoxious.'

Then they all stood up and argued that the ringleaders of these incidents should be punished, and that in the future it should be made impossible for anyone to initiate such a state of anarchy. Anyone who did so, they said, should be liable to the death penalty; the generals were to ensure that all the offenders came to trial, there were also to be hearings about every other offence that had been committed since the time of Cyrus' death, and the company commanders were to act as jurors for all these trials. Xenophon, with the support of the diviners, proposed that the army should be purified;* this motion was carried and the purification took place.

[8] Another proposal, that the generals should undergo an assessment of their past conduct, was also carried. When the inquiry took place, Philesius and Xanthicles were fined twenty mnas—the amount of the loss—for their failure to protect the merchant cargoes,* and Sophaenetus was fined ten mnas for having neglected the duties of the post to which he had been elected.*† Some men brought a charge against Xenophon too. They claimed that they had been beaten by him and they framed the charge as one of assault.* Xenophon asked the first of his accusers to say at what stage of the journey he had been beaten, and he replied: 'It was when we were dying of cold and the snow lay very deep on the ground.'*

'Well,' Xenophon said, 'if the weather was as bad as you say, and we had run out of food, and we couldn't get even the faintest whiff of wine, and we were exhausted from all our hardships, and we had the enemy on our heels—if under these circumstances I assaulted you, I must admit to being a more assiduous assaulter than the proverbial ass, which is said to be so fond of assault that it never gets tired. But do please tell us why you were beaten. Was it that I had asked you for something and beat you when you didn't give it to me? Was it a loan you were supposed to return? Were we fighting about a boy we fancied? Was I so drunk that I was spoiling for a fight?'

'No, it wasn't for any of these reasons,' the man said.

'Were you serving as a hoplite?' Xenophon asked.

'No,' said the man.

'As a peltast, then?' Xenophon asked next.

'No, not a peltast either,' he replied. 'I was acting as a mule-driver. I'd been given the job by my comrades, although I'm a free man.'

Xenophon recognized him then and asked: 'You're the one who carried one of the invalids, aren't you?'

'Yes, that's right,' he said. 'You forced me to carry him, and you tossed my comrades' equipment all over the place.'

'What tossing?' Xenophon asked. 'I'll tell you more or less what happened: I got various men to carry various bits of the baggage, and I told them to give it back to me afterwards. When I'd got it back, I returned it all to you safe and sound, once you'd shown me the man you were carrying. But you should hear what really happened,' he said to the company at large. 'It's worth hearing. A man was starting to fall behind; he just couldn't go on any more. I didn't know him at all, except to recognize that he was one of us. I forced you to carry him, because otherwise he'd have died—the enemy were, after all, right behind us, I seem to remember.'

The fellow agreed, and Xenophon went on: 'So I sent you on ahead, but later I caught up with you again, as I came up with the rearguard, and found you digging a hole to bury the poor fellow. I stopped and thanked you for that, but as we were standing around the man flexed his leg and everyone there shouted out that he was alive. "Well," you said, "I don't care how alive he is. I'm not going to carry him." And you're right: that was when I hit you, because I got the impression that you had known he was still alive.'

'So what?' the man said. 'He still died, didn't he, after I'd shown him to you?'

'Yes,' said Xenophon, 'we're all going to die, but does that mean we have to be buried alive?'

As far as this man was concerned, everyone shouted out that

Xenophon had not beaten him enough. Xenophon then called on others to explain, one by one, why they had been beaten, but no one got to his feet. So Xenophon continued: 'My friends, I freely admit that I have struck men for lack of discipline. They were men who were happy to be kept safe by you—by the fact that, when you had to, you marched with discipline and fought in proper formation—but they preferred to leave the ranks and run ahead to get more than their fair share of booty. If we all behaved like that, we'd all be dead.

'Also, I did once strike a man for displaying weakness: he was refusing to get to his feet and was just waiting to fall into the enemy's hands, until I struck him and forced him to carry on. You see, I too sat down once for quite a long time in bitterly cold weather to wait for some men who were packing their baggage, and I noticed that it was hard to get back to my feet and stretch my legs. So afterwards, as a result of this first-hand experience, whenever I saw someone else sitting down and shirking his duties, I bullied him on. The point is that keeping resolutely in motion did tend to give a certain amount of warmth and suppleness, but I noticed that sitting and doing nothing led to the blood freezing and the toes rotting, which, as you well know, happened to a lot of us.

'Yes, and here's another case: it's quite possible that I once punched a man who was too lazy to keep up with the rest and was impeding both you in the van and us in the rear—that I struck him with my fist to stop the enemy striking him with their spears. In fact, that's why these people are still alive and have the opportunity to punish me now for any wrong I did them. But if they had fallen into the hands of the enemy, would they now be in a position to demand satisfaction for the huge wrong that would have been done to them?

'My argument is perfectly straightforward,' he went on. 'If I chastised anyone for their own good, I think I should be judged by the same criteria that are used to assess parents' treatment of their sons or teachers' punishment of their pupils. Even doctors cauterize and cut for the good of their patients. But if you're inclined to think that my actions constitute assault, you should bear in mind that now, thanks to the gods, I'm a more confident person than I was before, and more bold, and I drink more wine—but I don't hit anyone. Why? Because I can see that you are sailing in calm weather. But when there's a storm and the sea is running high, haven't you noticed that even a slight movement of the head arouses the anger of the prow-man against the crew in the front of the ship or the helmsman against the crew in the stern? And the reason for this is that in that kind of situation even small errors are enough to cause complete ruin.

'In fact, you've already acquitted me of the charge of unlawfully striking these men, because you were there, standing by with swords in your hands, not just votes, and you could have come to their assistance if you'd wanted to. To tell the truth, though, it's not just that you didn't help them, but you also didn't help me punish anyone for lack of discipline—and this lax attitude made it possible for the bad elements in the army to run riot. The point is that, if you care to look into the business, I'm sure you'll find that it's the men who were the worst cowards earlier who are now the worst criminals. Boïscus, for instance, the boxer from Thessaly, used in the past to resist carrying a shield on grounds of ill health, and now, I'm told, he has already stripped a number of citizens of Cotyora of their belongings. The sensible course of action would be for you to do to him the opposite of what people do to their dogs: they leash troublesome dogs by day and let them loose at night, but the sensible thing for you to do with Boïscus would be to tie him up each night and let him loose during the days.

'What really surprises me,' he concluded, 'is that you remember and bring up incidents when I was annoyed with one or another of you, while no one remembers occasions when I brought relief during bitter weather, or protected someone from an enemy attack, or helped to look after a man who was ill or in difficulties. You also completely fail to mention occasions when I praised someone for doing well or rewarded a man, to the best of my ability, for his courage. And yet remembering good rather than bad is the right thing to do; it is fair and moral, and it gives more pleasure to all concerned.'

People then got to their feet and began to bring up some of these other occasions, and everything turned out well.

BOOK SIX

[1] Afterwards, while they continued to wait, the Greeks supported themselves either by buying food from the market or by plundering the territory of the Paphlagonians. But the Paphlagonians repeatedly intercepted any stragglers, and at nights they did their best to wreak havoc on those who had pitched their tents some way from the main camp. The upshot of all this was that there was a state of unremitting hostility between the two sides. But then Corylas, who was the Paphlagonian ruler at the time, sent a delegation to the Greeks. The men brought horses and fine clothes, and a message to the effect that Corylas was ready to enter into a pact of mutual non-aggression with the Greeks. The generals replied that they would consult with their troops about the pact, and in the meantime they put on a banquet for the delegates, to which they also invited anyone else who seemed to deserve it. Once they had sacrificed some of the oxen they had captured, and other animals too, they laid on a satisfactory feast, but they reclined on palliasses to eat and drank from horn cups, which they had found locally.

They poured libations and sang a paean, and then two Thracians were the first to get to their feet. Still in their armour, they danced to the accompaniment of the pipes, lightly leaping high off the ground and thrusting with their swords. In the end one of them struck the other, and everyone thought the man had been wounded, though he fell in a somewhat contrived fashion. The Paphlagonians shouted out loud at the sight. Then the first man stripped the other of his arms and armour and left, singing the Sitalces,* while other Thracians carried the fallen man away as though he were dead, although in fact he was completely unscathed.

Next, some Aenianians and Magnesians stood up and began a dance in armour called the *karpaia*,* which goes like this: one man puts down his weapons and starts to sow grain and drive a team, while constantly turning this way and that as though in fear; a robber approaches and the farmer spots him, grabs his weapons, goes to meet him, and fights him to stop him stealing his team of oxen. They keep time throughout with the music of the pipes. In the end the robber ties up the farmer and steals the oxen, but sometimes the farmer ties up the robber and then puts him under the yoke next to the oxen with his hands tied behind his back and drives him on.

Next, a Mysian stepped forward with a light shield in each hand. As he danced, sometimes he pretended that he was fending off two opponents, but at other times he wielded both shields as though he were fighting just one man. Then he whirled and turned somersaults while keeping the shields in his hands, which made a beautiful display. Finally, he performed the Persian dance,* which involved clashing his shields together, while squatting and rising up again. He kept time throughout with the music of the pipes.

After the Mysian it was the turn of the Mantineans to step forward, and others from elsewhere in Arcadia also got to their feet. Dressed in the most splendid armour they could muster, they paraded in time with a martial tune played on the pipes, chanted a paean, and performed the same dance they put on during their religious processions.

The Paphlagonians found it strange that all the dances they had seen involved armour, and the Mysian, seeing how surprised they were, persuaded one of the Arcadians, who owned a dancing-girl, to let him dress her in the most beautiful costume he could find, give her a light shield, and then bring her on. She performed an elegant version of the Pyrrhic dance* and received loud applause. The Paphlagonians asked whether the women fought alongside them, and the Greeks said that these were the very women who had put the king to flight from his camp. And so the evening came to an end.

The next day they presented the delegates to the main body of the army, and the troops decided to enter into a pact of mutual non-aggression with the Paphlagonians. After the delegates had left, the Greeks, reckoning that they then had enough ships, put to sea and sailed for a day and a night on a fair wind, with Paphlagonia on their left. The following day they reached Sinope and anchored the ships at Harmene, the port of Sinope—a city, originally a colony of Miletus, in Paphlagonian territory. The Sinopeans sent the Greeks as tokens of their friendship 3,000 medimni of barley and 1,500 jars of wine.

While they were at Sinope, Chirisophus also arrived, on board a trireme. The soldiers expected him to bring them something, but he brought nothing except a message from Anaxibius, the Spartan naval commander, conveying his and everyone else's gratitude and promising them regular pay if they left the Euxine Sea. The army stayed at Harmene for five days.

Greece now seemed to be close, and the men began to wonder, with more urgency than before, how they might actually return to their homes with something in hand. They came to the conclusion that if they chose just one leader, a single individual might be able to make better use of the army, at any hour of the day or night, than a plurality of commanding officers. They thought, for instance, that if stealth were called for a single leader would be better at concealment, and that if haste were required he would be less likely to cause a delay, because one man's decisions could simply be implemented without having first to be discussed with others. Up until then, however, all the generals' actions had depended on a consensus.

The upshot of these thoughts was that they turned to Xenophon. The company commanders came to him and said that this was what the men wanted and each of them, with expressions of loyalty, tried to persuade him to accept overall command. From one point of view, Xenophon was inclined to accept, because he thought it would bring him more respect from his friends and make him better known in his home city; besides, he thought, he might perhaps be the agent of some good for the army. So considerations such as these aroused in him the desire to become sole commander, but then, when he bore in mind that no one can see into the future and that therefore he would run the risk of losing even the reputation he had already built up, he did not know what to do.

Since he was uncertain how to resolve the issue, he decided that it would be best for him to consult the gods. He brought up two victims and sacrificed them to Zeus the King—the god who had been named in the oracle he had been given at Delphi,* and the one who he thought had sent the vision he had seen in a dream at the time when he began to play a part in managing the army.* He was also bearing in mind that, as he was setting out from Ephesus to be introduced to Cyrus, he had heard an eagle cry to his right. The eagle had been perched, however, and the diviner who was seeing him on his way had said that although the eagle was magnificent, extraordinary, and glorious, nevertheless it signified suffering, because other birds were liable to attack an eagle when it was perched; moreover, it was not an omen of profit, he said, because the eagle generally got its food on the wing. Anyway, when Xenophon performed this sacrifice, the god made it perfectly plain that he should neither feel the need for further command nor accept it if the troops chose him. So that was how this turned out.

The troops held a general meeting, unanimously agreed to choose just one man to lead them, and as a result of this decision nominated Xenophon. It was clear that if the matter was put to the vote they were going to choose him, so he stood up and spoke as follows: 'Men, I am naturally as delighted as anyone would be at the high regard in which you hold me, and I'd like to thank you for it. I pray that the gods may grant me the opportunity to be the agent of some good for you. But I don't think it's in your best interests for me to be preferred by you as your leader when there's a Spartan available for the position, because then the Spartans would be less likely to give you anything you might want from them.* Nor do I think it would be altogether safe for me to accept the post. I was a witness to the fact that the Spartans didn't stop fighting the city of my birth until they had made the entire citizen body acknowledge them as their masters. As soon as this concession had been made, the Spartans stopped fighting and broke off their blockade of the city. So if I, who was a witness to all this, were taken to be undermining their authority wherever I could, I think I'd very quickly be brought to my senses. Now, your thinking is that the level of feuding will decrease if there's just one leader rather than a number of them, and so I want to assure you that if you choose someone else you won't find me stirring up trouble, because in my opinion anyone who jeopardizes a leader's authority in wartime is jeopardizing his own safety. However, if you choose me, I wouldn't be surprised if you found that this made someone angry with both you and me.'*

After this speech even more people got to their feet and said that he should be their leader, and Agasias of Stymphalus argued that the situation was absurd if it was as Xenophon had described it. 'Will the Spartans also be angry, then,' he said, 'if the guests at a symposium fail to choose a Spartan as their symposiarch?* I mean, if this is so, I guess the fact that we are Arcadians should debar us even from being company commanders.'* The troops roared out their approval of Agasias' words.

Xenophon could see that he needed to say something more, so he stepped forward and said: 'Men, I want you to be fully aware of the situation. I swear to you, by all the gods and goddesses, that when I learnt of your plan I sacrificed to see whether it would be better for you to entrust this command to me and for me to take it on, and through the entrails of the victims the gods indicated, in ways that even a non-diviner could recognize, that I should having nothing to do with this sole command.'

Under these circumstances, they chose Chirisophus. After he had been appointed to the post, Chirisophus stepped forward and said: 'Men, I want you to know that I wouldn't have stirred up trouble either, if you had chosen someone else. But I should tell you that you did Xenophon a favour by not appointing him, because Dexippus has already been blackening his name as much as he can to Anaxibius, despite my efforts to shut him up. He told Anaxibius that, in his opinion, Xenophon preferred to share the command of Clearchus' army with Timasion, a Dardanian, than with him, a Spartan. But anyway, you've chosen me, and I will do my best to act in your best interests. I want you now to get ready to put to sea tomorrow, if the weather is good for sailing. Our destination is Heraclea, and so everyone must try to come to land there. We'll talk over what to do next once we're there.'

[2] The next day they put to sea and sailed for two days on a fair wind along the coast. During this voyage, they saw Jason's Point, where the *Argo* is said to have landed,* and they also saw the mouths of the rivers—first, the Thermodon, then in order the Iris, the Halys, and the Parthenius.* Once they had sailed past the Parthenius, they came to Heraclea, a Greek city, originally a Megarian colony, which had been founded in the territory of the Mariandynians. They anchored by the Acherusian peninsula, where Heracles is said to have gone down to fetch the hound Cerberus.* At this spot nowadays they show the marks of his descent, to a depth of more than two stades. While they were there, the people of Heraclea sent the Greeks, as tokens of friendship, 3,000 medimni of barley, 2,000 jars of wine, 20 oxen, and 100 sheep. The Lycus river, about two plethra wide, flows through the plain at this point.

The troops held a meeting at which they discussed the remainder of their journey and specifically whether they should leave the Euxine by land or by sea. Lycon of Achaea got to his feet and said, 'Men, I'm surprised that our generals aren't making any attempt to get provision-money for us. These tokens of friendship won't feed the army for more than three days at the most, and there's nowhere here for us to stock up on supplies before setting out. So I think we should ask the people of Heraclea for at least 3,000 Cyzicene staters'—someone else suggested at least 10,000—'and that we should choose delegates straight away, while we're in session, and send them to the city. Then we can hear the report they bring back and discuss how to respond to it.'

They then set about nominating delegates, and the first to be proposed was Chirisophus, because he was their elected leader, and some people proposed Xenophon too. But Chirisophus and Xenophon disagreed vehemently with the plan, because they both felt that they should not be forcing a friendly Greek city to give something they had not freely offered. Given their obvious reluctance, the men sent Lycon of Achaea, Callimachus of Parrhasia, and Agasias of Stymphalus. This delegation went to the city and explained what the army had decided, and it was said that Lycon also threatened them with dire consequences if they refused to comply. After listening to the envoys, the people of Heraclea said that they would consult about what to do—and immediately set about gathering their livestock from the countryside. They packed up the market and moved it inside the city walls, the gates were shut, and armed men were to be seen on the walls.

Those who had caused this disruption of normal activity then blamed the generals for the failure of their plans, and the Arcadians and Achaeans held a meeting at which Callimachus of Parrhasia and Lycon of Achaea were particularly prominent. They argued that it was disgraceful for an Athenian, who had provided no troops for the army, to be in command of Peloponnesians and Spartans, and that it was wrong for others to profit from their hard work, especially since it was they who were responsible for the army's survival. In other words, they claimed that the army's survival was due to the Arcadians and Achaeans, while the rest of the army counted for nothing (and it was true that Arcadians and Achaeans made up more than half the army). It made sense, then, they said, for them to join forces, choose their own generals, continue the journey by themselves, and try to profit from it.

This proposal was carried, and all the Arcadians and Achaeans among Chirisophus' and Xenophon's troops left them and joined forces with their countrymen. They chose ten of their number to be their generals, and they decreed that these generals were to act on their own majority decisions. So Chirisophus' overall command came to an end five or six days after he had been chosen for the job. But Xenophon wanted to continue the journey with Chirisophus, because he thought that this would be safer than if each of them travelled on his own. Neon, however, tried to persuade Xenophon to carry on by himself, because he had heard from Chirisophus that Cleander, the harmost* in Byzantium, had promised to come to Calpe Harbour with triremes. The reason for Neon's advice to Xenophon, then, was that he wanted to exclude everyone else, so that he and Chirisophus and their men could leave the Euxine on board these ships; and Chirisophus was so depressed by what had happened and so filled with hatred for the men because of what they had done that he gave Xenophon permission to do whatever he liked.

At first, Xenophon did his best to extricate himself from the army and sail away home, but when he sacrificed to Heracles the Guide with the question whether it would be better and more honourable for him to continue to serve with those troops who remained or to leave them, the god indicated to him, by means of the victim's entrails, that he should continue his service with the army. The upshot was that the army broke up into three parts: there were the Arcadians and Achaeans, who numbered more than 4,500 and were all hoplites; Chirisophus had at most 1,400 hoplites and 700 peltasts, who were Clearchus' Thracians; and Xenophon had about 1,700 hoplites and about 300 peltasts. Xenophon, who was the only one with any cavalry, also had about 40 horsemen.

The Arcadians were the first to sail away, once they had managed to get some ships from the people of Heraclea. Their plan was to make a sudden assault on the Bithynians and to seize as much as they could, so they disembarked at Calpe Harbour, about halfway along the Thracian coast. Chirisophus set out by land straight away and took an inland route from Heraclea until he entered Thrace, when he travelled along the coast, since he was not well.* Xenophon got hold of some ships, disembarked at the border between Thrace and Heraclea, and then set out through the interior.

[3] This is how each division of the army fared. The Arcadians disembarked by night at Calpe Harbour and marched against the nearest villages, which were about thirty stades from the coast. At dawn, each general led his own company against one of the villages,

unless the village seemed rather large, in which case the generals combined two companies and led them in a joint attack on the village. They also agreed upon a hill where they were all to meet afterwards. Their assaults were unexpected, so they took a lot of prisoners and rounded up a lot of sheep and goats, but the Thracians who escaped began to form up—and, since they were peltasts evading hoplites, there were plenty of men who managed to slip right out of the Arcadians' grasp. Once they had regrouped, they first attacked the company of one of the Arcadian generals called Smicres, just as he was returning to the rendezvous point with all his booty. For a while the Greeks fought them off while marching, but when they were crossing a gully the Thracians put them to flight and killed every single one of them, including Smicres. Then from another company, commanded by Hegesander, one of the ten generals, the Thracians left only eight men alive, one of whom was Hegesander.

The remaining company commanders joined forces more or less easily, but after their successes the Thracians spent the night calling out to one another and resolutely mustering their forces. At dawn the next day they began to deploy around the hill where the Greeks had passed the night; their forces consisted not just of peltasts, but of large numbers of horsemen, and more men were constantly streaming in. They began to attack the hoplites, and because the Greeks had no archers, javelin-men, or horsemen, the Thracians were in no danger: they would run or ride up and throw their javelins, and they easily escaped every time the Greeks launched an attack against them. The Thracians also attacked from various directions. One side was taking a lot of wounds, the other none, and the upshot was that the Greeks were unable to move from their position. Eventually, the Thracians were making it difficult for them even to get water, and in these extremely hazardous conditions the Greeks began to negotiate for a truce. The two sides were agreeing on everything, but the Thracians refused to give the Greeks the hostages they demanded and the negotiations broke down over this issue. So that is how the Arcadians fared.

Chirisophus marched unmolested along the coast and reached Calpe Harbour, and as for Xenophon, while he was making his way through the interior his horsemen, who had ridden on ahead, came across some old men who were travelling somewhere or other. The men were brought to Xenophon, and he asked them whether they had heard anything of another Greek army. They told him the whole story and said that the Greeks were at that moment being besieged on a hill, and were surrounded by a Thracian force at full strength.

Xenophon had the men put under close guard, because he wanted them to show him where to go, and once he had posted lookouts he called the troops to a meeting and said: 'Men, some of the Arcadians have been killed and the rest are trapped on a hill. If they die, I think we will be in danger too, since there are so many of the enemy and they will be so elated by their victory. I think, then, that our best course of action is to go to help our comrades as quickly as we can. If they're still alive, we can fight alongside them and we won't be left to face a dangerous future alone and unaided. After all, there's nowhere we can safely escape to from here: it's a long way back to Heraclea, Chrysopolis is a long way ahead, and hostile forces are near by. The closest place is Calpe Harbour, where we take Chirisophus to be, if he has survived. It may be true that there are no ships there for us to sail away in and that there aren't enough supplies for us to stay there for even a single day, but we'll be worse off if the trapped troops are killed and we have to take our chances with only Chirisophus' men than if they are saved and we unite and work together for our safety. No, we must carry on with our minds made up that now we may either die famous deaths or achieve the glorious result of rescuing so many fellow Greeks.

'It may well be that this whole business is being directed by the god, in his desire to humble those who boasted and assumed that they knew best, and to grant us, who begin with the gods,* greater prestige than them. Nevertheless, you should follow my lead and be ready to carry out any order you receive. So let's now march on until we judge it to be time to prepare the evening meal, and then let's make camp. And while we're on the march, let's have Timasion ride ahead with the cavalry*—but not so far ahead that he loses sight of us—and reconnoitre what lies in front of us, so that we avoid any unpleasant surprises.'

With these words he began to lead the way forward. He deployed the most mobile of the light-armed men on the flanks and on the heights as escorts, so that they could warn the main body of the army of any threat they saw anywhere, and he gave the order that anything they came across which could be burnt was to be burnt. So the horsemen spread out over as wide an area as they sensibly could and set about burning things, while the peltasts set fire to everything combustible they found on the heights where they were marching parallel to the main army, and the rest of the troops set fire to anything they came across which had been overlooked. These measures had the effect of making the whole region seem ablaze and the army appear large.

When the time came, they climbed a hill and made camp. They could see the enemy's fires at a distance of about forty stades and they lit as many fires as possible themselves too. As soon as they had finished eating, however, the order came that all the fires were to be extinguished. Then they posted guards and lay down to sleep for the night. At daybreak, they prayed to the gods, fell in as if for battle, and marched on with all possible haste. Timasion and the cavalry rode on ahead with the guides and, without realizing it, reached the hill where the Greeks had been trapped, but, as they reported back to Xenophon and the main body of the army, they found no troops there, either friendly or hostile. They found only those who had been left behind there—some feeble old women and men, a few sheep and goats, and some oxen. At first, they were puzzled as to what might have happened, but then they were told by the people who had been left behind that the Thracians had left after nightfall and that the Greeks had done likewise at dawn; but they said that they did not know where the Greeks had gone.

When Xenophon and his men heard this, they ate their midday meal, broke camp, and set out, because they wanted to join the others at Calpe Harbour as soon as possible; and as they were marching along they could see the tracks of the Arcadians and Achaeans on the Calpe road. When the two contingents joined up, they were delighted to see one another and greeted one another like brothers. The Arcadians asked Xenophon and his men why they had put out their fires. 'At first,' they said, 'when we could no longer see your fires, we thought you were going to make a night attack on the enemy, and it occurred to us that it was fear of this that made the enemy leave too, because that was about when they left. But time passed and you still had not arrived, so we began to think that the information you had received about our situation had made you afraid, and that you had slipped away to the coast. It didn't seem a good idea for us to fall too far behind you, so we too made our way here.'

[4] They bivouacked that day right there on the beach by the harbour. The place where they were, Calpe Harbour, is in the part of Thrace which is in Asia. This part of Thrace, which is on the right as one sails into the Euxine Sea, starts at the mouth of the Euxine and goes up to Heraclea. For a trireme propelled by oars it is a very long day's journey from Byzantium to Heraclea, and there is no other friendly or Greek town between these two places, only Bithynian Thracians, whose treatment of any Greeks who fall into their hands as a result of shipwreck or whatever is said to be horrendous.

Calpe Harbour* is situated at the halfway point of the voyage from Byzantium to Heraclea or vice versa. It is a headland on the coast, and the bit which actually runs out into the sea is a sheer cliff, which at its lowest point is at least twenty fathoms high, while the neck, which connects the cape to the mainland, is about four plethra wide. The headland itself, beyond the neck, is large enough to accommodate ten thousand people. There is a harbour right under the cliff, with a west-facing beach and a freshwater spring which flows in generous quantities right by the sea and falls within the confines of the place. There is a great deal of timber of various kinds, but good-quality ship-building timber is especially abundant and grows right by the sea. A hilly ridge extends about twenty stades back into the mainland; the ridge itself is well covered with stone-free soil, while the land by the coast is thickly wooded for a distance of more than twenty stades with tall trees of all kinds. The rest of the region is fertile and plentiful, and there are a number of inhabited villages there, because the soil produces barley, wheat, all kinds of legumes, millet, sesame, a good number of figs, plenty of grapes which make a sweet wine, and so on and so forth—everything except olives.

This is what the region was like. The Greeks made their camp on the beach, by the sea, and demonstrated no desire to do so at the place which might have become a town. In fact, they thought that it had taken scheming, on the part of those who wanted to found a city there, even to come to this place. After all, most of the troops had set sail and undertaken this mercenary service not because they were hard up, but because they had heard of Cyrus' magnanimity. Some had brought men with them and in some cases had also spent money on the expedition, while others had slipped away from their fathers and mothers or had left children behind, on the assumption that by the time they returned home they would have made some money for them, because they had heard that the other men in Cyrus' service were doing very well for themselves. Since this is what they were like, they longed to get back safely to Greece.*

The day after the contingents had joined forces, Xenophon performed a sacrifice for an expedition, because they had to go out after provisions and he also intended to bury the dead. The omens were favourable, and the Arcadians went on the expedition with the rest. They buried most of the bodies right where they lay, because they had already been there for four days and it was no longer feasible to take them away. But they did collect some bodies from the roads and bury them as decently as circumstances allowed. There were still some bodies that they could not find, and for them they constructed a large cenotaph which they adorned with wreaths. Then they went back to the camp, ate their evening meal, and went to bed.

On the next day, the entire army assembled for a meeting, at the instigation above all of Agasias of Stymphalus, along with his fellow company commander Hieronymus of Elis and other senior Arcadians. The meeting resolved that in the future anyone who mentioned dividing the army should be put to death, and that the army should resume the structure it had before, with the former generals in command. By this time, Chirisophus had died after taking an anti-fever potion, so Neon of Asine took over his post.

Once these resolutions had been passed, Xenophon got to his feet and said: 'It now seems clear, men, that we should continue our journey by land, since we have no ships. And we must get going immediately, because there are no provisions for us if we stay here. So we will perform sacrifices and you had better prepare yourselves at least as well as at any other time for fighting, because the enemy's morale is high again.'

The generals then performed the sacrifice. The diviner who attended the sacrifice was Arexion of Arcadia, because by this time Silanus of Ambracia had slipped away on a boat he had hired at Heraclea. But when they sacrificed, the omens told against departure, so they performed no more sacrifices that day. Now, some people went so far as to say that, in his desire to found a settlement in the place, Xenophon had prevailed upon the diviner to say that the omens told against departure, so Xenophon had the herald announce that anyone who wanted to could attend the sacrifices the next day, and he ordered any diviners in the army to attend so that they could inspect the entrails alongside Arexion. Xenophon performed the sacrifices, then, with a large number of people present; but although he sacrificed three times to see about their departure, the omens continued to be unfavourable.

The troops were displeased at this, because the provisions they had come with had run out and no market had yet been set up there, so they held another meeting, and Xenophon addresssed them again. 'Men,' he said, 'as you can see, the omens still forbid our travelling, but since I can see that you need provisions I think we should make just that issue the object of our sacrifices.'

Someone stood up and said, 'It's hardly surprising that the omens are unfavourable: I for one was told by the crew of a ship that coincidentally arrived here yesterday that Cleander, the harmost based in Byzantium, is going to come here with merchant ships and triremes.'

A proposal to stay where they were was therefore unanimously carried, but they still had to go out for provisions. Once again, as many as three sacrifices took place with regard to whether or not such an expedition should be made, and once again the omens were not propitious. By then people were even coming to Xenophon's tent and complaining about their lack of provisions, but he refused to lead them out of the camp until the omens were favourable. Further sacrifices were carried out the following day, and almost the whole army gathered around the victims because everyone was concerned about the outcome. But the sacrifices failed to produce a propitious result.

The generals continued to refuse to lead the men out on a foraging expedition, but they convened them for a meeting, at which Xenophon said: 'It's possible that the enemy have formed themselves into an army, and that we shall have to fight. I'm wondering whether we should leave our baggage in the strongpoint, get ready for battle, and set out. Then, perhaps, the entrails will be more likely to give us a favourable result.' In response to this suggestion the men shouted out that there was no need to take them first to the strongpoint, but that the generals should just hurry up with the sacrifice. They had run out of sheep, but they bought a team of oxen and used them as the sacrificial victims. Xenophon asked Cleanor of Arcadia to initiate the sacrifice,† in case he could make a difference, but even under these circumstances the omens were unfavourable.

When Neon, who had replaced Chirisophus as general, saw how badly affected the men were by hunger, he wanted to do something for them. He found a man from Heraclea who told him that he knew of nearby villages where they could get provisions, and he had it announced that he would lead allcomers on a foraging expedition. About 2,000 men set out with poles, wineskins, sacks, and other containers. They came to the villages and were in the process of spreading out to gather provisions, when they were attacked by Pharnabazus' cavalry, in the first place. These horsemen, who had come to help the Bithynians because they wanted to see if they could stop the Greeks reaching Phrygia, killed at least 500 men from the Greek army, while the remainder took refuge on the hills.

Some time later, one of the fugitives managed to bring the news back to the camp. Since the sacrifices had not turned out to be favourable that day, Xenophon took an ox from a team, for want of any other suitable victims, and, once he had sacrificed it, he and all the men below thirty years of age went to help their comrades. They rescued the survivors and got back to the camp. By then the sun was going down and the Greeks were preparing their evening meal in a state of deep despondency, when suddenly some Bithynians emerged from the woods and attacked the sentries; those they did not kill were chased back to the camp. Hearing shouts, all the Greeks ran to get their weapons, but decided that neither setting out in pursuit of the Bithynians nor moving camp in the darkness was a safe option, given that the region was so thickly wooded. So they posted a good number of sentries and spent the night under arms.

[5] At dawn, after a night spent like this, the generals led the way to the strongpoint and the men gathered their weapons and baggage and followed them. Before making time for their midday meal, they protected the way into the strongpoint with a trench and they also constructed a palisade which extended all along the trench, except that they left three gateways. A ship also arrived from Heraclea and brought them barley, sacrificial victims, and wine.

Xenophon got up early the next day and performed a sacrifice for a sortie, and with the first victim the omens were favourable. Also, just as the ritual was coming to an end, the diviner, Arexion of Parrhasia, saw an eagle in a position which boded well, and he told Xenophon that the sortie could go ahead. They crossed the trench and waited under arms, and the generals announced that, once they had finished eating, the troops were to march out, armed and ready, while the camp followers and the slaves were to be left behind. So the entire army marched out, except for Neon, since they had chosen him to stay behind to protect the camp and the people and property there. But his company commanders and soldiers began to desert him, because they were ashamed not to be involved in the sortie along with everyone else, so the generals left in the camp only those who were over forty-five years old.

While these men stayed behind, then, the rest marched out. Before they had gone fifteen stades, they began to come across corpses. Once the rear of the column had reached the first corpses to turn up, they set about burying all the bodies now encompassed by the column as a whole. After burying the first batch of bodies, they carried on until the rear had again drawn level with the first of the bodies which remained unburied, and then in the same way they set about burying all the bodies encompassed by the army. And when they reached the road out of the villages, where the bodies lay thick on the ground, they gathered the corpses together for mass burial.

By the early afternoon the army had reached the countryside outside the villages and was in the process of foraging for supplies, with each man collecting whatever he spotted within the area covered by the phalanx, when they suddenly saw a large force of enemy horsemen as well as foot soldiers coming over some hills in front of them in battle formation. It was in fact Spithridates* and Rhathines, who had been sent there by Pharnabazus with this body of men. Once the enemy had caught sight of the Greeks, they came to a halt about fifteen stades away. Arexion, the Greek diviner, lost no time in performing a sacrifice, and with the first victim the omens were favourable.

At this point Xenophon said to his fellow generals: 'I think it would be a good idea to post some companies in reserve, as a precaution, so that they can help the front lines if help is needed at any point. The enemy, who will be in disarray, will then be attacking men who are still fresh and in battle formation.' Everyone agreed that this was a good idea,* and Xenophon went on: 'You should set out towards our opponents, because now that we've been spotted and can see the enemy, we don't want to remain halted. I'll join you once I've deployed the companies in the rear in keeping with your plan.'

So the rest of the men advanced in silence, while Xenophon

detached the three final companies, each consisting of 200 men. He instructed one of the units, under the command of Samolas of Achaea, to come up behind the right of the front lines at a distance of about a plethron, and he deployed the second unit, under Pyrrhias of Arcadia, behind the centre, and the last one, with Phrasias of Athens in command, on the left.

As the Greeks advanced, the front line reached a deep ravine, where the going was awkward. They halted, uncertain whether or not they should cross it, and passed the word back for the generals and company commanders to come up to the front. Xenophon was puzzled: he did not know why their progress had been checked and as soon as he received the message he rode up as quickly as he could. When they were all together, Sophaenetus, the oldest of the generals,* said that there was no point in trying to cross such a difficult ravine.

Xenophon responded forcefully. 'Men,' he said, 'you know that I've never deliberately brought you into the presence of danger. After all, as I see it, your goal is to stay alive; you don't need to enhance your reputation for courage. But look at the situation we're faced with: we can't get away from here without a fight, because if we don't take the fight to the enemy, they'll just follow us and attack us when we leave. So what do you think? Is it better to advance against them with our weapons levelled or to have our weapons reversed* and watch them come at us from behind? But you know that no man of honour retreats from the enemy, and that pursuit makes even cowards confident. I for one would prefer to attack at half-strength than retreat with double our numbers, and I know that, if we attack, even you do not expect our opponents to stand up to us, whereas we're all aware that if we retreat they'll have the courage to pursue us.

'In fact, crossing a difficult ravine and putting it behind us is actually an unmissable opportunity, isn't it? I'd prefer the *enemy* to think they have easy terrain to cross—to retreat across, that is— while we should let the terrain teach us that our only chance of safety lies in victory. But I'm surprised that anyone would consider this ravine more formidable than the rest of the countryside we've just marched through. I mean, how is the plain to be crossed unless we defeat their cavalry? How are we to get back over the mountains with so many peltasts on our heels? And if we do get back safely to the sea, look at the size of the ravine that is the Euxine, since we have neither ships there to carry us away nor food to sustain us if we stay.

In fact, the sooner we get back there, the sooner we shall have to leave again in search of provisions. It's better, then, for us to fight now, with food already in our stomachs, than to fight tomorrow on empty stomachs. Men, the entrails were favourable, the birds of prey boded well, and the sacrificial victims left nothing to be desired. Let's attack! Now that they've seen us, they must never again be allowed to enjoy a pleasant meal or to camp wherever they choose.'

The company commanders then told him to lead the way forward, and none of the generals raised an objection. So Xenophon took the lead, and he ordered every man to cross at the point of the ravine where he happened to find himself. His thinking was that the army would reach the other side en masse more quickly that way than if they filed across the bridge which spanned the ravine.

Once they had reached the other side, Xenophon rode along the lines and said: 'Men, remember all the major battles in which you've engaged the enemy and defeated them, with the help of the gods, and remember what happens to those who flee from their foes. Bear in mind also that we are at the very threshold of Greece. With Heracles the Guide before you, encourage your companions by name. It is indeed a source of pleasure that anyone who now displays his courage and virtue by his words or his deeds will make his mark on precisely those people by whom he wants to be remembered.'

With these words, spoken as he rode along the line, he began to lead the troops forward in battle formation, and with the peltasts positioned on both flanks they set out against the enemy. The men had been told to keep their spears on their right shoulders until the trumpet sounded, when they were to lower them for attack, and their orders were to pursue the enemy at a steady pace, without breaking into a run. Next, the watchword was passed along the line: 'Zeus the Saviour, Heracles the Guide.' The enemy, thinking they had a favourable position, stood their ground. When there was little space between the two sides, the Greek peltasts raised a cry and charged at the enemy before any order to do so had been given, and the enemy troops—both the cavalry and the horde of Bithynians—raced to meet the peltasts and routed them. But the hoplite phalanx continued to advance at a brisk pace, and blasts rang simultaneously from the trumpet; the Greeks struck up a paean, and then they raised the battle-cry and lowered their spears at the same time; and at this the enemy formation crumbled and they turned to flight.

Timasion and the cavalry set out in pursuit and killed as many men as such a small force could. But although the enemy's left wing, against which the Greek horsemen had been deployed, was scattered straight away, the right wing, which was not being very vigorously pursued, rallied on a hill.

When the Greeks noticed that this enemy detachment was standing its ground, they decided that the easiest and least risky plan was to attack it straight away. They immediately struck up the paean and launched an assault. The enemy troops gave way and then it was the turn of the Greek peltasts to set out in pursuit, until the right wing had been dispersed. They did not inflict many casualties, however, because they were frightened of the enemy cavalry, which was a sizeable force. Nevertheless, when the Greeks saw that Pharnabazus' cavalry was still together, and that Bithynian horsemen were also joining them and surveying events from a hill, they decided that, despite their exhaustion, they had to launch the strongest possible attack on the cavalry too, to stop them resting and recovering their morale. So they regrouped and advanced on them—and then, just as if they were being chased by men on horseback, the enemy horsemen raced away downhill. There was a glen where they could find shelter, although the Greeks were not aware of it and broke off their pursuit early;* it was, after all, late in the day. They returned to where they had first engaged the enemy and set up a trophy, before withdrawing to their camp on the coast, about sixty stades away, as the sun was setting.

[6] After this, the enemy steered clear of the Greeks and took both their slaves and their livestock as far away as possible. The Greeks waited for Cleander and the triremes and ships which were supposed to be coming, but every day they left the camp with the yoke-animals and the slaves and fearlessly fetched wheat and barley, wine, legumes, millet, and figs; the only desirable product the land lacked was olives. Even when the army stayed in the camp and rested, individuals were allowed to go out foraging. On these private expeditions, individuals kept what they took, but it was resolved that when the whole army went out, anything anyone got hold of, even if he had gone off on his own, was to be common property.

Before long, they had a generous stock of everything, because traders arrived from Greek communities all over the place, and people sailing past were glad to come to shore, since they had heard that a city was being founded and that there was a harbour there. Even the hostile inhabitants of nearby settlements kept sending delegations to Xenophon (who they had heard was founding the colony) to ask him what they had to do to be on friendly terms with him. Xenophon always let the troops see these envoys.*

Meanwhile, Cleander arrived with two triremes but not a single merchant ship. It so happened that the army was away from the camp when he arrived, and certain individuals, who had gone foraging here and there in the hills and had captured a lot of sheep and goats, talked to Dexippus* (the man who had slipped away from Trapezus with the fifty-oared warship), because they were afraid that their booty would be taken away from them, and asked him to keep the sheep and goats safe for them, on the understanding that he could keep some for himself and return the rest to them later. Dexippus immediately began to shoo away some soldiers who were standing around and arguing that the sheep and goats were common property, and then he went straight to Cleander and told him that the soldiers were trying to steal the sheep and goats.

Cleander told Dexippus to bring him the thief. Dexippus seized one of the men and started to take him to Cleander, but Agasias met them and made Dexippus release the man he had arrested, who was a soldier in Agasias' company. The other soldiers who were there started throwing stones at Dexippus and calling him 'traitor'. A lot of sailors from the triremes became afraid and ran to the shore, and Cleander wanted to leave too, but Xenophon and the other soldiers tried to stop him. They told Cleander that there was no real problem and explained that it was the army's regulation which was responsible for what had happened. But Cleander, egged on by Dexippus and angry of his own accord at having been frightened, said that he would sail away and would direct every city to treat them as enemies and refuse them shelter. Now, at that time all Greeks were ruled by the Spartans, so this was a bad business, in the opinion of the Greek soldiers, and they begged Cleander not to carry out his threat. He replied that nothing would change unless they handed over the man who had instigated the stone-throwing and the one who had removed the prisoner from Dexippus. It was Agasias he was asking for, and Agasias had been a friend of Xenophon from the beginning —which was exactly why Dexippus was trying to get him into trouble.

No one really knew what to do, and so the commanding officers assembled the troops. Some of them were inclined to discount Cleander, but Xenophon did not regard the business as trivial, and he got to his feet and said: 'Men, I think it would be a serious matter if Cleander were to leave with the intention of hurting us as he threatened. After all, the Greek cities are now not far away, and the Spartans are the masters of Greece and, collectively or individually, are in a position to accomplish whatever they like in the cities. So if Cleander, in the first place, bars us from Byzantium and then commands all the other harmosts to refuse us entry into their cities on the grounds of our unruliness and disobedience to Spartan orders, and if, in the second place, this report about us reaches Anaxibius, the Spartan naval commander, then staying put and sailing away from here will both be equally hard, since at the moment the Spartans are supreme both on land and at sea.

'Now, the rest of us must not be prevented from reaching Greece by concern for one or two men. We have to obey any and every Spartan command, because our native cities are obedient to Sparta. Dexippus, I'm informed, is telling Cleander that Agasias would never have done what he did unless I had ordered him to do so, and therefore, for my part, I hereby absolve you collectively, and Agasias in particular, from any blame, if Agasias himself says that I was responsible for what happened. And I hereby pronounce my own sentence: if I initiated the stone-throwing or any other act of violence, I deserve the ultimate penalty and I shall submit to it. I also think that anyone else Dexippus accuses of these crimes ought to make himself available to Cleander for judgement, since that will mean that no blame will be attached to the rest of you. But as things stand at the moment, it will be hard if we, who expected to meet with praise and prestige in Greece, find instead that we're worse off than everyone else, with the Greek cities closed to us.'

Agasias was the next to get to his feet. 'Men,' he said, 'I swear by all the gods and goddesses that neither Xenophon nor anyone else here ordered me to rescue the man. When I saw a good man, one of my own company, being taken away by Dexippus—who betrayed you, as you know—I couldn't stand it, and I freely admit that I rescued him. You don't have to hand me over; as Xenophon suggests, I shall make myself available to Cleander for judgement and he can deal with me as he sees fit. Don't make this a reason to incur the

Spartans' hostility; no, each of you must get back, alive and well, to his chosen destination. But I'd like you to select some of your own number to go with me to Cleander, so that if I leave anything out of my defence, they can speak on my behalf and come to my support.'

In response the army allowed him to choose for himself whoever he wanted to accompany him, and he chose the generals. Agasias then made his way to Cleander, along with the generals and the man he had rescued. The generals said: 'We are here, Cleander, on a mission from the army. Here's their request. If you're accusing all of them collectively of the crime, they would like you to assess the case yourself and deal with them as you see fit. But if you're accusing one or two or a few individuals, they're asking these men to make them-selves available to you for judgement. So if you're accusing any one of us, here we are; if you're accusing someone who isn't here just now, tell us his name and he will appear before you, as long as he's prepared to do as we say.'

Then Agasias stepped forward and said: 'Cleander, it is I who rescued the man Dexippus had arrested and who gave the order to rough Dexippus up. You see, I know that the man is a good soldier—and I also know that when Dexippus was chosen by the army to take charge of the fifty-oared warship which we requested from the people of Trapezus, on the understanding that he would use it to collect merchant ships for us to sail safely home in, he slipped away and betrayed his comrades in arms, who had been instrumental in keeping him alive. As far as the Trapezuntians are concerned, we are criminals who stole their warship—and it was Dexippus' doing. But for all he cares we might as well be dead ourselves. After all, he had heard, along with the rest of us, how difficult it was going to be for us, if we continued by land, to cross the rivers and get safely home to Greece. So this is the man from whom I rescued the soldier. If it had been you or any of your officers who had arrested the man, and not one of our deserters, you can be sure that I wouldn't have done a thing. You should bear in mind that, if you put me to death, you will be killing a good man because of an untrustworthy coward.'

After listening to these speeches, Cleander said that although Dexippus' actions—if he had done what Agasias said—did not meet with his approval, nevertheless, even if Dexippus were an out-and-out criminal, violence should still not have been used against him. 'He should first have been tried,' he said, 'which is, after all, what you're asking of me now, and then have been punished. Leave this man with me and go away for the time being, and then present yourselves for his trial when I call for you. I no longer hold the army as a whole or any other individual responsible, now that he has admitted that he took the man away from Dexippus.'

The man who had been rescued by Agasias said: 'Cleander, just in case you think that I had been arrested for some offence, I'd like you to know that I didn't hit or throw stones at anyone. All I did was say that the sheep and goats were common property, because it was the decision of the assembled army that booty taken by an individual when the army was out foraging was to be common property. That's what I said, and then this man Dexippus grabbed hold of me and started to take me away, because he didn't want anyone to say anything. He wanted to keep the booty safe for the thieves—after taking his share—in violation of the decree.'*

'Since you're so keen,' Cleander said, 'you can stay behind, so that we can decide what to do in your case too.'

Cleander and his staff then ate their midday meal, while Xenophon assembled the troops and advised them to send a delegation to Cleander to plead for their comrades. The troops decided to send the generals and company commanders, along with Dracontius the Spartiate* and anyone else who seemed right for the job, to do all they could to get Cleander to release the two men.

So Xenophon went to Cleander and said: 'Cleander, you have the men, and the troops have left it up to you to do what you think best with them and indeed with the army as a whole. But now their urgent request is that you should give them the two men and not kill them, because both of them have in the past worked long and hard for the army. If you grant this request of theirs, they in turn guarantee that if you want to be their commander and if the gods look favourably upon your holding such a position, they'll give you clear proof of their discipline and will show you that they're capable of fearlessly facing their enemies, with the help of the gods, while obeying their leader's commands. And they have one more request: that when you have come and taken over command of the army, you should deal with Dexippus and the rest of them as they deserve, once you have first-hand experience both of his character and of theirs.'

'By the Twin Gods,'* said Cleander in reply, 'you won't have to wait long for my response to this request. I hereby return the two men to you, and I will come to join you. If the gods make it possible, I shall lead you home to Greece. What you've just said is quite different from what some people have been telling me about you—that you wanted your army to defy Spartan authority.'

After this, the delegates thanked him and left with the two men, and Cleander began to sacrifice for the return journey. He and Xenophon spent some time together, got on well, and agreed to be each other's guest-friend.* When Cleander saw that the men carried out their orders in a disciplined manner, he wanted even more to be their commander, but although he sacrificed for three days, the omens were not favourable. So he called the generals to a meeting and said: 'The omens do not favour my leading you away from here, but don't let this make you downhearted. It is your lot, apparently, to take the army onward. Carry on, then, and when you reach your journey's end, we will make you as welcome as we can.'

After this, the soldiers decided to give him the sheep and goats which were common property, and he accepted the gift, but gave it back to them. Then he sailed away, and once the troops had sold the grain they had collected and the rest of their booty they set out through Bithynia. But the direct route failed to produce the kind of contacts which would allow them to reach friendly territory with something in hand, so they decided to turn around and march in the opposite direction for a day and a night. This enabled them to capture a great many slaves, sheep, and goats, and five days later they arrived in Chrysopolis, in Chalcedonia, where they stayed for seven days selling their booty.

BOOK SEVEN

[1] Then Pharnabazus became afraid that the army might attack his province, so he sent word to Anaxibius, the Spartan naval commander, who happened to be in Byzantium, and asked him to ferry the army out of Asia; in return, he promised to do anything Anaxibius asked.* Anaxibius summoned the generals and company commanders to Byzantium and promised that their men would be hired for pay if they crossed the strait. The rest of the officers said that they would give their reply after talking the matter over, but Xenophon said that he wanted to leave the army and sail home straight away. Anaxibius, however, suggested that he should first cross over with the army and then leave, and Xenophon agreed to do so.

Meanwhile, Medosades arrived with a request from Seuthes of Thrace* that Xenophon should do his best to see that the army made the crossing, and the assurance that he would not regret doing so. 'Well,' Xenophon replied, 'the army is going to cross anyway, so there's no reason for Seuthes to pay me or anyone else for that, and by the time the army is over on the other side, I'll have left. There'll be others who stay on in positions of authority, however: have Seuthes approach them, however he likes.'

After this, all the troops crossed over to Byzantium. Not only did Anaxibius refuse to pay them, but he also publicly ordered them to take their weapons and baggage and leave the city; he was going to dismiss them, he announced, and assess their strength at the same time. This made the men angry, because they did not have the money to stock up on provisions for the journey, and it was with some reluctance that they set about packing up their gear.

Meanwhile, Xenophon went to see Cleander, the harmost, whose guest-friend he had recently become;* he wanted to say goodbye, since he was on the point of sailing back home. But Cleander said to him, 'I wouldn't do that, if I were you. Some people are already holding you responsible for the slow departure of the army, and if you leave it will all be laid at your door.'

'But it's not my fault,' Xenophon said. 'It's just that the shortage of supplies is making the men sullen at the prospect of leaving.'

'All the same,' Cleander said, 'I advise you to make it look as though you're accompanying the men out of the city, and extricate yourself from the army only when you have all left.'

'All right, then,' said Xenophon, 'we'll go to Anaxibius and see if we can agree on this plan.'

They went to Anaxibius and told him their thoughts. He agreed and said that the men were to pack up as quickly as possible; he also published another order, to the effect that anyone who failed to turn up for the review and the assessment would have himself to blame for the consequences.

So they left the city, with the main body of the army led by the generals, and before long almost all of them were outside, with Eteonicus* in position by the gates, ready to shut them and drive home the cross-bar when the last few men had left. Then Anaxibius invited the generals and the company commanders to a meeting, at which he said: 'Get your provisions from the villages of Thrace, which have everything you need, including barley and wheat. Once you've done that, march on to the Chersonese, where Cyniscus will give you your pay.'

Some of the men overheard this, or the news was spread around by one of the company commanders, and while the generals were trying to find out whether Seuthes was friend or foe and were debating whether they should march over the Sacred Mountain* or take the roundabout route through the middle of Thrace, the soldiers grabbed their weapons and sprinted back to the gates, with the intention of getting back inside the city walls. But when Eteonicus and his men saw the hoplites running towards them, they shut the gates and drove home the cross-bar. The soldiers began to beat on the gates and to protest at the utter injustice of throwing them out into hostile territory, and they said that if the gates were not freely opened up for them, they would smash them down. Meanwhile, others ran to the shore, made their way along the breakwater, and clambered into the city that way, while some of their comrades, who were still inside, saw what was happening at the gates and hacked through the cross-bar with axes. As soon as they threw the gates open, the men poured inside.

Xenophon was terrified that the army would turn to looting and that irredeemable harm would be done, not just to the city but also to himself and to the troops, so as soon as he realized what was going on he ran up and joined the crowd of soldiers who were pouring into the city. The sight of the troops forcing their way into the city made the people of Byzantium evacuate the marketplace and run for their ships or their homes, while those who were indoors ran out into the streets and others set about launching the city's war fleet, trusting the triremes to keep them safe. In short, everyone imagined that they were lost, as if the city had fallen into enemy hands. Eteonicus took refuge on the acropolis, while Anaxibius ran down to the shoreline, sailed around to the acropolis on a fishing-boat, and immediately sent for the garrison from Chalcedon, since he doubted that the troops he had on the acropolis were enough to bring the situation under control.

When the soldiers spotted Xenophon, a lot of them rushed over to him and said: 'Xenophon, here's your chance to prove yourself a real man. You have a city, triremes, money, and plenty of troops. Here's your chance, then: if you so choose, you can do us good and we can make you great.'

Xenophon wanted to calm them down, so he replied: 'I like the way you're thinking and I shall do as you suggest. But if that's really what you want, fall in with your weapons grounded.' In addition to giving this order personally, he had the order to ground weapons passed on as well. The hoplites fell in without any further instructions, and before long they were arrayed in eight ranks and the peltasts had run over to one wing or the other. The place where they were, which is called the Thracian Field, is perfectly suited for marshalling troops, since it is flat and has not been built on. Once they had grounded their weapons and settled down, Xenophon instigated a general meeting and spoke as follows:

'Men, I don't find your anger and your feeling that you've been deceived and abused at all surprising. But if we let anger get the better of us—if we punish this lot of Spartans for their underhand methods and sack the city when it is blameless—you should consider the outcome, which is that we'll be represented as enemies of the Spartans and their allies. As for the war that would follow, we can guess what that would be like, because we've witnessed recent events and can easily recall them. We Athenians entered the war against the Spartans and their allies with no fewer than 300 triremes at sea or in our shipyards; we had a huge reserve of money in the city and an annual income from home and abroad of at least 1,000 talents.* We had an empire consisting of all the islands, many of the Asian communities, and many towns and cities in Europe too, including Byzantium, the very place where we are now—and yet we suffered, as you are all aware, a thoroughly humiliating defeat. So what do you think would happen to us now, when the Spartans not only still have all their old allies, but have been joined by the Athenians and all their former allies too, when Tissaphernes and all the rest of the coastal barbarians are hostile to us, and when we have as our arch-enemy the king of Persia, since we came to wrest his throne from him and to kill him, if we could? With all these opponents united in their hostility towards us, is there anyone so stupid as to imagine that we could prevail against them? In the name of the gods, let's keep our wits about us. Let us not die despicable deaths as the enemies of our homelands and of our own friends and relatives, all of whom are inhabitants of communities which would be involved in campaigns against us. And our opponents would have right on their side, if after deliberately refraining from occupying any barbarian city even though we came as their conquerors, we ransack the first Greek city we've come to.*

'For my part, I pray that I may be swallowed into the deepest bowels of the earth before I see you do this; and my advice to you is that, as Greeks, you should try to get justice while remaining obedient to those who are the Greeks' masters. If that doesn't work, we must not lose Greece as a result of the injustice we have suffered. I think we should send a delegation to Anaxibius with this message: "We have not entered the city with the intention of committing acts of violence, but to see whether you Spartans might offer us some help. But at the very least, we want to make it clear that we're leaving out of obedience to your wishes, not as dupes." ' This proposal was carried, and they sent Hieronymus of Elis as their spokesman, along with Eurylochus of Lusi and Philesius of Achaea. So off they went to deliver this message.

While this session of the army was still going on, Coeratadas of Thebes* came up to them. He was travelling from place to place, not because he was in exile from Greece, but because he wanted to be a general and was offering himself to any city or people that needed one. So on this occasion he came up and said that he was prepared to lead the men to the part of Thrace known as the Delta,* where they would find plenty of everything they needed, and that until they got there he would keep them supplied with more than enough food and drink. This offer came at the same time as Anaxibius' response, in which he said that they would not regret their obedience and that he would be delivering a report of these events to the authorities back home, while personally trying to find a way to do what he could to help them. The soldiers therefore took on Coeratadas as their general and pulled back outside the city walls. Coeratadas arranged to join them the next day and to bring them sacrificial victims and a diviner, and food and drink.

Once the troops had left the city, Anaxibius shut the gates and had it proclaimed that any soldier found inside the walls would be sold into slavery. The next day Coeratadas arrived with the victims and the diviner, and with a train of twenty men carrying barley, another twenty with wine, three with olives, one with as big a load of garlic as he could manage, and another with onions. He put these things on the ground for later distribution and proceeded to perform a sacrifice.

Xenophon arranged a meeting with Cleander and asked him to find a way for him to be allowed inside the city so that he could leave Byzantium by ship. When Cleander came back, he said: 'It wasn't at all easy, but I've sorted things out for you. Anaxibius didn't like the idea of having the soldiers just outside the city walls and you inside them. Moreover, there's political feuding going on in Byzantium at the moment, and people are at one another's throats. But despite all this, he has given you permission to enter the city, if you're planning to accompany him on his voyage home.' So Xenophon said goodbye to his troops and left, entering the city walls with Cleander.

Meanwhile, Coeratadas failed to get favourable omens on the first day and gave the troops none of their rations. The next day, the victims were standing by the altar and Coeratadas was wearing a wreath in preparation for sacrificing, when he was approached by Timasion of Dardanus, Neon of Asine, and Cleanor of Orchomenus. They told Coeratadas not to bother with the sacrifice, because he was not going to be the leader of the army unless he handed out the provisions. He told them to distribute the food, but it fell far short of providing each man with food for a day. Coeratadas therefore gathered together his sacrificial victims, resigned from his post as general, and left.

[2] Responsibility for the army now lay with the remaining

generals, Neon of Asine, Phryniscus of Achaea, Philesius of Achaea,
Xanthicles of Achaea, and Timasion of Dardanus.* They set out for
some Thracian villages near Byzantium and set up camp there. But
there was disagreement among the generals: Cleanor and Phryniscus
wanted to take the army to work for Seuthes (who had been helping
them make up their minds with gifts of a horse to one of them and a
woman to the other), while Neon wanted to go to the Chersonese
(where, he thought, if the army were taken on by the Spartans, he
would get supreme command), and Timasion wanted to cross back
over to Asia (because he thought that he would be accepted back by
his native city). The soldiers supported Timasion, but as time went
by many of them either sold their arms and armour and found some
way to set sail for their various homes or began to get involved in the
life of the nearby communities. Anaxibius was delighted to hear what
was going on—that the army was falling apart—because he thought
that nothing would please Pharnabazus more.

At Cyzicus, during his voyage home from Byzantium, Anaxibius
was met by Aristarchus, who was on his way to take over from
Cleander as harmost of Byzantium; it was also said that Polus,
who was to take over as naval commander, had almost reached the
Hellespont. Anaxibius ordered Aristarchus to sell into slavery all the
soldiers from Cyrus' army whom he found still in Byzantium—
Cleander had not sold a single one, and in fact had felt sorry for those
who were ill and had taken care of them by insisting that they be
billeted in people's homes—and the first thing Aristarchus did on
arriving was sell at least 400 men. Meanwhile, Anaxibius sailed on to
Parium, where he sent a message to Pharnabazus, asking him to
honour their agreement.* But when Pharnabazus found out that
Aristarchus had arrived in Byzantium to be the new harmost and that
Anaxibius was no longer the naval commander, he ignored Anaxibius
and began to hold with Aristarchus the same kind of discussions
about Cyrus' army which he had previously held with Anaxibius.

Anaxibius therefore summoned Xenophon and urged him, using
every device and resource at his disposal, to sail back to the army
without the slightest delay, in order to keep it from falling apart and
to collect as many as he could of those who had gone their separate
ways; and then, he suggested, Xenophon should take the army along
the coast to Perinthus and cross over to Asia as quickly as possible.
He also gave him a thirty-oared warship and written authorization,

and sent along with him a man who was to tell the Perinthians to help Xenophon on his way to the army without delay by furnishing him with horses. So Xenophon sailed across the strait and returned to the army. The troops welcomed him back with open arms, and they immediately and happily accepted his leadership for the crossing from Thrace to Asia.

When Seuthes heard that Xenophon had returned, he sent Medosades to him again, by sea; he asked Xenophon to bring the army to him and made every promise he could think of that might win him over. But Xenophon replied that it was quite out of the question, and Medosades left after hearing what Xenophon had to say. When the Greeks reached Perinthus, Neon detached his troops (there were about 800 of them) and made a separate camp, while the rest of the army stayed together in the same place by the city walls.

Xenophon next began to negotiate for ships, so that they could cross the strait at the earliest possible opportunity. While this was going on, Aristarchus, the harmost based in Byzantium, arrived with two triremes. In deference to Pharnabazus' wishes he ordered the shipowners not to ferry the Greeks across and, on a visit to the army, told the soldiers that they were not to cross over into Asia. Xenophon explained that Anaxibius had given him a direct order, 'and sent me here to organize the crossing', he said. But Aristarchus replied: 'Well, Anaxibius is no longer the naval commander. I am the harmost here and I will sink any of you I catch at sea.' And with these words he went back inside the city walls.

The next day, Aristarchus sent for the army's generals and company commanders. They were just approaching the city walls when someone warned Xenophon that if he entered the city he would be arrested, and would either come to grief there and then or be handed over to Pharnabazus. On hearing this, Xenophon sent the others on ahead, telling them that he wanted to perform a sacrifice. He went back to the camp and sacrificed to see whether the gods might allow him to attempt to take the army to Seuthes, since he could see that it was unsafe to cross the strait when the person who wanted to stop them doing so had triremes at his command, and at the same time he did not want to go to the Chersonese and have the army find itself trapped and short of everything in a place where they would have to obey the local harmost and where they would get none of the supplies they needed.

While he was busy with the sacrifice, the generals and company commanders came back from Aristarchus with the news that he had told them to leave for the time being and to come back again in the late afternoon—which just seemed to make his underhand intentions more obvious. But the omens appeared to suggest that it would be safe for Xenophon and the army to go to Seuthes, so Xenophon enlisted Polycrates of Athens, who was one of his company commanders, and took from each of the generals (apart from Neon) one man whose reliability was vouched for by each of them, and set out under cover of darkness on the journey of sixty stades to Seuthes' army. When they got close, he found fires but no people by them. At first he thought Seuthes had left and gone elsewhere, but then there was a noise and he heard Seuthes' men signalling to one another, and he realized that Seuthes had deliberately lit fires in front of his sentries. This meant that while the darkness would make it impossible to see how many sentries there were or their whereabouts, no one could stealthily approach without becoming visible in the light.

Xenophon had a translator with him, so once he realized what was going on he sent him ahead with instructions to tell Seuthes that Xenophon had come and wanted to meet him. The sentries asked whether he was the Athenian from the army, and when he said that he was, they leapt onto their horses and raced away. Before long, about 200 peltasts appeared and took Xenophon and his men to meet Seuthes, who was well protected in a tower. Around the tower there were horses, already bridled, because Seuthes was so nervous that he fed his horses during the day and at night kept them bridled as a precaution. For it was said that in times past Seuthes' ancestor Teres* had gone there with a large force of men, and had suffered heavy losses fighting the local inhabitants—the Thynians, who were said to be the most warlike people in the world, and especially good at night-fighting*—and had all his baggage stolen too.

Xenophon and his men drew close to the tower and Seuthes told Xenophon to come inside with two men of his choice. When they were inside, they first greeted each other and drank horns of wine to each other's health, as is the Thracian custom. Seuthes also had Medosades there with him, the man who always acted as his representative on missions. After the preliminaries, Xenophon was the first to speak. 'The first time you sent this man Medosades to me, Seuthes,' he said, 'was when I was at Chalcedon. You asked me to do my best to get the army across from Asia, and you promised to be generous if I was successful. At any rate, that's what Medosades told me.' Then he asked Medosades whether what he had said was right, and Medosades agreed that it was.

'Then he came to me again,' Xenophon continued, 'after I had crossed the strait from Parium to rejoin the army, with the promise that if I brought you the army you would treat me as your friend and brother, and especially that I would receive from you all the places on the coast which you currently control.' With this he again asked Medosades if that was what he had said, and Medosades again agreed.

'Well, then,' Xenophon said, 'tell Seuthes how I replied to you in Chalcedon on the first occasion.'

'You said that the army was going to cross over to Byzantium anyway, so there was no need to pay you or anyone else for that, and you added that after the crossing you were going to leave. And that's exactly what happened.'

'And what did I say,' Xenophon asked, 'when you came to me at Selymbria?'

'You said that it was out of the question, and that you were going to Perinthus to cross over to Asia.'

'Well, here I am now,' said Xenophon, 'and this man here is Phryniscus, one of my fellow generals, and this one is Polycrates, one of my company commanders. Outside there are highly trusted representatives of each of the generals except Neon of Sparta. If you'd like our negotiations to be more secure, invite them to join us. Polycrates, why don't you go and tell them from me that they are to leave their weapons behind? And you too had better leave your sword there before coming back inside.'

After listening to Xenophon's words, Seuthes said that he would never distrust an Athenian; after all, he said, he understood that he and the Athenians were related,* and he regarded them as loyal friends. Next, once those who were to join them had come inside, Xenophon initiated the proceedings by asking Seuthes what he wanted the army for. Seuthes replied as follows: 'The kingdom of my father, Maesades, included the Melanditae, the Thynians, and the Tranipsae. When things turned bad for the Odrysians,* he was expelled from this country, and while in exile he died of an illness. I was brought up as an orphan in the household of Medocus, the present king, but when I grew up I found it impossible to live as a beggar at someone else's table. So I sat myself down next to Medocus and implored him to give me as many men as he could spare, so that I could make life as difficult as my resources allowed for those who had expelled us and so that I would not have to live as a beggar at someone else's table. He then gave me the men and horses you'll see for yourselves tomorrow morning, and my current way of life is that I keep these men with me and raid my own ancestral land. But if you come and join me, I'm sure that, with the help of the gods, I could easily recover my kingdom. That's what I want you for.'

'Well,' said Xenophon, 'if we did come, what would you be able to offer the rank and file, the company commanders, and the generals? Tell us, so that these men here can report back to the army.' Seuthes promised to pay each soldier the monthly rate of one Cyzicene stater, with the company commanders getting double that amount and the generals four times as much; he also promised them all the land they might want, teams of oxen, and a fortified stronghold on the coast.

'What if we don't succeed in our attempt to win over the men?' Xenophon asked. 'What if they are too frightened of the Spartans? Will you give shelter in your land to any soldier who wants to leave the army and come to you?'

Seuthes said that he would. 'In fact,' he said, 'I'll make them my brothers, they will sit by my side, and they will share in all our acquisitions. As for you, Xenophon, I shall also give you my daughter, and if you have a daughter, I'll buy her as we do in Thrace.* And I shall give you Bisanthe, the most attractive of my coastal properties, as a place to live.'

[3] After this conversation, the two parties shook hands on the arrangements and the Greeks rode away. They got back to the camp before daylight and each of them reported back to the general who had sent them on the mission. Early in the morning, Aristarchus again summoned the generals and company commanders to a conference, but they decided to forget about going to Aristarchus and chose to assemble the troops instead. All the men assembled, except for those under Neon's command, who remained about ten stades away. Once they were all there, Xenophon stood up and said: 'Men, with Aristarchus here using his triremes to stop us sailing over to where we want to go, it's risky for us to take to the sea. He would have us force our way into the Chersonese over the Sacred Mountain.*

If we take the mountain and reach the Chersonese, he promises that he will stop selling you into slavery as he did in Byzantium, that you will stop hearing lies but will be paid instead, and that he will stop turning a blind eye as he does at the moment to the fact that you are short of provisions.

'That's what he says. At the same time, Seuthes is promising to make it worth your while to go and work for him. Now, the immediate question for you to decide is whether you want to stay and think about what to do next or go out after provisions first. My own view is that, since here at Perinthus we don't have the money to buy goods and at the same time they're not allowing us just to take what we need without paying for it, we should start by going out to the villages where it *is* possible for us to take provisions, since they're weaker than us. Once we've replenished our supplies, you can be told there what each of these men wants you for, and then choose whichever option strikes you as best. If you agree with this motion, raise your hand.' Everyone raised their hands. 'Go and pack up, then,' Xenophon said, 'and when the order is given, follow your commanding officer.'

Next Xenophon took the lead and the men followed. Neon and some of Aristarchus' men tried to persuade them to turn back, but they refused to listen to them. After they had gone about thirty stades, Seuthes appeared. When Xenophon saw him, he asked him to ride up to the troops so that he would have as large an audience as possible when he told him what they had decided was in their best interests. Once Seuthes had drawn close, then, Xenophon said: 'Our destination is wherever the army will be able to get hold of food. Once we've reached such a place, we shall listen to you and to the Spartan's men and decide which option seems best for us. So if you take us to a place where provisions are in plentiful supply, we will gain a favourable impression of your hospitality.'

'I know of a large cluster of villages with everything you need,' Seuthes said. 'They aren't far from here: you'll just be in time to enjoy your midday meal when you get there.'

'Show us the way, then,' said Xenophon.

It was well after noon when they reached the villages. The troops assembled and Seuthes addressed them. 'Men,' he said, 'I'd like you to serve alongside me. If you do so, I guarantee a Cyzicene stater a month for the rank and file, and the usual pay for company commanders and generals; over and above this pay, I shall reward those who deserve it. You will get your food and drink by foraging, as you did today, but I shall expect to keep for myself any property you capture, so that I can pay you with what I raise by disposing of it. We already have the ability to pursue and track down anyone or anything that tries to escape or run away, but with your help we shall endeavour to overcome any resistance.'

'How far inland do you expect the army to come with you?' asked Xenophon.

'Never more than seven days' march,' Seuthes replied, 'and often less.'

After this the floor was given to anyone who wanted to speak, and quite a few people voiced the same view, that Seuthes' proposals were exactly what they needed: now that it was winter, those who wanted to sail back home could not do so; there was no way they could survive in friendly territory if they had to buy the necessities of life; and it would be safer for them to spend time and get their food in hostile territory with Seuthes than on their own. The fact that they were going to get paid, on top of all these advantages, was generally held to be a lucky bonus.

After the speeches Xenophon said: 'If anyone has any objections, let's hear them now. Otherwise, let's put it to the vote.'

No one raised any objections, so he put the proposal to the vote. It was carried and he immediately told Seuthes that they would serve with him. The rest of the men then bivouacked in their separate units, while Seuthes invited the generals and company commanders to dine with him in a nearby village he had taken over. But when they reached his threshold and were just about to go inside for dinner, they were met by a man called Heraclides of Maronea, who accosted everyone he thought had anything to give to Seuthes. First, he went up to some men from Parium who had come to negotiate an alliance with Medocus, the king of the Odrysians, and had brought gifts for him and his wife. Heraclides told them that while Medocus was twelve days' journey inland from the coast, Seuthes would make himself the ruler of the coast, now that he had gained this army. 'As your neighbour, then,' he said, 'he'll be perfectly placed to do you either good or harm. So the sensible thing would be for you to give him the gifts you've brought. You'll be better off if you do that than if you give them to Medocus, who lives so far away.'

After he had tried this argument out on them, he went up to
Timasion of Dardanus, because he had been told that Timasion
had some goblets and eastern carpets, and said that it was customary for Seuthes' dinner guests to give him something. 'Besides,' he
said, 'if Seuthes becomes important here, he'll be in a position
either to get you taken back by your native city or to make you a
rich man here.'

These were typical of the approaches he made to people. He came
up to Xenophon too, and said: 'You're from a very powerful city and
your standing with Seuthes is very high. You may well be expecting
to follow in the footsteps of some of your fellow countrymen* and be
given fortresses here and land, but in that case you ought to show
your regard for Seuthes in a particularly magnificent manner. I'm
looking after your best interests in giving you this advice, because I
know for certain that the greater the gifts you give him, the greater
the good you will get from him.' But his words left Xenophon in a
quandary, because he had crossed over from Parium with nothing
but a slave and enough money to cover his travelling expenses.

The dinner guests included the most high-ranking of the Thracians
who were there, the Greek generals and company commanders, and
envoys from various communities. Once they had gone inside, they
were seated for the meal in a circle, and then three-legged tables were
brought in for everyone. There were about twenty of these tables and
they were laden with slices of meat joined by skewers onto huge
loaves of risen bread. For the most part, the tables were placed,
according to Thracian custom, by each of the guests.

Seuthes initiated the proceedings as follows: he picked up the
loaves which had been served in front of him, broke them into small
pieces, and tossed the pieces to whichever of the guests he felt like.
Then he did the same with the meat, leaving himself only morsels.
Once he had finished, everyone else who had a table placed near by
did the same. But an Arcadian called Arystas, who had a prodigious
appetite, could not be bothered with throwing pieces of food around:
he just picked up a three-choenix-sized loaf, put some meat on his
knees, and began to eat. Horns of wine were also being offered
around and everyone took one, except for Arystas: when the cup-
bearer brought him a horn, Arystas noticed that Xenophon had
finished eating and said: 'Give it to that man there. He's got time for
it, but I haven't yet.' When Seuthes heard him speak he asked the

cup-bearer, who understood Greek, what he had said, and there was laughter when the cup-bearer told him.

As the drinking continued, a Thracian man came in, leading a white horse. He took a full horn and said: 'Here's to you, Seuthes! This horse is my gift to you. On its back you will catch anyone you pursue and in retreat you need not fear the enemy.' Someone else brought in a slave and gave him to Seuthes in the same way, with a toast to his health, and someone else brought clothes for his wife. Timasion also drank his health and gave him a silver goblet and a carpet worth ten mnas, while an Athenian called Gnesippus stood up and praised the ancient tradition that those who had possessions should show their regard for the king by giving, while the king should do the giving in the case of those who had nothing. 'Then I too will have something to give you,' he explained, 'to show my regard for you.'

Xenophon did not know what to do, seated as he was in the place of honour right next to Seuthes. But then Heraclides told the cup-bearer to hand him the horn and Xenophon, who was by then a little tipsy, took the horn, boldly stood up, and said: 'As for me, Seuthes, I give you myself and my comrades here to be your loyal friends. None of them has the slightest doubts; all of them look forward with even more pleasure than I do to being your friends. And so they've come to you now, not because they have anything further to ask of you, but because they're ready and willing to exert themselves and face danger for you. With their help and the consent of the gods, you will recover huge tracts of your ancestral land and gain more besides— not just land, but large numbers of horses, and plenty of men and beautiful women. And you will not need to seize them as booty, because my comrades will bring them to you as gifts.'

Then Seuthes got to his feet, and together he and Xenophon drained the horn and scattered the last drops of wine.* Afterwards, musicians came in and played horns (similar to the ones they use for sending signals) and trumpets covered in untreated oxhide, which they used not only to keep time, but also like a magadis.* Later, Seuthes also stood up on his own, yelled out a war-cry, and with great agility performed a vigorous dance which simulated the dodging of missiles. There was also a performance by comedians.

At sunset the Greeks got to their feet, explaining that it was time for them to post sentries and give out the watchword. They also recommended Seuthes to instruct his Thracians not to enter the Greek camp after dark: 'You see,' they explained, 'our enemies are Thracians and so are you, our friends.' As they were leaving, Seuthes got up too, without showing the slightest sign of being drunk, and once they were outside he called the generals aside to a private conference and said: 'My friends, our enemies don't yet know about our alliance. If we attack them before they've protected themselves against capture or taken any steps to keep us at bay, I have not the slightest doubt that both men and livestock will fall into our hands.'

The generals agreed that this was a good idea and suggested that he show them the way. 'Get ready, then,' he said, 'and wait for me. I'll come to you when it's time. I'll lead the way with my horsemen, and I'll take my peltasts as well as you.'

Xenophon said: 'All right, but if we're going to march at night, you should ask yourself whether it might not be better to go about it in the Greek fashion. When we march during the daylight hours, the army is led by whichever division—the hoplites, the peltasts, or the cavalry—is best suited to the terrain on that particular occasion. But at night it is Greek practice that the slowest element of the army should take the lead, because that hugely reduces the possibility of the various divisions becoming separated and of men losing touch with one another without realizing it. And accidental meetings between units which have become separated from the main army commonly result in injuries to both sides, if they fail to recognize one another.'

'That's a good idea,' said Seuthes. 'I'll follow your practice. I'll provide you with guides, some of my older men who know the country very well, and I myself will bring up the rear with my horsemen. After all, I'll be able to get up to the front quickly in an emergency.' They settled on 'Athena' as the watchword, in honour of their kinship, and then they went to rest.

Seuthes came back around midnight with his horsemen already wearing their cuirasses and his peltasts equipped for battle. Once he had delivered the guides, the hoplites led the way, with the peltasts behind them and the cavalry bringing up the rear. At daybreak, Seuthes rode up to the front and said how much he liked the Greek practice. 'Often in the past,' he said, 'when marching at night with even a small force, I and my horsemen have lost touch with the foot soldiers, but now here we are all together at daybreak, as we should be. Anyway, why don't you wait here and rest, and I'll come back once I've assessed the situation.'

With these words he took a trail which wound its way through the mountains and rode off. He came to a place where there was deep snow, checked for human footprints heading either up or down the trail, and once he had assured himself that the path was unused he came back and said: 'All will be well, my friends. God willing, we'll take our opponents by surprise. I'll lead the way with the cavalry, so that we'll be able to prevent anyone we see from escaping and warning the enemy. You bring up the rear, and if you fall behind, just follow the tracks of the horses. We'll find many prosperous villages on the other side of the mountains.'

Around midday he reached the top of the mountain range and looked down on the villages. He rode back to the hoplites and said: 'I'm going to let my horsemen gallop down to the plain straight away, and have my peltasts attack the villages. You come along as quickly as you can, so that you can deal with any resistance.'

Xenophon dismounted from his horse at these words, and Seuthes asked: 'Why are you dismounting? We need to get a move on.'

'I'm sure I'm not the only one you need,' Xenophon replied, 'and the hoplites will be faster and more willing if their leader is on foot as well.'

Then Seuthes left, taking Timasion and about forty Greek horsemen with him. Xenophon ordered all the most mobile men below thirty years of age to leave their companies and join him, and then he set off at a run with them, while Cleanor took command of the rest of the troops. When they reached the villages, Seuthes rode up with about thirty horsemen and said: 'It's just as you said, Xenophon: my horsemen have gone off on their own here and there in pursuit of fugitives, and even though we've taken over the villages, it might well be possible for the enemy to form themselves into a coherent body somewhere and do us harm. I'm worried about that, but some of us have to stay in the villages as well, because they're teeming with people.'

'I'll take my men and occupy the high ground,' said Xenophon. 'You tell Cleanor to form a long line across the plain by the villages.' As a result of these operations, about 1,000 captives were herded together, along with 2,000 oxen and 10,000 sheep and goats as well. Afterwards, they spent the night there.

[4] The next day Seuthes burnt the villages to the ground, leaving not a single house standing, as a warning to everyone else of what would happen to them if they did not submit. Then he returned to his headquarters. He sent Heraclides to Perinthus to dispose of the booty and raise money with which he could pay the troops, while he and the Greeks encamped on the plain where the Thynians usually lived, except that they had taken refuge in the mountains. The snow lay deep on the ground and it was so cold that the water they fetched for their meals tended to freeze, and so did the wine in its jars. Also, a lot of Greeks got frostbite on their noses and ears. This made them understand why the Thracians wear fox-skin hats which protect their ears as well as their heads, why their clothes cover not only the trunks of their bodies but their thighs too, and why when riding they wear long cloaks* down to their feet rather than short ones.

Seuthes sent some of the captives into the mountains with a message from him that if the Thynians did not come down and live on the plain as his subjects, he would burn their villages as well, and their grain, so that they would starve to death. As a result of this ultimatum the women, the children, and the elderly came down to the plain, but the younger men continued use the villages in the lee of the mountain as their base. When Seuthes found out about this, he told Xenophon to follow him with the youngest of the hoplites, and they set out at night-time and reached the villages at dawn. The proximity of the mountains allowed most of the Thynians to escape, but Seuthes ruthlessly had his men kill with their javelins all those who fell into their hands.

There was in the army a man from Olynthus called Episthenes who was attracted to boys.* He noticed that a good-looking boy, carrying a light shield,* who had just reached the period of bloom,* was about to be put to death, and he ran over to Xenophon and begged him to rescue the beautiful boy. Xenophon went up to Seuthes and asked him to spare the boy's life; he explained Episthenes' character and told him how he had served with distinction in a military unit he had formed, the sole criterion for entry into which was the attractiveness of the men.

'Would you really be willing to die for this boy's sake, Episthenes?' asked Seuthes.

Episthenes exposed his neck and said: 'Strike, if the boy tells you to. Anything to make him happy.'

Seuthes asked the boy if he should execute Episthenes instead of him, but the boy said no and begged him to kill neither of them. Then Episthenes embraced the boy and said: 'Seuthes, you'll have to fight me for him, because I'm not going to let him go.'

Seuthes laughed and let the matter drop. He decided to bivouac there, to stop the men in the mountains getting food from these villages either,* so while he went back down to the plain and established his camp there, Xenophon took his elite troops and billeted them in the uppermost of the villages in the lee of the mountain, while the rest of the Greeks set up their tents near by, among the mountain-dwelling Thracians, as they are called.

A few days later the Thracians on the mountain came down and entered into discussions with Seuthes about a truce guaranteed by hostages. This coincided with a visit Xenophon paid to Seuthes, to complain about the poor location of his camp and the proximity of the enemy. Xenophon said he would prefer to have his men pitch their tents in defensible spots out in the open rather than have them indoors where their lives were in danger. Seuthes told Xenophon not to worry and showed him the hostages the enemy had given. Moreover, some of the Thracians on the mountain came down and asked Xenophon, too, in person to help them negotiate an end to the hostilities. He agreed to help them; he told them not to worry and guaranteed that they would come to no harm if they did what Seuthes asked them to do. But it turned out that this request of theirs was only a cover for their spying.

The night following the day of these events, the Thynians emerged from the mountains and launched an attack. The masters of each household acted as their guides, because otherwise it would have been hard to enter the villages in the dark and locate the houses, which were surrounded by stockades of tall stakes to protect the sheep and goats. Whenever they came to the threshold of a house, they hurled their javelins inside or set to with their clubs, which they carried, it was said, in order to knock the heads off spears. Others set houses on fire, and at Xenophon's house they called on Xenophon by name and invited him to come out and get killed or be burnt to death where he was.

Flames were just beginning to be visible through the roof, and Xenophon and his men were inside, with their breastplates on and equipped with shields, swords, and helmets. Then Silanus of

Macistus, who was about eighteen years old, blew a blast on his trumpet and they immediately dashed out of the house with their swords drawn. The Greeks in the other houses did the same, and the Thracians ran away, with their shields swung round on their backs, as is their custom.* Some of them got their shields snagged on the stakes as they tried to leap over a stockade and were caught hanging there; others were killed because they could not find a way out of the village. The Greeks continued the pursuit beyond the village, but in the darkness some of the Thynians turned around and threw their javelins at their pursuers as they were running past a burning house—throwing from darkness into light. They wounded two company commanders, Hieronymus of Epitalium†* and Theogenes of Locri, but no one was killed. Some men, however, lost their clothing and baggage in the fires.

Seuthes arrived, bringing reinforcements in the form of seven horsemen, in the first instance. He was also accompanied by his Thracian trumpeter, and from the moment he realized what was going on, for the whole time that he was riding over to help, he had the trumpeter sound his horn, which helped to panic the enemy. Once he got there, he shook their hands and said that he had expected to find a lot of them dead.

After this episode, Xenophon asked Seuthes to give him the hostages and either join him on an expedition to the mountains, if he wished to do so, or give him permission to go by himself. So the next day Seuthes gave Xenophon the hostages (who were elderly men, reputed to be the most important of the mountain-dwelling Thracians) and set out with him. Seuthes brought his whole army with him, and by this time he had three times as many men as before, because a lot of Odrysians, hearing of Seuthes' successes, had come down from the interior to join his ranks. When the Thynians looked down from the mountain and saw how many hoplites, peltasts, and horsemen there were, they came down and begged Seuthes to make a truce with them; they would do whatever he wanted, they said, and they urged him to accept their pledges. Seuthes called Xenophon over, explained what they were saying, and said that he would not make a truce with them if Xenophon wanted to punish them for the attack. But Xenophon said: 'For my part, I think the fact that they are now going to exchange freedom for slavery is recompense enough.' But he also advised Seuthes in the future to take as hostages those with the potential of causing the most trouble and to leave the old men at home. And so the entire population of the region came to terms with Seuthes.

[5] They crossed the mountains and entered the Delta, as it is called, in the country of the Thracians north of Byzantium, which was no longer part of Maesades' kingdom, but was ruled by Teres the Odrysian.* Heraclides met up with them there with the money he had raised by selling the booty. Seuthes brought out three pairs of mules (which is all he had) and teams of oxen as well, and invited Xenophon to take what he wanted and to give the rest to the generals and company commanders. 'Well,' Xenophon said, 'speaking for myself, I'm happy to wait. Why don't you give them to my companions, the generals here and the company commanders?' So Timasion of Dardanus, Cleanor of Orchomenus, and Phryniscus of Achaea each took one of the mule teams, while the teams of oxen were shared out among the company commanders.

Seuthes paid the troops, but only for twenty days of the month that had passed by then, with Heraclides claiming that he had not made any more than that from the sale of the booty. This made Xenophon angry, and he said to Heraclides with an oath: 'I don't think you care for Seuthes as you should. If you did, you'd have brought our pay in full, even if the only option had been borrowing some money or selling your own clothes.'

This made Heraclides angry, but he was also afraid of falling out of Seuthes' favour, and from that day on he did all he could to make Seuthes think badly of Xenophon. At the same time, the troops blamed Xenophon for the shortfall in their pay and Seuthes was angry with him for his strenuous insistence that he pay the men. Up until then, Seuthes had constantly been mentioning that on his return to the coast he was going to give Xenophon Bisanthe, Ganus, and New Fort, but from then on he never mentioned any of them, because one of Heraclides' snide suggestions had been that it was dangerous to give fortresses to a man with an army.

So while Xenophon was thinking about how best to conduct the campaign further inland, Heraclides arranged a meeting between the other generals and Seuthes, and told them to let Seuthes know that they could lead the army just as well as Xenophon; he also promised that before many days had passed they would be paid in full for two months, and he urged them to continue to serve with Seuthes. 'Well, speaking for myself,' Timasion replied, 'I'm not going to campaign without Xenophon even for five months' pay.' Phryniscus and Cleanor agreed with Timasion. This made Seuthes tell Heraclides off for failing to invite Xenophon to the meeting as well. In the end, they invited Xenophon to a meeting by himself, but because he was aware of Heraclides' malicious desire to stir up trouble between himself and the other generals, he brought all the generals and company commanders with him.

All the officers were won over by Seuthes and carried on in his service. Keeping the Euxine on their right, they marched through the land of the Thracians known as the millet-eaters and came to Salmydessus. A lot of ships sailing into the Euxine run aground and are wrecked there, because there are extensive shoals in the sea. The Thracians who live in this region set up marker-stones and each group of them plunders the wrecks that fall within their plot. It was said that in times past, before they set up these markers, they often used to kill one another on their plundering raids. Discoveries there include large quantities of all the kinds of items which shipowners transport in wooden chests, such as couches, boxes, and written scrolls.*

They subdued the local inhabitants and then marched back again. By then, Seuthes' own army was larger than the Greek force, because more and more of the Odrysians had joined him from the interior and because every time he conquered a tribe, these new subjects of his supplied him with men for his army. They set up camp on the plain above Selymbria, about thirty stades from the coast. There was still no sign of any pay, and not only were the soldiers furious with Xenophon, but Seuthes had stopped being cordial with him. Whenever Xenophon came and asked for a meeting, Seuthes suddenly found a number of matters that required his time and attention.

[6] By this time almost two months had passed. Just then, Charminus of Sparta and Polynicus came to them with a message from Thibron, saying that the Spartans had declared war on Tissaphernes and that Thibron had set sail to take charge of the war effort.* Thibron wanted their army, they said, and promised to pay each man a daric a month, with the company commanders getting double that amount and the generals four times as much.

Heraclides found out about the arrival of the Spartans the

moment they came for the army, and he encouraged Seuthes to think of it as a highly favourable event. 'After all,' he said, 'the Spartans need the army, while you don't any more. You will get into their good books by giving them the army, and the soldiers will stop demanding their pay from you and will leave the country instead.'

After listening to Heraclides, Seuthes told him to fetch the Spartans. They told him they had come for the army, and he said he would give it to them and that he wanted to be their friend and ally. He invited them to dine with him and entertained them lavishly. However, he did not invite Xenophon or any of the other generals, and when the Spartans asked what kind of a man Xenophon was, Seuthes replied that although basically he was not a bad man, he liked to be on good terms with the troops. 'And that makes things more difficult for him than they might be,' he said.

'Do you mean that he panders to their wishes?'* asked the Spartans.

'Yes, exactly,' said Heraclides.

'Then won't he try to stop us taking them away?' they asked.

'All you have to do is call them together and offer to pay them,' Heraclides replied, 'and they'll run off with you and hardly listen to him.'

'How should we go about convening them?' they asked.

'We'll take you to them tomorrow morning,' said Heraclides, 'and I'm sure that at the sight of you they'll run to the assembly point without the slightest hesitation.'

So this day came to an end. The next day, Seuthes and Heraclides took the Spartans to the army, and the men assembled. Once the two Spartans had announced the Spartan decision to make war on Tissaphernes—'the man who wronged you', as they put it—they went on: 'So if you join us, not only will you punish your enemy, but each of you will get a daric a month, with company commanders getting double that amount and generals four times as much.'

The troops were delighted to hear this, and an Arcadian got to his feet straight away in order to criticize Xenophon. Seuthes had come because he wanted to know what would happen, and though he had a translator with him, he found himself a place within earshot, because he was actually fairly fluent at Greek as well. Then the Arcadian spoke as follows: 'You Spartans should know that if it had been up to us, we'd have joined you long ago, but Xenophon won us over to his designs and brought us here. We've spent an appalling winter here on active service which has continued day and night without a break, while Xenophon profits from our efforts. As for Seuthes, he has given Xenophon a personal fortune while robbing us of our pay. Speaking for myself, then, if I could see Xenophon stoned to death in retribution for having dragged us all over the place, I'd consider myself paid in full and I wouldn't mind all the hard work I've put in.'

After him, other speakers got up and voiced the same sentiments, and then Xenophon spoke as follows: 'So, then, it seems that a man should never be surprised at what happens in life. After all, here I am, being criticized by you when I feel certain—within myself, at any rate—that I displayed absolute commitment to you. I was already on my way home, but I turned back. Why? Not, I assure you, because I'd heard that you were doing well, but because I was told that you were in difficulties, and I wanted to do what I could to help you.* After my return, Seuthes here kept sending me messages* and promising me all kinds of rewards if I could persuade you to come to him, but, as you're well aware, I made no attempt to do that. What I did was take you to a place from where, I expected, your crossing to Asia would be expedited, partly because I thought that was the best thing for you and partly because that was what you yourselves wanted to do. But once Aristarchus had arrived with his triremes and stopped us sailing over, at that point—and I really can't see how this could be considered inappropriate—I called a meeting so that we could discuss what to do. So you listened as Aristarchus ordered you to march to the Chersonese, and you listened as Seuthes tried to talk you into serving with him, and then you all spoke in favour of going with Seuthes and you all voted to do just that. Was I wrong in this, then, when all I did was take you where you all wanted to go?

'The time came when Seuthes began to cheat you of your pay. Now, if I put in a good word for him, you'd be right to criticize me and hate me; but since I've completely fallen out with him, when previously I was his closest friend, how can it be right for me to be criticized by you for what I fell out with him over, for choosing you rather than him? But it's still possible, you may argue, that this is all just a trick and that Seuthes has already given me what is rightfully yours. If so, it obviously follows that Seuthes did not pay me— assuming for a moment that he did so—in order to pay you more, over and above what he gave me. No, if he had paid me, I suppose he'd have done so on the understanding that he'd give me less in order to avoid giving you more. But in that case all you have to do is get your money from him and you'll have totally sabotaged his and my deal. I mean, Seuthes will obviously tell me to return whatever I received from him, and he'll be right to make this demand, since I failed to bring the scheme to the successful conclusion for which I was bribed.

'In actual fact, I'd have to say that, so far from my having what's rightfully yours, I don't even have what Seuthes promised me for myself. I swear to you by all the gods and goddesses that this is the truth. Seuthes is here in person to hear my words, and he knows whether I'm lying. And you'll be even more surprised to hear that I also swear that I haven't even been given what some of the company commanders have received, let alone the other generals.*

'Why, then, did I do what I did? Because, my friends, I thought that the more I helped him through his period of poverty, the more friendly he'd be to me once he gained power. But the sight of him prospering immediately brought recognition of his true intentions. "Aren't you ashamed at having been taken in like an idiot?" someone might ask. I can assure you that I most certainly would be ashamed if I'd been taken in by someone who was an enemy, but when the other person is a friend it seems to me to be more shameful to deceive than to be deceived. I mean, in so far as precautions play a part in a friendly relationship, I know that we took every possible precaution to avoid giving him a reasonable excuse for not paying us what he promised. After all, we did him no wrong, we didn't mishandle his project, and of course we didn't shirk any task, however dangerous, when he asked for our help.

'You might say that at the time I should have got pledges to ensure that he couldn't have deceived me even if he'd wanted to. In order to respond to this suggestion, I have to say things I'd never have said in front of him, but what strikes me as your utter lack of sensitivity or perhaps ingratitude towards me leaves me no choice. Remember how difficult your situation was at the time, and remember also that my taking you to Seuthes extricated you from these difficulties. Didn't Aristarchus of Sparta shut the gates of Perinthus* and stop you entering the city whenever you approached it? It was the middle of winter and you were camping in the open air outside the city; moreover, you were dependent on there being provisions to buy, though you could see that there was little for sale and though you had little money with which to make purchases. But you had no choice about staying in Thrace, because there were triremes moored there to stop you sailing across to Asia. And to stay there was to stay in hostile territory, with large numbers of horsemen and peltasts ranged against you. It's true that we had hoplites and that if we had gone out en masse against the villages we might perhaps have been able to get hold of food (though not in large quantities), but we didn't have the kind of troops with whom we could chase and catch either slaves or livestock, because on my return I found that you no longer had any organized units of cavalry or peltasts.*

'Since this was the predicament you found yourselves in, even if I'd arranged an alliance with Seuthes without demanding any pay whatsoever, would you have thought that I was failing to take your best interests into consideration? After all, he had horsemen and peltasts, precisely what you lacked, and as you know, once you joined forces with them, you not only found larger quantities of food in the villages, because the Thracians were compelled to evacuate them in greater haste, but you also captured more livestock and slaves. Moreover, once we had cavalry with us, we didn't see a single enemy soldier, whereas previously enemy troops had brazenly dogged our heels and had used their horsemen and peltasts to stop us splitting up into small raiding parties and so getting larger quantities of supplies. Now, if the person who gave you this security didn't also pay you well for it, is that so terrible a disaster? Is that sufficient reason for you to think that there's no way you can leave me alive?

'As things stand at the moment, what sort of condition will you be in when you leave here? Haven't you had plenty of supplies to see you through the winter? Isn't anything you got from Seuthes just a bonus, since you've been living at the enemy's expense and have been doing so without seeing any of your comrades being killed and without losing any of them alive either? Haven't you preserved intact all your fine achievements against the barbarians in Asia? Haven't you even added to them by having now gained further glory thanks to your conquest of the European Thracians against whom you campaigned? Personally, I think that in all fairness you ought to thank the gods for the things that are making you angry with me, and count them as blessings.

'That's all I want to say about *your* situation, but in the name of the gods I would ask you to take a look at mine too. Earlier, when I set out for home, I went with your thanks ringing in my ears and with the certainty that you had made me famous throughout Greece. Moreover, I had the confidence of the Spartans, because otherwise they wouldn't have sent me back to you. But now I'm leaving with the Spartans thinking badly of me because of what you've been telling them and with Seuthes hating me for having defended your interests. And Seuthes was the man by whom I hoped to be settled in a safe haven—somewhere nice for me and for my children, if I should have any—as a reward for the help I had given him, with your assistance. After all this, how can you—the very people for whose sake I've earned the unrelenting hatred of men who are far more powerful than I, the very people whose interests I am still serving even now—how can you be planning to do this to me?

'Well, you have me in your power, and you didn't have to catch me: I'm no fugitive or deserter. If you carry out your plan, you should know that you'll have killed a man who often passed sleepless nights for your sakes, who often endured more than his fair share of the troubles and hazards we faced together, who often joined you, when the gods were favourable, in setting up trophies* to celebrate our victories over barbarians, and who gave his all to stop you making enemies of even a single fellow Greek. In fact, you can now travel in safety wherever you choose, by land or by sea.

'And now, just when your difficulties have substantially vanished and you're sailing for the destination which has long been your hearts' desire, just when the mightiest people on earth are requesting your help and payment is within sight, just when the Spartans, who are held to be the best military men in the world, are coming to take command of the army—do you really think that this is the best moment for you to hurry me off for execution? You have unrivalled memories, so you'll remember how different things were when we were beset by difficulties and uncertainty. You called me "father" then and promised that you'd always remember me as your benefactor. In truth, the men who've now come to fetch you are actually not insensitive and so, I think, your treatment of me will not improve their opinion of you either.'

He finished speaking at this point, and then Charminus of Sparta stood up and said: 'By the Twin Gods, men, I have to say that personally I don't think it's right for you to be angry with this man. You see,

I have some testimony to give on his behalf myself too: when Polynicus and I asked Seuthes what kind of a man Xenophon was, Seuthes replied that he had nothing bad to say about him, except that he was too fond of being on good terms with the troops; this, he said, made things more difficult for Xenophon when he was dealing with us Spartans and with him.'

Next Eurylochus of Lusi got to his feet and said: 'Yes, and in my opinion, the first task you Spartans have to undertake as our generals is to get our pay from Seuthes, with or without his consent; and I don't think you should take us away from here until you've done that.'

Then, at Xenophon's instigation, Polycrates of Athens said: 'Men, here's Heraclides, right before my eyes. He's the one who took the valuables we struggled to acquire, and sold them but failed to hand the proceeds over to either Seuthes or us. He stole the money and kept it for himself. Good sense suggests that we should seize him. After all, he's no Thracian; this man who is wronging Greeks is himself a Greek.'

Terrified by these words, Heraclides went up to Seuthes and said: 'And in our case good sense suggests that we should leave here and get away from their sphere of influence.' They mounted their horses and rode back to their own camp.

From the safety of his own camp, Seuthes sent his translator, Abrozelmes, to Xenophon, with the request that he should retain a force of 1,000 hoplites and stay with him, and he promised to give him the coastal strongholds and everything else he had promised before. He also mentioned something he had heard from Polynicus—and he made out that this was privileged information—that if Xenophon fell into the hands of the Spartans, he would certainly be put to death by Thibron.* A lot of other people also sent word of this to Xenophon, adding that his name had been blackened and that he ought to be careful. In response to this information, Xenophon took two victims and sacrificed them to Zeus the King, to find out whether it was better and more advantageous for him to stay with Seuthes on Seuthes' terms or to leave with the army. The god told him to leave.

[7] After that, Seuthes moved his camp further away, while the Greeks bivouacked in villages where they could stock up on supplies before moving to the coast. These villages, however, had been given

by Seuthes to Medosades, and he became angry when it came to his attention that the Greeks were draining the villages of all their provisions. He enlisted the help of a high-ranking Odrysian, one of those who had come from the interior, and about thirty horsemen, and came and summoned Xenophon from the Greek quarters. Xenophon took some of his friends, including some of the company commanders, and approached Medosades. 'This plundering of our villages is a crime,' Medosades said. 'I speak for Seuthes and my companion here has come from Medocus, the king in the interior, and we hereby order you Greeks to leave the land or face the consequences: if you damage our land we will regard you as enemies and we will defend ourselves against you.'

Xenophon heard him out and then said: 'It's hard even to frame a reply to this kind of ultimatum. But I will respond, for the sake of this young man here, because I want him to see what you are like and what we are like. Before we became your friends, we marched wherever we wanted in this land. We stole crops if we felt like it and we burnt them if we felt like it. As for you, Medosades, whenever you came to us on a mission from Seuthes, you pitched your tent by ours and never felt threatened by any enemy, whereas previously, on the rare occasions when you and your men came here, you behaved as if you were in the territory of a stronger people and kept your horses already bridled in your camps. But then you became our friends and, with the help of the gods, we have ensured that this territory is under your control—and now you want to drive us out of this land, which we held by force of arms (as you yourself know, the enemy proved incapable of driving us out) and gave to you.

'Not only do you not have the decency to speed us on our way with rewards and concrete expressions of thanks for our assistance, but in so far as it's in your power to stop us, you're not even allowing us to bivouac here in the course of our journey home. In issuing this ultimatum, do you not feel shame, before this man here, if not before the gods? After all, although he can now tell that you're well off, he used to know you before your friendship with us, in the days when, as you yourself have admitted, you used to make a living as a brigand.

'In any case,' he went on, 'why are you even bothering to issue the ultimatum to me? I'm no longer in command here; the Spartans are. It was you and your men who handed the army over to them, for them to lead it away. Astonishingly, you didn't even invite me to the meeting and give me the opportunity to recover their favour by returning the army to them, which would have cancelled out the hostility I aroused in them when I took the army to you.'

After listening to this, the Odrysian said: 'Speaking for myself, Medosades, Xenophon's words fill me with so much shame that I wish the earth would swallow me up. If I'd known all this before, I wouldn't even have come with you. I'm leaving now. King Medocus would never thank me for banishing those who have helped him.'

With these words, he mounted his horse and rode away, and all but four or five of the other horsemen left with him. But Medosades, who was still upset by the plundering of the land, asked Xenophon to fetch the two Spartans. Xenophon took the most suitable men as his companions, went to Charminus and Polynicus, and told them that Medosades was asking for them. He warned them that Medosades intended to issue the same ultimatum to them that he had to him, that they should leave, and then went on: 'Now, I expect you could recover all the army's back pay. All you have to do is say that the men have asked for your help in collecting their pay from Seuthes, with or without his consent, and have said that they'd be happy to follow you away from here once they've got what's owing to them. You should add that, in your opinion, the troops' request is entirely justified, and that you gave them your word you wouldn't leave until they had what's rightly theirs.'

The Spartans said that they would act on this suggestion and would use other arguments as well, the most persuasive ones they could muster. Then they immediately left with all the high-ranking officers. When they got there, Charminus said: 'If you have anything to say to us, Medosades, say it. Otherwise, we've got something to say to you.'

Thoroughly cowed, Medosades replied: 'Seuthes and I are of one mind on this. We don't want to see those who have become our friends suffering at your hands. Any harm you do to them is harm done to us, because they are our subjects.'

'Well,' the Spartans continued, 'we'll leave when the men who brought about this state of affairs for you have been paid. Otherwise, we're going to lend them our immediate support and punish the oath-breakers who have wronged them. If you and Seuthes are in that group, our quest for justice will start with you.'

'Medosades,' said Xenophon, 'would you be prepared to let the inhabitants of this land, who you claim are your friends, vote on whether it would be appropriate for you or us to leave their territory?'

Medosades refused to go along with this, but he strongly encouraged the two Spartans to go and see Seuthes about the soldiers' pay, and he said that he thought they might get Seuthes to comply with their wishes. If they did not want to go themselves, he suggested that they let Xenophon go as his companion, and he promised Xenophon his support. He also begged them not to burn the villages.

Following this discussion, they sent Xenophon with an escort of the men most suited to the task. When Xenophon arrived, he said to Seuthes: 'I haven't come here with a list of demands, Seuthes. I want to explain to you, if I can, that you were wrong to hate me for taking the soldiers' part and forcefully demanding from you what you had promised them. It was my considered opinion, you see, that it was just as good for you to pay them as it was for them to be paid.

'In the first place, I know that, after the gods, it was the soldiers who raised you to your current position of prominence, since they made you the ruler of vast tracts of territory and huge numbers of men. Now, one of the consequences of your prominence is that everything you do, moral or immoral, is in the public eye. I thought it was important for someone in your position not to be held to have churlishly dismissed people who had helped you, and I thought it was important for you to be spoken of in glowing terms by 6,000 men.* But the most important thing of all, in my view, was that you should not let people feel that your word is anything less than your bond. It's plain to me that the shifty words of untrustworthy men have no purpose, authority, or value, whereas the words of those who are known for their cultivation of truth are as effective as the physical strength of others at getting them whatever they want. If they want to restrain certain people, I'm convinced that the mere threat of action from them is just as effective as actual punishment from others; and a promise from such a man is no less effective than an immediate gift from someone else.

'I'm sure you too remember how much you paid us up front to gain our support for your campaign. It was nothing, as you well know, but because you were thought to be honest and reliable you induced all those men to serve with you and to gain for you a kingdom which is worth many times more than the thirty talents* they currently think they should recover. So the first point I want to make is that this is the amount of money for which you are selling your credibility, the quality that gained you your kingdom.

'I would remind you how important it seemed to you at the time to gain the land which is now yours by right of conquest. I'm perfectly sure that you'd have prayed for this outcome rather than for many times this amount of money. Now, failing to retain your gains seems to me to be more painful and more disgraceful than failing to have got them in the first place, just as it is harder to exchange wealth for poverty than never to have been wealthy, and more painful to be publicly deposed from a throne than never to have occupied a throne at all. You understand that the people who've just become your subjects weren't persuaded to accept you as their ruler out of friendship towards you: they had no choice in the matter. You know, then, that fear is all that keeps them in check and stops them trying to regain their freedom. So in which of the following two situations do you think they'd be more afraid and more likely to be submissive towards you? One possibility is that they could see that the troops hold you in such regard that they would stay here if you asked them and would hurry back if you needed them, and they could also see that others, having heard nothing but good reports from the troops, would soon come and join you whenever you wanted them. Alternatively, they might come to believe not only that the distrust generated by what has just happened meant that no more soldiers would join you, but also that the men already here felt more inclined to co-operate with them than with you.

'Again, their submission to you was not due to our outnumbering them, but to their lack of effective leadership. So there's also danger here for you: they might find leaders among those who consider themselves to have been wronged by you. Or they might even get better leaders: they might get the Spartans. That is, the troops might promise to commit themselves more fully to active service under the Spartans on the condition that the Spartans now get their money from you, and the Spartans might be forced by their need of the army to agree to this condition. At any rate, it's certain that the Thracians who've just been conquered by you would be far more motivated to fight against you than to fight alongside you, because as long as you win they remain slaves, but if you lose they gain their freedom.

'Moreover, since the land is yours, it's possible that you might already want to take some thought for its future. In which of the following two situations, then, do you think the territory would be less burdened by troubles? Either these soldiers can be paid their claim and depart, leaving a state of peace behind them, or they can stay and treat the land as enemy territory, while you try to recruit another army to take the field against them, an army which would have to be larger and would need maintaining. And which of these two situations would be more expensive: if they are paid what is owed them, or if this debt remains outstanding and you still have to hire another, stronger army?

'Heraclides, however, believes, as he used to try to explain to me, that the soldiers are asking for too much money. In actual fact, however, it is now a far smaller amount for you either to get or to pay than a tenth of the amount would have been before we came to join you. I mean, it's not the mere figure which determines what is a large amount and what is little, but the resources of the giver and the receiver. And your annual revenue will now surpass the value of all your property and holdings before.

'Speaking for myself, Seuthes, I have been looking out for you in this, as I would for a friend. I wanted people to think that you deserved the good fortune the gods have granted you. At the same time, I didn't want to lose my status in the army. I mean, you should know that, as things are, if I wanted to use this army to injure an enemy, I wouldn't be capable of doing so, and if I wanted to come to your assistance again, I wouldn't be in a position to do so. That's how bad things are between me and the troops. And yet I have you (along with the gods, who know the truth) to attest that not only have I not received from you anything for the troops, but I've also never asked for what's rightfully theirs to be given to me for my personal use. In fact, I haven't asked you to make good on your promises to me, and I swear to you that even if you had been offering to do so, I wouldn't have accepted unless the troops were also going to get their back pay. It would have been shocking behaviour for me to settle my own affairs while ignoring the terrible state theirs were in, especially since I was highly regarded by them at the time.

'Now, Heraclides believes that everything pales into insignificance compared with getting money, whatever it takes to do so, but it's my view, Seuthes, that there's no possession which brings greater honour and glory to a man, especially if he's in a position of leadership, than courage, justice, and generosity. The man who possesses these qualities is rich not just because of all his friends, but because there are always others who would like to become his friends. If he does well, he's surrounded by people who share his pleasure, and if he meets with a setback, he's not short of people to help him out.

'But if my actions didn't make you understand that I was your true friend, and if my words fail to make you realize this too, you might at least bear in mind what the soldiers said. After all, you were there and you heard the complaints of my critics. They not only accused me in front of the Spartans of preferring you to Spartans, but, speaking for their own interests, they also charged me with concentrating more on your success than theirs. They also said that I'd been bribed by you. Now, do you think they accused me of accepting these bribes from you because they had noticed some hostility in me towards you, or because they saw how highly committed I was to you?

'It's universally held, I suppose, that such loyalty is reserved for the man who has bribed a person, but even before I'd done anything for you, you were delighted to make me welcome with kind looks and words and banquets, and you couldn't make enough promises about the future to satisfy yourself. But now that you've got what you wanted and are standing as high as I could raise you, can you hardheartedly leave me so out of favour with the troops? No, I'm sure you'll decide to pay them—that time will teach you and that you yourself won't be able to stand the sight of men who gave liberally of themselves in your service bringing charges against you. All I ask, then, is that when you pay the troops, you do your best to make them think of me as they did when you engaged me.'

Seuthes' response to this speech was to curse the person who was responsible for the fact that the troops had not been paid long before, and everyone suspected that he meant Heraclides. 'You see,' Seuthes said, 'it was never *my* intention to deprive them of their wages. I will pay them.'

'Since you're intending to pay them,' Xenophon said in response, 'I'd ask you to pay them through me. Don't leave me with this difficult relationship with the men, when it was you who changed it from what it was when we came to you.'

'All right,' said Seuthes, 'I won't be responsible for any decline in your standing in the army. Also, if you keep just 1,000 hoplites and stay with me, I'll give you the strongholds and everything else I promised you.'*

'That's impossible,' Xenophon replied. 'You had better just send us away.'

'But I'm also sure', Seuthes went on, 'that it will be safer for you to stay with me than to go away.'

'Thank you for your thoughtfulness,' Xenophon replied, 'but I can't stay. Instead, I'd ask you to consider it in your interests as well as mine if my prestige is enhanced, wherever I may find myself.'

Then Seuthes said: 'I don't have much money at the moment—just a talent—and you can have it. But I have 600 oxen, about 4,000 sheep and goats, and about 120 slaves. Take them, in addition to the hostages of the men who used such unfair tactics against you,* and be on your way.'

Xenophon laughed and said: 'If this doesn't add up to the full amount of their back pay, who shall I say the talent is from?* Since I'm really in some danger, wouldn't it be better for me to watch out for stones when I leave here?* You heard the threats.' So he stayed where he was for the rest of the day.

The next day, Seuthes gave them what he had promised and assigned drovers to accompany them. By then, the soldiers were starting to say that Xenophon had gone off to live with Seuthes and to get what Seuthes had promised him, but when they saw him approaching, they were delighted and they ran to meet him. When Xenophon saw Charminus and Polynicus, he said: 'Thanks to you,* these things have been kept safe for the army, and I hereby pass them over to you. It's up to you to sell them and distribute the money among the troops.'

The Spartans took over the booty and set about raising money by appointing quartermasters to do the selling. They incurred a great deal of criticism for their actions in this matter. Meanwhile, Xenophon stayed away and made no secret of the fact that he was getting ready to go home—for there was no sign yet in Athens of any proposal that he should be officially banished.* But his friends in the camp came and asked him not to leave until he had led the army away and turned it over to Thibron.

[8] They next sailed across to Lampsacus, where Xenophon was met by Euclides, the diviner from Phlius, whose father was the

Cleagoras who painted the murals in the Lyceum.* Euclides expressed his delight that Xenophon had made it back safe and sound and asked him how much money he had. Xenophon told him that, unless he sold his horse and the few possessions he had on him, he would not even be able to cover the costs of his journey home, but although he swore an oath to the truth of this statement, Euclides did not believe him. Later, however, the people of Lampsacus sent Xenophon tokens of friendship and he let Euclides stand next to him while he was sacrificing to Apollo, and at the sight of the entrails Euclides said that he now believed that Xenophon was broke. 'But it looks to me', he said, 'as though something turns up to frustrate you whenever you're due to get money—and that you frustrate yourself, if nothing else does.'

Xenophon agreed and Euclides went on: 'Yes, and in the present instance Zeus the Compassionate* is the obstacle. Have you sacrificed to him already—you know, the kind of whole-victim sacrifice I used to perform at home for you Athenians?'

When Xenophon said that he had not sacrificed to Zeus the Compassionate since he had left home, Euclides advised him to revive his old habit of sacrificing to him and said that he would gain from it. The next day, on arriving at Ophrynium, Xenophon performed the traditional sacrifice of whole pigs and received favourable omens. And in fact that same day Biton and Nausiclides arrived with money for the army. Xenophon made them welcome and they gave him back his horse, which he had sold in Lampsacus for fifty darics.* They bought the horse back because they suspected that he had sold it only because he was hard up and they had heard that he liked it. Xenophon offered to pay them back, but they would not hear of it.

They marched from Ophrynium through the Troad and across Mount Ida, and then made Antandrus their first stopping-point. After that, they marched along the coast to the plain of Thebe in Mysia. From there, travelling via Adramyttium and Certonium and past Atarneus, they came to Pergamum in Mysia, on the plain of the Caïcus river.

In Pergamum, Xenophon was made welcome at the house of Hellas,* the wife of Gongylus of Eretria* and mother of Gorgion and Gongylus. Hellas told him of a Persian called Asidates, who was living in the plain, and suggested that a night attack with 300 men would enable him to capture Asidates, his wife, his children, and his plentiful livestock. To show him the way, she sent not just her own cousin, but also Daphnagoras, of whom she thought very highly. With these two men by his side, Xenophon performed a sacrifice, and the diviner Basias of Elis, who was there, described the omens as highly favourable and said that the Persian would be easy to capture.

After dinner, then, Xenophon set out with his closest friends from the company commanders and others who had constantly demonstrated their reliability, because he wanted to do them a good turn. But they were joined by about six hundred others as well, who insisted on being included. The company commanders tried to get rid of them, because they did not want the booty, which they regarded as already in the bag, to be shared out among so many people.

It was close to midnight when they reached the place. The slaves, who were kept around the outside of the tower, ran away, as did most of the livestock, but the Greeks ignored them because they wanted to capture Asidates himself and his personal belongings. But the tower, which was massive and tall, fortified with battlements, and well defended by large numbers of good fighters, proved impossible to take by direct assault. Instead, they attempted to tunnel into the tower through the wall, which was eight clay bricks thick. By daybreak, they had created an opening, but no sooner had they broken through than someone inside the tower stabbed an ox-spit right through the thigh of the first man in the hole, and after that the defenders began to fire arrows through the opening, which made it unsafe even to approach it. Then, in response to the cries and beacons of the defenders, Itabelis† came to their assistance with a force consisting not just of his own troops, but Assyrian hoplites from Comania, about eighty Hyrcanian horsemen (who were mercenaries hired by the Persian king), and about 800 peltasts as well, who were supported by more peltasts from Parthenium and others, including horsemen, from Apollonia and other nearby places.

The Greeks therefore had urgently to decide how to get away from there. They formed a square and set out, driving all the cattle, sheep and goats, and slaves they had inside the square. They did this not because they were concerned about the booty as such, but because they thought that, if they left all these goods behind, their retreat would turn into a rout, since their opponents' confidence would be increased while their own men would be disheartened.

With this formation, however, they showed that they were ready to fight for the booty as they retreated.

When Gongylus saw that the Greeks were well outnumbered by their attackers, he wanted so much to play a part in the action that, despite his mother's protests, he came out with a troop of his own men. He was joined in this relief effort by Procles of Halisarne in Teuthrania, the descendant of Damaratus.* By this time Xenophon and his men were finding it very difficult to defend themselves against all the arrows and sling-shot. Marching in a circular formation, so as to keep their shields between themselves and the arrows, they only just managed to cross the Carcasus river, with about half of them wounded. Among those who were wounded at this time was Agasias, the company commander from Stymphalus, who had constantly been fighting back against the enemy. So they got back safely, with about two hundred slaves and enough sheep and goats for sacrifices.

The next day, after performing a sacrifice, Xenophon led the whole army away under cover of darkness. He wanted to get as far as he could into Lydia, so that Asidates would not be alarmed by his proximity and would relax his guard. But on being told that Xenophon had sacrificed with a view to attacking him and was on his way with the entire army, Asidates left and set up camp at some villages which lay below the town of Parthenium. Xenophon and his men came across him there and captured him, his wife, his children, his horses, and everything he had. And so the omens of the earlier sacrifice turned out to be true.

After that they went back to Pergamum, where Xenophon paid his respects to the god, because the Spartans, the company commanders, his fellow generals, and the troops together arranged things so that Xenophon should get the pick of the booty—the horses, teams of oxen, and so on—which meant that he was at last in a position even to do someone else a favour. Meanwhile, Thibron arrived and took over the army. He combined it with the rest of the Greek forces under his command and started to make war on Tissaphernes and Pharnabazus.

APPENDIX

WEIGHTS AND MEASURES

Values varied somewhat from place to place within the Greek world; what follows is just one system.

Measuring Distance

16 fingers (breadth) = 4 palms = 1 foot

12 fingers = ½ cubit = 1 span (the distance between the tips of the thumb and the little finger when the hand is fully spread)

1¼ feet = 1 pygon (the distance from the elbow to the bottom joint of the little finger)

1½ feet = 1 cubit (the distance from the elbow to the tip of the middle finger)

6 feet = 1 fathom (the distance from the fingertips of the left hand to those of the right hand when the arms are stretched out horizontally)

100 feet = 1 plethron

600 feet = 1 stade

30 stades = 1 parasang (see the note to p. 5)

1 foot on the Attic scale has been estimated to be 29.6 centimetres (11.65 inches). Therefore:

1 finger = 1.85 centimetres (0.73 inches)

1 palm = 7.4 centimetres (2.91 inches)

1 span = 22.2 centimetres (8.74 inches)

1 pygon = 37 centimetres (14.57 inches)

1 cubit = 44.4 centimetres (17.5 inches)

1 fathom = 1.776 metres (1.94 yards)

1 plethron = 29.6 metres (32.38 yards)

1 stade = 177.6 metres (194.29 yards)

1 parasang = 5.328 kilometres (3.33 miles)

Money, or Measuring Weight

Greek coinage was not on the whole fiduciary, but was worth its weight. Hence measures of weight are at the same time monetary measures.

1 talent = 60 mnas = 6,000 drachmas = 36,000 obols

1 obol = 722 milligrams (0.025 ounces)

1 drachma = 4.332 grams (0.15 ounces)
1 mna = 433.2 grams (15.16 ounces)
1 talent = 25.992 kilograms (57.31 pounds)

Measuring Capacity

Liquid measures: 1 amphora ('jar') = 12 choes ('pitchers') = 144 cotylae ('cups') = 864 cyathi ('spoons'). Since 1 amphora = about 39 litres (68.64 pints, 8.58 gallons), then 1 chous = 3.25 litres (5.72 pints), 1 cotyle = 270 millilitres (0.48 pints), and 1 cyathus = 45 millilitres (0.079 pints, 1.58 fluid ounces).

Dry measures: 1 medimnus = 48 choenixes = 192 cotylae. Since 1 cotyle = 270 millilitres (0.48 pints), then 1 choenix = 1.08 litres (1.90 pints), and 1 medimnus = 51.84 litres (91.24 pints, 11.40 gallons).

EXPLANATORY NOTES

References to modern works included in the Select Bibliography are given in shortened form. *FGH* stands for F. Jacoby, *Die Fragmente der griechischen Historiker* (15 vols.; Berlin and Leiden, 1923–58). For more detailed guidance on topography, see O. Lendle, *Kommentar zu Xenophons Anabasis* (Darmstadt, 1995), V. M. Manfredi, *La Strada dei Diecimila: Topografia e geografia dell'Oriente di Senofonte* (Milan, 1986), and R. J. A. Talbert (ed.), *Barrington Atlas of the Greek and Roman World* (Princeton, 2000).

BOOK ONE

3 *two sons*: according to Plutarch, Darius II and Parysatis (who was Darius' half-sister) also had two other sons, both younger than Cyrus, Ostanes and Oxathres (*Artaxerxes* 1.2); Xenophon himself later mentions a half-brother leading a contingent of Artaxerxes' army (2.4.25). Plutarch also alleges that Cyrus' claim to the throne was that he was the first son born after Darius II had become king (*Artaxerxes* 2.4), but his account may have been inspired by Herodotus' account of how Darius I chose Xerxes as his heir after being advised by the exiled Spartan king Damaratus that it was Spartan practice for the eldest son born in the purple to accede to the throne (7.2–3). Herodotus' account is suspicious: Xerxes was the eldest son born to Darius I by Atossa (the daughter of Cyrus II), and there were political reasons why Darius should have favoured a son born to her. Xenophon's claim that Parysatis supported Cyrus recalls Herodotus' account of Atossa's support for Xerxes: the Greeks liked to imagine that the Persian royal women were powerful at court. See P. Briant, *From Cyrus to Alexander: A History of the Persian Empire*, trans. P. T. Daniels (Winona Lake, Ind., 2002; Fr. orig. 1996), 518–22.

satrap: governor of one of the regions (twenty, according to Herodotus 3.89.1) into which the Persian empire was divided; Cyrus' area of command was greater than that of a regular satrap, though the details are controversial (see C. J. Tuplin, 'The Persian Empire', in R. Lane Fox (ed.), *The Long March* (New Haven, 2004), 162).

the Plain of Castolus: east of Sardis, a regular place of assembly (see also 1.9.7, and *Hellenica* 1.4.3). Xenophon also mentions Persian annual military reviews at *Oeconomicus* 4.6.

up country: the Greek word *anabainei* is cognate with the title of the work, *Anabasis*; the force of the *ana-* prefix is 'away from the sea'.

hoplites: heavily armed foot soldiers: see Introduction, pp. xxvii ff.

barbarians: Greek *barbaroi*, the regular word for non-Greeks; not necessarily a hostile term.

by the king: these cities were within Cyrus' area of command. On one view, the gift to Tissaphernes need not mean that Cyrus had been deprived of his satrapy: for the grant of cities to individuals, see notes to pp. 33, 191 below. The Ionian cities may have been granted to Tissaphernes when Sparta's treaty with Persia was renegotiated in 407 BC (the 'Treaty of Boeotius' inferred by D. M. Lewis, *Sparta and Persia* (Leiden, 1977), 120–5, granting the cities autonomy along with a financial obligation to the king). On another view, however, Ionia may have been transferred to Tissaphernes when Cyrus was first summoned back to Babylon (C. J. Tuplin, 'The Treaty of Boiotios', in H. Sancisi-Weerdenburg and A. Kuhrt (eds.), *Achaemenid History II: The Greek Sources* (Leiden, 1987), 133–53).

4 *a Spartan exile*: see 2.6.2–4 for the circumstances of Clearchus' exile. His presence in the Thracian Chersonese (the Gallipoli peninsula) suggests that his support for Cyrus may have been sanctioned by Sparta (a Spartan governor is mentioned in the Chersonese at 7.1.13); other sources claim that Clearchus was officially sent by Sparta (Isocrates 8.98, Plutarch, *Artaxerxes* 6.5) or even (absurdly) that the Spartans persuaded Cyrus to make his expedition (Isocrates 12.104, in a strongly anti-Spartan speech). On Clearchus and his background, see L. Tritle, *From Melos to My Lai: War and Survival* (London and New York, 2000), 55–78; S. R. Bassett, 'The Enigma of Clearchus the Spartan', *Ancient History Bulletin*, 15 (2001), 1–13; T. Braun, 'Xenophon's Dangerous Liaisons', in Lane Fox (ed.), *Long March*, 97–130, at 97–107.

darics: a Persian gold coin, worth just under 26 Attic drachmas.

guest-friend: Greek *xenos*, a term that implies 'a bond of solidarity manifesting itself in an exchange of goods or services between individuals originating from separate social units' (G. Herman, *Ritualised Friendship and the Greek City* (Cambridge, 1987), 10).

5 *acropolises*: the citadels in the Ionian cities had to be protected against Tissaphernes, see 1.1.6.

peltasts: lightly armed troops who carried a crescent-shaped shield (*peltē*), see Introduction, p. xxix; contrast the ordinary light-armed troops (*gumnētes*) mentioned just above (but Xenophon sometimes uses 'peltasts' to mean light-armed troops more generally).

parasangs: Persian measure of distance, rated by Herodotus (2.6.3) at thirty Greek stades (about three and a third miles), by other Greek authorities at up to or even more than sixty stades (Strabo 11.11.5; Posidonius F 203 Edelstein and Kidd). The later Ottoman and Persian *farsang* or *farsakh* was often used as a measure of the distance that can be covered in one hour, but there is no evidence that the Greeks regarded the parasang as a variable unit, and one proposed etymology for the word has suggested the possibility that there were parasang markers (like milestones) along some Persian roads. See C. J. Tuplin, 'Achaemenid Arithmetic: Numerical Problems in Persian History', *Topoi*, Suppl. 1

(1997), 404–17. Xenophon's detailed figures for stages and parasangs probably presuppose some sort of notes kept during the expedition; a written source such as the account of the Persian empire in Ctesias' *Persica*, which included stage and parasang figures (*FGH* 688 F 33) is proposed by G. L. Cawkwell, 'When, How, and Why did Xenophon Write the *Anabasis*?', in Lane Fox (ed.), *Long March*, 47–67, at 55–9, but it seems unlikely that such sources would have covered the unusual routes taken by Cyrus and subsequently by the Ten Thousand in their retreat.

5 *an inhabited city, prosperous and large*: first instance of a formulaic phrase. The meaning of 'inhabited' (*oikoumenē*) is debated: it may indicate particularly large cities, or else imply a contrast with cities that had been deserted. L. Geysels, '*Polis oikoumenē* dans l'Anabase de Xénophon', *Études classiques*, 42 (1974), 29–38, argues that it denotes some degree of autonomy.

large park: Greek *paradeisos*, a loanword from Old Persian (**paradaida*), first attested in Xenophon, and source of the English word 'paradise'. There was at least one paradise in each satrapy (cf. *Cyropaedia* 8.6.12); some were used for hunting, others for the cultivation of trees and plants. They were part of the royal ideology of the king as bringer of fertility; cf. *Oeconomicus* 4.4–14. See Briant, *From Cyrus to Alexander*, 442–4; C. J. Tuplin, *Achaemenid Studies* (Stuttgart, 1996), 80–131.

6 *Great King*: common Greek title for the king of Persia.

Marsyas ... had lost: Marsyas challenged Apollo to a contest with the lyre. The story is also mentioned by Herodotus (7.26.3), with a small difference (Apollo puts the skin up in the marketplace, not the cave).

the famous battle: the Battle of Salamis (480 BC).

Cretan bowmen: Cretan archers are also attested in Athenian armies (Thucydides 6.25.2, 43; cf. Aristophanes, *Frogs* 1346) and in Alexander's army (Arrian, *Anabasis* 2.9.3).

Agias: the manuscripts all read 'Sophaenetus', but Xenophon probably wrote—or meant to write—'Agias', since Sophaenetus has already come with his contingent. The general Agias would otherwise be mentioned only at his death (2.5.31, 2.6.30). No matter whether the manuscript reading or the emendation is adopted, there is a problem with the number of Greek troops Xenophon gives for the battle of Cunaxa (1.7.10).

athletic contest: in honour of Zeus Lycaeus, an important Arcadian deity (Lycaeus is a mountain in Arcadia). There was a close connection between the cult of Zeus Lycaeus and Arcadian ethnic identity (fifth-century BC Arcadian coins depicting Zeus Lycaeus are inscribed *Arkadikon*): the festival and games here are a sign that the Arcadian mercenaries retained their ethnic identity (T. H. Nielsen, 'The Concept of Arkadia: The People, their Land, and their Organisation', in id.

Explanatory Notes
199

and J. Roy (eds.), *Defining Ancient Arkadia* (Copenhagen, 1999), 16–79). Athletic games at the Lycaea are attested by fourth-century BC inscriptions.

golden crowns: more plausible as prizes than 'golden strigils' (used by athletes for wiping off oil and sweat), another possible translation of the Greek. The usual prizes in the Lycaea at home were bronze implements such as tripods that would have been hard to carry on a military expedition: the value of the prizes at these games suggests that they were donated by Cyrus (J. Roy, 'The Ambitions of a Mercenary', in Lane Fox (ed.), *Long March*, 279).

Syennesis: a hereditary title for the rulers of Cilicia: cf. Aeschylus, *Persians* 326–7; Herodotus 5.118.2. Ctesias (*FGH* 688 F 16) and Diodorus (14.20.3) claim that Syennesis played a double game by sending a message to Artaxerxes warning of Cyrus' advance.

7 *by adding wine to the spring water*: attracted by the satyr Silenus' reputation for wisdom, Midas captured him by making him drunk (cf. Theopompus *FGH* 115 F 75; Pausanias 1.4.5). Silenus then gave Midas the gloomy opinion that it is best for mortals not to have been born (Aristotle fr. 44 Rose; Cicero, *Tusculan Disputations* 1.48; for another version, see Theopompus). The spring was also placed in Macedonia (Herodotus 8.138.3), at Inna between the Maedi and the Paeonians (Athenaeus, *Deipnosophists* 2.45 G), and at Ancyra in Phrygia (Pausanias).

red cloaks: particularly associated with the Spartan army (Plutarch, *Lycurgus* 27.2; Aristophanes, *Lysistrata* 1140): it was alleged that it was the most warlike and least feminine colour (*Constitution of the Spartans* 11.3). They are also found on allied contingents (*Agesilaus* 2.7). Note that Xenophon does not mention body armour: the translation 'cloak' (rather than 'tunic') for the Greek *chitōn* allows for the possibility that armour was worn under the cloak. Xenophon's failure to mention the armour can be explained by his stress on the hoplite's visual effect (M. Whitby, 'Xenophon's Ten Thousand as a Fighting Force', in Lane Fox (ed.), *Long March*, 218–20). A different view is that the hoplites wore tunics and that many of them did not in fact wear body armour, unlike the cavalrymen, who were not protected by shields (note the vignette at 3.4.47–8, the special provision of cuirasses for the new cavalry unit at 3.3.20, and the infantryman shot through a corslet at 4.1.18; but these passages are not conclusive).

shields uncovered: normally, soldiers on the march would have their shields covered to stop them from tarnishing. Shield-bags are attested at Anacreon F 388.4 Page; Aristophanes, *Acharnians* 574; Caesar, *Gallic War* 2.21.5; for a vase illustration, see B. A. Sparkes, 'Illustrating Aristophanes', *Journal of Hellenic Studies*, 95 (1975), plate XIII.

the merchants in the market: the Greek troops had to buy their provisions themselves, either from the traders who were among the non-combatants following the army or from local inhabitants.

7 *hostile territory*: it was hostile because Cyrus had now crossed the boundary of the area he had been allotted by his father.

8 *royal secretary*: an inscription from Cyprus has shown that the rare noun *phoinikistēs* means 'scribe' or 'secretary' (the Greek alphabet was derived from the Phoenician), not 'wearer of the royal purple', as it had sometimes been taken; see Lewis, *Sparta and Persia*, 25 n. 143. Such secretaries are also attested at Herodotus 3.128.3.

triremes: fast-sailing ships. The arrival of Spartan triremes (with 700 hoplites: see 1.4.3) is the only hint Xenophon offers that Cyrus' expedition had official Spartan backing (see Introduction, p. xxi).

9 *at the king's court*: gift-giving played a fundamental role in Persian royal ideology (Briant, *From Cyrus to Alexander*, 304–7). A calibrated system of honour determined the king's gifts of clothes and jewellery: cf. *Cyropaedia* 8.2.7–8, 8.3.1–3; Herodotus 3.84.1 (annual gift of a Median robe for Otanes and his descendants); Aelian, *Various History* 1.22, 32 (mentioning robes, horses with gold-studded bridles, bracelets). Cyrus is already assuming for himself the position of king.

the friendship of the barbarians: Clearchus is appealing to the feelings of his Greek audience by claiming that he will put their interests even above his reciprocal attachment with Cyrus. His definition of his relationship with Cyrus in terms of the Greek ethic of reciprocity obscures the imbalance in the relationship: Cyrus' gift to Clearchus was made specifically with the expedition in mind, and not as a free gift which Clearchus is returning. Clearchus makes it seem more impressive that he is putting the Greeks first. In fact—as Xenophon brings out in what follows—he is manipulating his audience to make them stay with Cyrus.

10 *I think of you as my homeland*: compare Andromache's words to her husband Hector ('you are father and honoured mother and brother to me', Homer, *Iliad* 6.429–30), also echoed by Tecmessa at Sophocles, *Ajax* 518 ('what homeland would I have without you?').

defend myself against an adversary: the common Greek ethic of helping friends and harming enemies, often seen as the definition of justice (as by Polemarchus at Plato, *Republic* 332a–d).

11 *the one for which he was using mercenaries before*: his earlier journey to see his father, accompanied by 300 Greek hoplites (1.1.2).

12 *Abrocomas*: a Persian general sent by the king to Phoenicia, perhaps in preparation for an expedition to Egypt (Isocrates 4.140 mentions that he was later one of the commanders of an army sent to put down the Egyptian revolt, date uncertain); problems in Egypt may explain why the king was late in responding to Cyrus' expedition and also why Cyrus chose this time to attack. Diodorus states that Cyrus told the Greeks that he was leading them against a satrap of Syria (14.20.5).

Pythagoras of Sparta: Xenophon elsewhere gives the name of the Spartan admiral as Samius (*Hellenica* 3.1.1).

13 *300,000 men*: Xenophon later states that the Persian king had four commanders in the battle against Cyrus, each with 300,000 troops, but that
Abrocomas arrived five days too late (1.7.12).

marching against the king: see 1.3.7.

14 *or doves either*: Xenophon is the earliest Greek source to mention the
Syrian reverence for fish and doves; it is a standard element in many later
Greek accounts of the Syrian goddess, e.g. Lucian, *On the Syrian Goddess*
14, 54. An explanation is offered by Diodorus: the Syrian goddess Derceto
was turned into a fish after jumping into a lake, and her abandoned
daughter Semiramis was kept alive by doves (2.4.2–6). The respect for
fish and doves is supported by Syrian evidence, though Xenophon is
wrong to claim that the Syrians regarded fish as gods; for discussion, see
J. L. Lightfoot (ed.), *Lucian: On the Syrian Goddess* (Oxford, 2003), 65–72
on fish and 513 on doves.

girdle-money: compare also the villages of Parysatis mentioned at 2.4.27;
estates belonging to Parysatis are also attested in Babylonian tablets.
Such ownership by royal women was surprising to the Greeks (cf. Plato,
Alcibiades I 123b5–c3). What the Persian king was granting was in fact
part of the revenue from the land, not proper ownership. See M. Brosius,
Women in Ancient Persia (559–331 BC) (Oxford, 1996), ch. 5; Briant,
From Cyrus to Alexander, 461–3.

Belesys: the same as the Bēlšunu—earlier a governor of Babylon—known
from Babylonian inscriptions. A non-Iranian, he left office between 16
January 401 BC and Cyrus' arrival that summer (Tuplin, 'Persian
Empire', 163; M. W. Stolper, 'Bēlšunu the Satrap', in F. Rochberg-
Halton (ed.), *Language, Literature, and History: Philological and Historical
Studies Presented to Erica Reiner* (New Haven, 1987), 389–402).

five mnas of silver: a one-off payment (equivalent to about twenty
months' pay at the regular rate), rather than an increase of pay. It has also
been suggested that Cyrus started to supply food as part of the terms
of service (R. Descat, 'Marché et tribut: L'approvisionnement des
Dix-Mille', in P. Briant (ed.), *Dans les pas des Dix Mille: Peuples et pays du
Proche-Orient vus par un grec = Pallas*, 43 (1995), 99–108, at 103–4), but the
evidence for this new contract is weak (C. J. Tuplin, 'On the Track of the
Ten Thousand', *Revue des études anciennes*, 101 (1991), 331–66, at 343–4).

15 *until he got them back to Ionia*: another mark of Cyrus' generosity:
normally mercenaries were paid only for the campaign, and would have
to make their own way home.

since he was destined to be king: the falseness of the omen suggests that the
belief was genuine, not retrospective. Compare how the Pamphylian sea
was said to have yielded to Alexander (Arrian, *Anabasis* 1.26.1–2, and
Callisthenes *FGH* 124 F 31); and stories of the Euphrates falling for
the Roman general Lucullus (Plutarch, *Lucullus* 24.2–3) and rising
for Vitellius when he was making an expedition to reinstate Tiridates
(Tacitus, *Annals* 6.37).

16 *Gates*: location uncertain, perhaps at Beqaa ('Gate' in Arabic) near
Ramadhi, where the Euphrates narrows (Manfredi, *Strada*, 132).

by eating meat: that is, by a diet of meat alone, probably from worn-out
pack animals—a mark of their difficulties (cf. Caesar, *Gallic War* 7.17.3,
and Tacitus, *Annals* 14.24). The price of grain in the Lydian market is
equivalent to 120 drachmas per medimnus, forty times the normal price.
Cyrus did not use the reserves of flour mentioned at 1.10.18 to ease the
position. On the measures used, see Tuplin, 'Persian Empire', 172.

17 *bracelets on their arms*: the wearing of jewellery in the Persian court was
honorific (see note to p. 9). Compare the Spartan general Lysander's
astonishment when he first meets Cyrus and discovers that the
bejewelled prince had himself planted some of the trees in his garden
(*Oeconomicus* 4.20–5).

sudden offensive: this statement has sometimes been seen as a sign of
the panhellenic orientation of the *Expedition of Cyrus*: see Introduction,
p. xxxi. Xenophon does not explicitly state that Cyrus was marching by a
shorter route than usual, even though he does mention that Abrocomas—who had a head-start—arrived at the battlefield five days later than
Cyrus.

19 *altar of Artemis*: presumably Artemis of Sardis, a goddess attested in
fourth-century BC Lydian inscriptions (Briant, *From Cyrus to Alexander*,
703–4).

21 *I would choose freedom over all my wealth*: the Greeks imagined that every
Persian apart from the king himself was a slave, using the Greek term
doulos to cover the Persian *bandaka*. See A. Missiou, 'Δοῦλος τοῦ
βασιλέως: The Politics of Translation', *Classical Quarterly*, 43 (1993),
377–91.

22 *10,400 hoplites and 2,500 peltasts*: the numbers do not quite fit the figures
Xenophon has given so far (see also note to p. 6).

said to number 1,200,000: an absurd exaggeration, comparable with
Herodotus' figures for Xerxes' invasion of Greece: the fact that Xenophon
was an eyewitness shows how ingrained in the Greek mentality the perception of Persia's vast resources was (Xenophon does later let Ariaeus
make the point that the king's large forces are slower and face problems
with provisions). Ctesias, who was present on the Persian side, numbered
the king's army at 400,000 (*FGH* 688 F 22), but even that figure is a
great exaggeration: modern estimates are closer to 60,000.

Median Wall: described at 2.4.12.

23 *Late in the morning*: literally 'at full-market time'. This is one of the signs
that Cyrus' army set off during the night.

24 *things went well*: for the controversy over whether Clearchus was right to
disobey Cyrus' order, see Introduction, p. xxiii. On the progress of the
battle, see J. M. Bigwood, 'The Ancient Accounts of the Battle of
Cunaxa', *American Journal of Philology*, 104 (1983), 340–57; G. Wylie,
'Cunaxa and Xenophon', *L'Antiquité classique*, 61 (1992), 119–34.

Xenophon of Athens: the first appearance of the author. He always uses third-person forms when describing his own actions as a character.

25 *watchword*: a watchword was necessary because enemy troops were not easy to distinguish (the Athenians suffered greatly in the night battle on Epipolae when the enemy learnt their watchword: Thucydides 7.44.4). As at 6.5.25, the watchword has two parts—presumably question and answer. It was passed along the lines and then back to ensure that it was not overheard and that it was correctly communicated (cf. *Cyropaedia* 3.3.58, 7.1.10). See F. S. Russell, *Information Gathering in Classical Greece* (Ann Arbor, 1999), 182–5.

paean: a common Greek battle-chant (*iō paian*).

Enyalius: a god of war, often equated with Ares.

as king: the homage known as *proskunēsis*. Persian images suggest that this involved bowing slightly while blowing a kiss; the Greeks tended to think that it involved falling to one's knees, and to take it as a mark of oriental slavishness (Briant, *From Cyrus to Alexander*, 222–3).

26 *'table-companions'*: an official title denoting courtiers of a high status (Briant, *From Cyrus to Alexander*, 308); Xenophon also presents them as brave in war at *Cyropaedia* 7.1.30. The title is found also at Herodotus 3.132.1 and Ctesias *FGH* 688 F 14 §41.

the authority of Ctesias the doctor: *FGH* 688 F 21. On Ctesias, see Introduction, pp. xxiv–xxv.

under the eye: Plutarch in his *Life of Artaxerxes* reports variant accounts of Cyrus' death (for discussion, see S. R. Bassett, 'The Death of Cyrus the Younger', *Classical Quarterly*, 49 (1999), 473–83). While Xenophon says that Cyrus was bare-headed and struck under the eye, Ctesias reported that Cyrus was wearing a tiara which fell from his head and that he was struck in the temple beside the eye (*FGH* 688 F 20). Xenophon's account has been seen as apologetic: 'Xenophon portrays Cyrus as being wounded where a javelin could have struck if he had been wearing a helmet, rather than being bare-headed because his tiara had fallen off' (Bassett, p. 477). The fourth-century BC historian Dinon of Colophon (*FGH* 690 F 17) claimed that Cyrus wounded the king's horse, not the king himself, and that the king then wounded Cyrus: this account may be derived from Artaxerxes' propaganda or from Dinon's own imagination.

Cyrus the Elder: Cyrus II, king of Persia 559–530 BC, and subject of Xenophon's own *Cyropaedia*.

29 *slave*: see above, note to p. 21.

30 *Phocaean concubine*: for the presence of Greek concubines in Persian armies, cf. Herodotus 7.83.2, 9.76.1; Briant, *From Cyrus to Alexander*, 278–80. Later historians told many stories about Cyrus' concubine, whose name they give as Aspasia (or Milto): it was said that she won Cyrus over by her modesty and refused extravagant presents from him; that Cyrus changed her name to Aspasia after Pericles' famous mistress;

that she later became a favourite of Artaxerxes, who dressed her up in the clothes of his favourite eunuch when he died; and that when his son asked for her, Artaxerxes made her a priestess of Anaita in Ecbatana (Plutarch, *Pericles* 24.11–12, *Artaxerxes* 26.5–27.5; Aelian, *Various History* 12.1; Justin 10.2.2–4; Athenaeus, *Deipnosophists* 13.576 D).

31 *the Greek left wing*: the left wing in the original battle formation: now that the Greeks had advanced and turned to face the Persians who were moving back along their original line of advance, the original left wing was in fact at the right of the Greek army.

as far as a village: perhaps the village of Cunaxa, after which the battle was named (Plutarch, *Artaxerxes* 8.2).

a golden spread eagle on a shield: the classical Greeks did not have standards, though Xenophon saw the point of them (*Cyropaedia* 8.5.13). Xenophon also mentions the Persian royal standard at *Cyropaedia* 7.1.4 (cf. also Philostratus, *Imagines* 2.31). The eagle was prominent in Achaemenid royal ideology: Aelian, *On the Nature of Animals* 12.21, reports a story that Achaemenes had been fed and raised by an eagle. It has been argued that what Xenophon took for an eagle was in fact an image of Ahura Mazda, the god represented on winged discs in Achaemenid reliefs (C. Bonner, 'The Standard of Artaxerxes II', *Classical Review*, 61 (1947), 9–10). See in general C. Nylander, 'The Standard of the Great King—A Problem in the Alexander Mosaic', *Opuscula Romana*, 14 (1983), 19–37.

32 *the evening meal*: it was now early evening. The troops would eat two meals a day, in the late morning and the early evening.

BOOK TWO

33 *Damaratus of Sparta*: king of Sparta, exiled in 491 BC. He fled to Persia and appears several times in Herodotus as an adviser of Xerxes during his invasion of Greece in 480 BC. Teuthrania was the name of both a city and a region in Mysia; at *Hellenica* 3.1.6 Xenophon states that Damaratus had been given Teuthrania and Halicarne as a gift for accompanying Xerxes on his expedition to Greece. Procles appears again at the end of *The Expedition of Cyrus*, helping Xenophon on a raid (7.8.17); he may well have served with Cyrus as a subordinate ruler in Cyrus' province (Tuplin, 'Persian Empire', 164) and then gone over to Artaxerxes after Cyrus' death.

deserters from the king's army: see 1.10.6. Xenophon mentions these deserters only when the Persian king recovers them, not when they originally desert.

34 *a single Greek*: contrast Ctesias' claim that he was one of the envoys (*FGH* 688 F 23, disbelieved by Plutarch, *Artaxerxes* 13.5–7).

Theopompus: some manuscripts attribute the reply to Xenophon himself, but this reading was probably a gloss, based on the unnecessary supposition that the name Theopompus (which means 'god-sent') was a pseudonym for Xenophon.

35 *if he wanted to use them for a campaign there*: Persian control in Egypt was weak (Egypt was in revolt at the time when Cyrus made his expedition, and Persian control was restored only in 343 BC).

36 *signal for rest*: Clearchus was exploiting the fact that the enemy could hear the signals; compare 3.4.36 and 4.3.29.

38 *a talent of silver*: the same ruse for stopping panic is found in different contexts; see Aeneas Tacticus 27.11, Polyaenus 3.9.4 (used by the Athenian general Iphicrates).

40 *beat him*: typically arrogant Spartan behaviour, using the stick carried by Spartan officers; see S. Hornblower, 'Sticks, Stones, and Spartans: The Sociology of Spartan Violence', in H. van Wees (ed.), *War and Violence in Ancient Greece* (London, 2000), 57–82.

riddled with obstacles: whether Clearchus' suspicions were justified depends on the time of year: the ditches would often have been filled with water for irrigation and drainage.

the cabbage of the palm: Xenophon's observation is slightly confused. It is not removing the part that is commonly cut off and eaten that causes the palm to wither, but removing the succulent leaf-bearing part at the top of the trunk—a delicacy that is eaten only when the tree has to be removed anyway (Tuplin, 'On the Track of the Ten Thousand', 356).

king's wife's brother: by referring to him only by his relationship to the king, and not by name, Xenophon stresses the importance of family links in the Persian royal household. Xenophon's account is at odds with Ctesias' claim (*FGH* 688 F 15) that Artaxerxes had had all of his wife's brothers executed.

41 *in your camp*: this statement is inconsistent with Ctesias' report that the king withdrew to a hill after he had been wounded (*FGH* 688 F 20).

42 *hand-tokens*: physical objects that took the place of handshakes for parties wanting to make pledges without being in each other's presence (cf. *Agesilaus* 3.4). Some examples in the shape of actual hands survive from later in antiquity. See Herman, *Ritualised Friendship and the Greek City*, 50–4.

43 *we won't be able to save anyone*: because cavalry would be used to pursue and kill them if they were defeated.

his wife: Orontas was satrap of Armenia, cf. 3.5.17. His wife's name was Rhodogyne (Plutarch, *Artaxerxes* 27.7; W. Dittenberger (ed.), *Orientis Graeci Inscriptiones Selectae* (Leipzig, 1903–5), 391–2).

Median Wall: the topography is uncertain: see R. D. Barnett, 'Xenophon and the Wall of Media', *Journal of Hellenic Studies*, 83 (1963), 1–26; Tuplin, 'On the Track of the Ten Thousand', 351–3.

44 *Sittace*: it is often thought that Xenophon got Sittace and Opis (2.4.25)

the wrong way round. For discussion, see C. J. Tuplin, 'Modern and Ancient Travellers in the Achaemenid Empire: Byron's *Road to Oxiana* and Xenophon's *Anabasis*', in H. Sancisi-Weerdenburg and J. W. Drijvers (eds.), *Achaemenid History VII: Through Travellers' Eyes* (Leiden, 1991), 51–4.

44 *He did not ask for Meno*: Xenophon hints that Meno was implicated in the attempt to deceive the Greeks.

45 *Physcus river*: Xenophon's account of the rivers between here and the Zab is confused: he omits two of the Diyala, the Adheim, and the Lesser Zab. Physcus is probably the Diyala if Xenophon did not confuse Opis and Sittace (see above), the Adheim if he did confuse them. Sophaenetus (*FGH* 109 F 3) mentioned a town Physcus as well as a river.

the villages belonging to Parysatis: for such villages, cf. 1.4.9 and note to p. 14; the prohibition on taking slaves may point to the importance of the tribute paid to the king from such villages (Briant, *From Cyrus to Alexander*, 459–60), but it may just be that 'human booty would simply mean more mouths to feed' (Tuplin, 'Persian Empire', 170). For the favour shown by Parysatis towards Cyrus, see 1.1.4.

46 *waiting to take us on*: Greek *ephedros*—a wrestling metaphor, used of the competitor who would take on the victor in a bout.

48 *the crown that is in his heart*: Tissaphernes is hinting that he may have ambitions himself and so be particularly eager to have the Greeks' support. It is unlikely that he did have any such ambitions. He is, rather, pandering to the Greeks' sense of themselves as kingmakers (compare their earlier offer to Ariaeus).

49 *strongly insistent*: Ctesias, by contrast, says that Clearchus went to Tissaphernes' tent against his will (*FGH* 688 F 27).

murdered: Xenophon presents the arrest and execution of the generals and the killing of their followers as an act of Persian perjury. The Greeks may, however, have placed themselves in the wrong by foraging (they did not have sufficient money to buy all their provisions from the market Tissaphernes was supplying). Tissaphernes seems to have exploited the Greeks' weakness (as well as the tensions among the Greek generals) and made them swear to terms they would not be able to keep: see S. R. Bassett, 'Innocent Victims or Perjurers Betrayed? The Arrest of the Generals in Xenophon's *Anabasis*', *Classical Quarterly*, 52 (2002), 447–61.

50 *Proxenus and Meno*: while there have been hints of Meno's duplicity (note to p. 44), the unexplained mention of Xenophon's friend Proxenus is surprising: it could be a Persian attempt to instil distrust among the Greeks, but Ctesias (*FGH* 688 F 27) states that Proxenus was involved in the plan to trap the other Greek generals.

beheaded: Ctesias (*FGH* 688 FF 27–8) reports that the generals were

Explanatory Notes

207

taken to Babylon and that he was able to help Clearchus there as a service
to Parysatis. If this is true, they were not executed at once (Xenophon
does say later that Meno was kept alive for a year). Ctesias also reports
that while the other generals' bodies were torn apart by dogs and birds, a
sudden wind caused a mound to rise up over Clearchus' corpse and a
grove of trees later grew on the mound (F 28, reported sceptically by
Plutarch, *Artaxerxes* 18.7). This story (with its hint of the Persian king's
association with fertility) perhaps stems from pro-Cyrus propaganda put
out by Parysatis (Briant, *From Cyrus to Alexander*, 238–9).

51 *at war with the Athenians*: the Peloponnesian War (431–404 BC).

ephors: the five leading officials at Sparta, who served for one year.

Hellespont: Clearchus' governorship of Byzantium is also attested by
Diodorus 14.12.2–7 and Polyaenus 2.2.7.

recorded elsewhere: an unexplained cross-reference: no such account is
found in this work. Perhaps Xenophon forgot that he had not been more
explicit earlier. Another hypothesis is that Xenophon wrote the obituary
notices before the rest of the narrative.

52 *Gorgias of Leontini*: famous philosopher and teacher of rhetoric
(*c*.480–380 BC), whose extant works include *The Encomium of Helen* and
The Defence of Palamedes.

53 *Meno of Thessaly*: the hostility of Xenophon's obituary of Meno was
explained in antiquity (Marcellinus, *Life of Thucydides* 27) as due to
rivalry over their links with Plato (this Meno is the eponymous character
in Plato's *Meno*).

in the bloom of youth: the Greek adjective *hōraios* denotes 'the age at
which one is most attractive and desirable' (K. J. Dover, *Greek Homosexuality* (London, 1978), 69)—for the Greeks, the age just before the
beard started to appear. For Aristippus, see 1.1.10, 1.2.1.

54 *mature enough to have a beard*: normally it was the older man who had the
younger as his 'boyfriend' (*paidika*). Meno's reversal of the norm was
meant to seem shocking (cf. Dover, *Greek Homosexuality*, 87)—and it did
shock: it was the one item in Xenophon's abuse of Meno recalled by
Diogenes Laertius in his life of Xenophon (*Lives of the Philosophers* 2.50).

BOOK THREE

55 *the famous Socrates of Athens*: Xenophon was a pupil of Socrates, and he
also wrote Socratic dialogues (Introduction, p. viii).

against the Athenians: Cyrus helped to finance the Spartan fleet after he
had been appointed by his father to a special command in western Asia
Minor in 407 BC. In the event, Xenophon was exiled by the Athenians,
but his exile may have been because he later accompanied Agesilaus
rather than because of his support for Cyrus (see Introduction, p. xv).

208   *Explanatory Notes*

55 *whether or not he should go*: the oracle at Delphi was commonly consulted
not just by cities planning to found a colony, for instance, or fight a war,
but also by individuals seeking advice on their own problems; questions
about journeys were especially common (R. C. T. Parker, 'One Man's
Piety: The Religious Dimension of the *Anabasis*', in Lane Fox (ed.), *Long
March*, 131–53, at 147 with n. 45). Xenophon manipulated the question
because he wanted to go anyway.

56 *except Clearchus*: Diodorus, by contrast, states that all the generals knew
that Cyrus was marching against the king (14.9.19).

Zeus the King: for the comparison between Zeus and the Persian king,
compare Gorgias' description of Xerxes as 'Zeus of the Persians'
(H. Diels and W. Kranz (eds.), *Die Fragmente der Vorsokratiker*, 82 B5a).
In the *Interpretation of Dreams* by Artemidorus (second century AD), a
dream of lightning striking a house is thought to foretell exile (2.9
p. 110.20–2 Pack).

57 *How old do I have to be?*: Xenophon was probably still under 30 at this
time. His question perhaps reflects the fact that in Athens 30 was the age-
limit for holding some offices and for jury service (Pseudo-Aristotle,
Constitution of the Athenians 30.2, 63.3).

full brother: translating the Greek adjective *homomētrios*, literally 'sharing
the same mother'—a word commonly used to distinguish full brothers
from half-brothers.

58 *easier to wound and kill*: because the Persians were not as heavily armed as
Greek hoplites.

59 *ears pierced, Lydian-style*: the Greeks thought it a sign of softness for a
man to have his ears pierced, and the Lydians were commonly regarded
as a luxurious and soft people (Herodotus 1.155.4). Apollonides was
perhaps an ex-slave, like the Macronian peltast at 4.8.4.

62 *someone sneezed*: sneezing was regarded as an omen, and here it is a
good omen because Xenophon had just uttered the word 'survival'. Cf.
Telemachus' sneeze at Homer, *Odyssey* 17.541, after Penelope has just
talked of the possibility of Odysseus' return home.

did homage to the god: the Greek term is *proskunēsis*; see note to p. 25.

beat them: at Marathon (490 BC). The Athenians did in fact receive help
from Plataea, but they later prided themselves on having fought alone.

annual sacrifice: Herodotus puts the number of Persian dead at 6,400
(6.117.1): Xenophon's allusion implies a much higher figure (compare
Plutarch, *On the Malice of Herodotus* 862 BC, who cites this sacrifice in a
criticism of Herodotus' figure). The sacrifice was held on the sixth day of
the Athenian month Boedromion; one later source puts the number of
victims at only 300 a year (Aelian, *Various History* 2.25). Another version
was that the Athenians vowed to sacrifice oxen, but changed to goats after
the battle (scholia on Aristophanes, *Knights* 660).

63 *on land and sea*: on land at Plataea (479 BC), on sea at Salamis (480 BC).

trophies: at the spot where a battle had turned, victorious Greek armies dedicated trophies (*tropaia*)—wooden frames on which they hung weapons and armour captured from the enemy.

64 *Lycaonians*: see 1.2.19 for the Lycaonians; for other autonomous peoples within the Persian empire, see 2.5.13, and *Memorabilia* 3.5.26 (Mysians and Pisidians).

as the lotus-eaters were: an allusion to Homer, *Odyssey* 9.83–104: the lotus-eaters were one of the tribes encountered by Odysseus on his return to Ithaca; those of his companions who ate the lotus plant forgot about their journey home. In the classical era geographers located a tribe of lotus-eaters on the north coast of Africa (Herodotus 4.177).

66 *a Spartan*: because the Spartans were the supreme power in Greece at this moment. Chirisophus was also leader of the 700 hoplites sent out by the Spartans (1.4.3). It has been claimed that Xenophon obscures the fact that Chirisophus was elected overall leader (Diodorus 14.27.1). It is more likely that Diodorus is oversimplifying, just as later he contradicts Xenophon by saying that Xenophon was chosen general in Thrace (14.37.1).

67 *Zapatas river*: Xenophon does not say how the army crossed this river, some 400 feet in breadth.

68 *men from Rhodes*: Rhodians were renowned as slingers. The creation of a unit of slingers has been taken to show the versatility of the hoplite, but the unit may in fact have been formed from the camp followers; this would explain why Xenophon offers a special inducement (Whitby, 'Xenophon's Ten Thousand', 217–18).

69 *Clearchus' men*: the forty horsemen with Miltocythes who deserted to the king (2.2.7).

passed muster: Xenophon uses a verb cognate with *dokimasia*, the term used at Athens for the examination of magistrates before they entered office.

70 *mutilated the corpses of the dead*: in battles between Greeks, by contrast, it was customary to return corpses under treaty.

inhabited by Medes: Larisa is Nimrud, the Calah/Kalhu of Genesis 10: 11. Probably the best explanation for the name Xenophon gives is that it is derived from 'āl šarrūti', 'royal city', and that Xenophon assimilated what he heard to Larisa, which is also the name of several Greek cities. The physical description matches the site well (C. J. Tuplin, 'Xenophon in Media', in G. B. Lanfranchi, M. Roaf, and R. Rollinger (eds.), *Continuity of Empire (?): Assyria, Media, Persia* (Padua, 2003), 351–89, at 374–6).

The Persian king: Cyrus the Great, who conquered the Median empire in 550 BC. Xenophon obscures the fact that Larisa/Nimrud, like Mespila/Nineveh, mentioned immediately afterwards, was an Assyrian city. Both cities had been conquered and partly destroyed by the Medes in 614–612 BC. The only other evidence for a specific Persian attack on these cities is Amyntas *FGH* 122 F 2, an account of the conquest of Nineveh by Cyrus.

It is likely that the cities were still inhabited after the Median conquest and possible that the Persian conquest of these cities is historical. There is no reason to suppose that Xenophon himself has transferred stories from the Median conquest of Babylon to the Persian defeat of the Medes: he was presumably using local sources who were either ignorant of, or had political reasons for wanting to suppress, the Assyrian past. For a full discussion, see Tuplin, 'Xenophon in Media', 379–85.

70 *hid the sun from sight*: Xenophon is not referring to an eclipse, but to a meteorological event (like the thunder at Mespila, see below): at some times of the year clouds would be rare. Tuplin, 'Xenophon in Media', 381, compares the prophecy against Egypt at Ezekiel 32: 7: 'I will cover the sun with a cloud.'

the Medes: Mespila is Nineveh: see above on Xenophon's failure to mention the Assyrians. The name has been connected with Mosul (the city across the river from Nineveh) or with 'mušpalu' ('lower city'). The physical description is slightly less satisfactory than the description of Nimrud (Tuplin, 'Xenophon in Media', 376–9).

Medea, the king's wife: the last Median king was Astyages. The name Medea means 'Median woman'.

72 *section commanders under them*: the Greek terms are *lochagoi* (leading 100 men), *pentēkontēres* (leading 50), and *enōmotarchoi* (leading 25). Both the terms and the principle of subdivision are specifically Spartan (cf. *Constitution of the Spartans* 11.4; Thucydides 5.68.3), but the exact relation to the organization of the Spartan army is unclear (there is nothing to correspond to the Spartan *mora*, and in any case the evidence for the Spartan army is hard to interpret). On one view, the arrangement corresponds to Spartan practice ('Presumably Chirisophus knew how the various technical terms were actually used at Sparta, and this is not therefore a case of professional soldiers wanting to sound like Spartans but not really understanding the Spartan military vocabulary', J. K. Anderson, *Military Theory and Practice in the Age of Xenophon* (Berkeley, 1970), 234); others hold that the Spartan *pentēkontēr* was not a group of fifty soldiers (like the units set up in the Ten Thousand), but a fiftieth part of the army (e.g. J. F. Lazenby, *The Spartan Army* (Warminster, 1985), 5–10).

section by section: the solution to the disruption caused by narrowing of the path was to identify 'six companies of a hundred men each who would drop behind the square whenever the flanks were compressed and then fill up any size of gap which might appear as the formation spread out' (Whitby, 'Xenophon's Ten Thousand', 233).

urged on by whips: the Greeks liked to contrast the enforced obedience in the Persian army with their own willing obedience to authority (cf. Herodotus 7.223.2, whips at Thermopylae).

73 *eight doctors*: 'Presumably only orderlies, who did what they could in the way of bandaging' (Anderson, *Military Theory*, 70). They were probably slaves.

76 *Two thousand skins*: the Rhodian seems to have learnt from the native inhabitants whom the Greeks had seen crossing rivers in this way: cf. 1.5.10, 2.4.28. In asking for a talent he was asking for a very large sum.

77 *spring and summer residences*: Greek sources present the Persian king migrating between his residences at Persepolis, Babylon, Susa, and Ecbatana according to the season (*Cyropaedia* 8.6.22; Athenaeus, *Deipnosophists* 12.513 F; Dio Chrysostom 6.1; Plutarch, *Moral Essays* 78 D, 499 AB, 604 C; Aelian, *On the Nature of Animals* 3.13, 10.6; scholia on Aristophanes, *Knights* 1089); they differ as to the details, but one constant is that Ecbatana (in mountainous Media) was the king's summer residence. See C. J. Tuplin, 'The Seasonal Migration of Achaemenid Kings: A Report on Old and New Evidence', in M. Brosius and A. Kuhrt (eds.), *Studies in Persian History: Essays in Memory of David M. Lewis* (Leiden, 1998), 63–114.

Carduchians: often thought to be the Kurds, who live in the same area— but who also now inhabit a much wider area than Xenophon's Carduchians.

when it seemed right to do so: normally the sacrifice would be performed immediately before departure.

BOOK FOUR

78 *the final watch*: it is not certain how many watches the night was divided into. Divisions between three and five watches are attested; the length of watch may have varied by season or else different cities at different times may have had their own conventions. Stars were used to determine the time at night (cf. *Memorabilia* 4.7.4). See Russell, *Information Gathering in Classical Greece*, 28–9.

83 *shield-bearer*: Greek *hupaspistēs*, probably a slave; hoplites were regularly accompanied by such attendants.

84 *loops*: the Greeks were improvising javelins for throwing: the loop would be wound around the index and middle fingers (as shown on some Greek vase-paintings) to give the javelin more force when thrown and also to stabilize the flight of the javelin by causing it to rotate around its own axis.

seven days: the narrative has explicitly covered only five days so far: Xenophon seems to have included the two days to come.

Chaldean: a name normally used of the priestly caste of the Babylonians, but also used of a tribe in the Black Sea region. Strabo (12.3.19) says that the Chaldeans were previously known as the Chalybians, but both tribe-names are found in Xenophon.

85 *whatever length of stride he wanted*: the verb for 'stride', *diabainein*, also means 'cross', and so the dream is a good omen.

86 *pour a libation*: of wine. Some wine would be poured from a hand-held jug before a prayer was made.

86 *a wreath on his head*: sacrifices were offered before armies crossed rivers, seas, and boundaries, and garlands were regularly worn by the officiator at a sacrifice. Here, the Greeks follow a Spartan custom of putting on wreaths before going into battle (*Constitution of the Spartans* 13.8; Plutarch, *Lycurgus* 22.4–5).

    kept women: Greek *hetairai*. *Hetairai* were more respectable than *pornai*, 'prostitutes': their dealings were conceived in terms of gift-giving, not in terms of cash payment for sex, and some of them lived in monogamous relationships (like Aspasia, the *hetaira* of the Athenian politician Pericles).

    ritual cry: Greek *ololugē*, a shrill cry uttered by women at the climax of animal sacrifices and some other religious occasions.

89 *governor*: Greek *huparchos*, a more general term regularly used by Herodotus for 'satrap'. Xenophon has already referred to Orontas as satrap of Armenia (3.5.17). His phrasing here could mean either that there was a separate satrapy of Western Armenia or that Tiribazus was governor of a sub-district within a single satrapy of Armenia. Tiribazus is mentioned mounting the king on his horse in Dinon's account of the battle of Cunaxa (*FGH* 690 F 17).

    greasing their bodies: for warmth and suppleness. Greeks also greased themselves before athletic exercise.

90 *Amazons*: a legendary tribe of women, localized to the north of the Black Sea, who were often depicted wielding a type of axe (*sagaris*).

91 *hunger faintness*: Greek *boulimia* ('ox-hunger'), used of an extreme hunger that caused faintness, not (as now) of an eating disorder. It was particularly thought to occur in cold weather (Aristotle, *Problems* 887^{b}37–888^{a}22).

93 *to take to the camp*: Xenophon subsequently beat a man who tried to bury one of the invalids while he was still alive—an incident he mentions only when he has to defend himself against the charge of violence (5.8.1–11).

    tribute for the king: Strabo (11.14.9) reports that during the Achaemenid period the satrap had to send 20,000 colts each year at the time of the festival of Mithras.

94 *diluted with water*: the Greeks generally diluted their wine with water; drinking unmixed wine was regarded as a mark of savageness.

95 *Sun God*: the Greeks tended to regard Mithras as the Sun God (Strabo 15.3.13); there was certainly a close relation between Mithras and the Sun, but they were probably not assimilated (Briant, *From Cyrus to Alexander*, 250–3). For horse sacrifices to the Sun, cf. *Cyropaedia* 8.3.12, 24; also Herodotus 1.216.4 (among the Scythians). Horse sacrifice was uncommon in Greece itself, as was cult of the Sun: the Sun received cult only in Rhodes, and Aristophanes could joke that the Sun would favour the barbarians rather than the Greeks (*Peace* 406–13).

    Phasis river: probably the Araxes (which flows into the Caspian Sea). It has sometimes been thought that the Ten Thousand mistook this river for the Phasis that flows into the Black Sea.

96 *from a very early age*: the Similars are the *Homoioi*, the elite at Sparta who were put through a famously demanding system of education, the *agōgē*, that included thieving and flogging for those who were caught (*Constitution of the Spartans* 2.6–9; Plutarch, *Lycurgus* 17.5–6). The thieving metaphor is also applied to war in a speech by the Spartan general Brasidas at Thucydides 5.9.5; in general, the use of ruses and deception in warfare was much more common than many ideologically slanted representations of hoplite fighting suggest (P. Krentz, 'Deception in Archaic and Classical Greek Warfare', in van Wees, *War and Violence*, 167–200).

97 *the thieves who were following us*: that is, the native inhabitants: Xenophon alludes occasionally to their attacks on the rearguard.

99 *Eurylochus of Lusi*: for an earlier act of heroism by this soldier, see 4.2.21. Here, as later (7.1.32, 7.6.40), he is mentioned together with captains: he may have been promoted in the meantime.

100 *Chalybian territory*: Aeschylus, *Prometheus Bound* 714–15, places the Chalybians to the north-east of the Scythians, that is, north of the Black Sea, but the ethnographic tradition places them, as Xenophon does, on the south coast (Hecataeus *FGH* 1 F 203; Herodotus 1.28; Strabo 11.14.5). They were famous among the Greeks as iron-workers, a reputation supported by modern archaeological finds.

twisted cords instead of flaps: Xenophon contrasts the Chalybians' armour with the Greek corslet, which at its lower edge was cut into a sort of skirt formed of narrow vertical flaps (*pteryges*, literally 'wings') which provided protection without impeding movement. Asiatic troops were often described or portrayed wearing stiffened and padded linen corslets (compare the Mossynoecian dress at 5.4.13); they were also used by Greek troops. In other respects the Chalybians' armour is strikingly similar to Greek hoplite armour.

a Laconian dirk: Greek *xyēlē*, a sickle-shaped tool used by the Spartans (inhabitants of Laconia). A sickle is mentioned by Plutarch in an anecdote about a fight between boys (*Spartan Sayings* 233 F), but the *xyēlē* is not shown in representations of Spartan adults fighting.

fifteen cubits long: about twenty feet long—probably an exaggeration.

101 *first men got there*: after these words some manuscripts have the phrase 'and saw the sea', but the addition of this clause destroys the suspense in the famous description that follows. The modern reception of this scene is discussed by T. C. B. Rood, *The Sea! The Sea! The Shout of the Ten Thousand in the Modern Imagination* (London, 2004).

103 *from the right wing*: the rear of the army formed the left wing during battle while the vanguard formed the right wing. So Xenophon is crossing from Chirisophus' position on the (more honoured) right wing to his own position on the left.

104 *on the point of death*: taking *apothneiskousi* as dative participle rather than present indicative (which would imply that some men actually died). The

poisonous honey in the area around Trebizond became famous (Pliny, *Natural History* 21.77), and it affected other armies too: Strabo reports that a local tribe, the Heptacometae, which he equates with a tribe Xenophon mentions, the Mossynoecians, used the poisonous honey to trap three of Pompey's squadrons (12.3.18). A toxic compound, andromedotoxin, was identified in the honey by a German scientist in 1889; the toxin occurs in the local yellow-flowered *Rhododendron luteum*, and is particularly a problem when the honey is very fresh. The time of the incident is fixed by the fact that the rhododendron flowers in the Pontic mountains in late May and early June; the high route along which the Ten Thousand were marching would also have been impossible much earlier in the year because of snow. A date in late May for this episode suggests that there may be a gap of up to three months in Xenophon's account. See A. Mayor, 'Mad Honey!', *Archaeology*, 48 (1995), 32–40, on the honey, and R. Lane Fox, 'Introduction', in id. (ed.), *Long March*, 1–46, at 36–46, on the 'snow lacuna' (developing the hypothesis of Manfredi, *Strada*, 211–15).

104 *the sacrifice they had vowed to make*: see 3.2.9, where Xenophon proposed to sacrifice to Zeus the Saviour when they reached a friendly land, and the vow just mentioned (4.8.16). The Greeks must have made other vows as well.

Dracontius the Spartiate: the Spartiates were the highest rank within the regimented Spartan society (see the note to p. 96 about Similars). The circumstances of Dracontius' exile recall Homer, *Iliad* 23.85–8 (Patroclus exiled for accidentally killing another child in a quarrel over a game). The implement used by Dracontius was the sickle-shaped *xyēlē*.

105 *the animal skins*: skins from the victims, presumably to be given as prizes (cf. Homer, *Iliad* 22.159–60).

more painful for the one who is thrown: a suitably laconic remark. Wrestling bouts were won by inflicting three falls on the opponent.

a long-distance race: Greek *dolichos*—known examples ranged from seven to twenty-four stades (between one and a half and four kilometres). The Cretans were renowned runners.

pancratium: a combat event involving boxing, wrestling, and kicking. See M. Poliakoff, *Combat Sports in the Ancient World* (New Haven, 1987), 54–63.

with their friends watching: the Greek could also mean with their 'kept women' (*hetairai*) watching—in which case the Ten Thousand were 'the first known beneficiaries of female cheer-leaders in the history of athletic sport' (R. Lane Fox, 'Sex, Gender and the Other in Xenophon's *Anabasis*', in id. (ed.), *Long March*, 184–214, at 203).

BOOK FIVE

106 *like Odysseus*: an allusion to Odysseus' deep sleep on board the Phaeacian ship that carries him back to Ithaca (Homer, *Odyssey* 13.79–80).

naval commander of Sparta: Greek *nauarchos*, an annual command. Chirisophus' proposal must be connected with the Spartans' official support for Cyrus' expedition (a fact which Xenophon obscures, see Introduction, p. xxi).

108 *a free Laconian*: Greek *perioikos* (literally 'one who lives around'), used of a class of Spartans who were not full Spartan citizens and lived in Laconia in the villages and towns surrounding Sparta.

109 *spearmen*: Xenophon has not mentioned this category of fighter before. It may be that they are camp followers who have armed themselves with spears.

trying to outdo one another in bravery: see their behaviour in the attack on the citadel of the Taochians at 4.7.11–12.

111 *Paphlagonian helmets*: Paphlagonia was a province further to the west along the Black Sea coast; the helmets resemble those worn by the Mossynoecians ('leather helmets in the Paphlagonian style, with the leather tufted around the middle so that it looked like nothing so much as a tiara', 5.4.13).

112 *the oldest of the generals*: Xenophon seems to be inconsistent: at the meeting of the Greek generals after the battle of Cunaxa, Cleanor is described as oldest (2.1.10), though Sophaenetus was presumably present (Philesius was elected general only later, 3.1.47). At 6.5.13 Sophaenetus is described as the oldest.

the prisoners of war: in wars against non-Greeks, prisoners of war were commonly sold as slaves.

Apollo and Artemis of Ephesus: it was customary in the Greek world to offer a tenth of the spoils of war to the gods. Ephesus was an important cult centre of Artemis, marked by strong influence from Asia Minor (see below, notes to p. 113 on *Megabyzus* and *the golden one in Ephesus*).

Neon of Asine: Asine was a town in Laconia—the description marks Neon out as a perioecus rather than a Spartiate.

the Athenian treasury in Delphi: from the sixth century BC onwards, Greek cities set up at the major panhellenic sanctuaries of Olympia and Delphi separate treasuries, *thēsauroi*, in the form of small temples to house offerings to the gods. Xenophon presumably made his offering before he was exiled from Athens. The Athenian treasury has been reconstructed by modern archaeologists.

113 *the expedition against Boeotia*: in 394 BC. Xenophon served with Agesilaus in Asia from 396 BC: it may have been his presence with Agesilaus at the battle of Coronea (when the Athenians were on the anti-Spartan side) that led to his exile.

113 *Megabyzus*: a cult-title given to the eunuch priest of Artemis at Ephesus (Strabo 14.1.23; Pliny, *Natural History* 35.93). The name is Persian, the Greek rendering of *Bagabuxša*, 'who serves the god'. For Persian respect for Artemis of Ephesus, cf. *Hellenica* 1.2.6; Thucydides 8.109.1; Strabo 14.1.5; Tacitus, *Annals* 3.61; Briant, *From Cyrus to Alexander*, 701–2.

After Xenophon became an exile: for the date and circumstances of Xenophon's exile, see Introduction, p. xv.

as a spectator: Greek *theōrēsōn*, also implying that he was a *theōros*, an official envoy sent by his home city to the festival.

the god: Apollo's oracle at Delphi.

joined in the feast: public festivals were commonly marked by the distribution of sacrificial meat (one of the few occasions on which Greeks would eat meat). Xenophon seems to have gained personal prestige from the festival he set up.

the golden one in Ephesus: remarkable marble statues of Artemis of Ephesus survive from the Roman era: the goddess is decorated with figures of animals and endowed with a pectoral of breast-shaped protrusions. It is not certain that the goddess's statue in Ephesus had the same appearance in Xenophon's day. For discussion of Xenophon's sanctuary, see C. J. Tuplin, 'Xenophon, Artemis and Scillus', in T. Figueira (ed.), *Spartan Society* (Swansea, 2004), 258–81.

114 *Mossynoecians*: the name means 'those who live in *mossynoi* (wooden towers)'.

the job of representing Mossynoecian interests: Greek *proxenos*, a word used of a citizen who looked after the interests of another state in his own city (the Greeks did not have consulates).

115 *like the two halves of a chorus*: not referring to theatrical or lyric choruses, but to dancers arranged in opposing lines (cf. *Symposium* 2.20). Xenophon also uses an analogy between an army and dancers at *Cyropaedia* 1.6.18.

because they were after booty: a sign of the growing indiscipline among the Ten Thousand as they got nearer to Greece: see Introduction, p. xxxiii.

117 *the wooden tower*: Xenophon writes 'the' wooden tower even though it has not been mentioned before, perhaps because the name 'Mossynoecians' itself means 'wooden-tower dwellers'.

118 *their own religious processions*: compare the Arcadian celebration of the Lycaea at 1.2.10. The ethnic splintering here perhaps anticipates the later Arcadian breakaway (6.2.16).

121 *what the saying describes as "sacred counsel"*: there was a proverb 'counsel is a sacred thing' (Plato, *Theages* 122b2–3).

123 *this idea of his*: 'Xenophon had consulted the gods before consulting the people, whereas the principle in a democracy or even a broad oligarchy was that, where matters of collective concern were at issue, the decision to consult the gods was itself collective; otherwise the decision might be

pre-empted' (Parker, 'One Man's Piety', in Lane Fox (ed.), *Long March*, 152).

the truth about the ten days: see 1.7.18.

124 *one Cyzicene stater*: common currency in the Black Sea region (Cyzicus was a city on the Asian shore of the Propontis), worth about 26 Attic drachmas. The pay offered is close to the average pay of a drachma a day.

Pharnabazus' domain: Pharnabazus was satrap of Hellespontine Phrygia, a satrapy that had been held by his great-grandfather, grandfather, and father. He had supported the Spartans in the Ionian War (the final part of the Peloponnesian War), when he had been a rival of Tissaphernes.

Dercylidas: Spartan general who had worked with Pharnabazus in the Ionian War, and later led the Spartan army (including the remnants of the Ten Thousand) in Asia, when he attacked Pharnabazus (*Hellenica* 3.1.8–2.20).

plenty of abundantly rich land in Greece: a paradox for most Greeks, who saw their own land as poor and Asia as rich. The proposal to settle in the Chersonese (the Gallipoli Peninsula) was unrealistic: there had been Athenian settlers in the Chersonese down to end of the Peloponnesian War, but it is scarcely likely that the Spartans would have simply let the Ten Thousand take it (Xenophon later mentions a Spartan officer there, 7.1.13).

125 *Aeëtes*: the same name as the mythical ruler of Colchis (the father of Medea).

126 *back to Phasis*: contrast the proposal 'to sail to Phasis': the addition of 'back' perhaps created the mistaken impression that the proposal was to sail back to the Phasis river in Armenia (4.6.4) rather than to the Phasis river in Colchis.

to escape to the sea: the incident is described by Xenophon in the speech that follows.

128 *the official representatives of their village*: Greek *presbeis*, who were conventionally protected (though not so strongly as heralds).

129 *treating the army abominably*: market officials (Greek *agoranomoi*) whose responsibilities would have included keeping order in the market (or agora) and collecting market dues.

130 *where we expected to win praise from everyone*: Greece.

purified: techniques of purification included sprinkling, fumigation, and sacrifice: in Macedonia, before the start of each campaigning season a dog was sacrificed and cut in half, and the army then marched between the two halves. The purification was a 'reassertion of the army's corporate identity as a disciplined unit' (R. Parker, *Miasma* (Oxford, 1983), 23); similar acts of purification are attested after instances of civil discord, and also in Alexander's army after a period of indiscipline (Curtius Rufus 10.9.11).

the merchant cargoes: see 5.1.16.

130 *had been elected*: see 5.3.1.

they framed the charge as one of assault: a charge of *hybris*, that is, malicious and violent assault designed to demean the victim.

the snow lay very deep on the ground: in Armenia (4.5).

BOOK SIX

134 *singing the Sitalces*: a Thracian war-song (Sitalces was a Thracian royal name).

karpaia: this is the only reference to this dance. The name is derived from *karpos*, 'fruit' or 'produce'.

135 *Persian dance*: Duris of Samos (*FGH* 76 F 5) reports that this was a vigorous dance thought to be useful for developing physical strength, and that during the festival of Mithras only the king was allowed to dance it. Cf. *Cyropaedia* 8.4.12; Briant, *From Cyrus to Alexander*, 252–3.

Pyrrhic dance: a famous war-dance, originally from Sparta.

136 *the oracle he had been given at Delphi*: see 3.1.5–8 (where the god is not named).

managing the army: the dream is recounted at 3.1.11–12.

137 *anything you might want from them*: for the importance of having a Spartan leader, cf. 3.2.37, with note to p. 66.

angry with both you and me: a clear hint at the Spartan Chirisophus.

symposiarch: the leader of a symposium, also sometimes known as the *basileus* ('king') or *prytanis* ('president'). His duties were to make sure that guests at the symposium were neither too sober nor too drunk (Plato, *Laws* 640c4–5).

from being company commanders: these Arcadian sensitivities soon lead to a short-lived Arcadian breakaway. There had been anti-Spartan feeling in Arcadia during the Peloponnesian War, and after the Spartan defeat at Leuctra in 371 BC the Arcadians achieved independence.

138 *where the Argo is said to have landed*: on Jason's voyage to Colchis to fetch the golden fleece.

Parthenius: in fact, the Parthenius is the only one of these rivers that lies to the west of Sinope. It has sometimes been suspected that the passage is an interpolation (prompted perhaps by the Sinopean Hecatonymus' remarks on these rivers at 5.5.9), but it is quite possible that Xenophon himself made the mistake.

to fetch the hound Cerberus: Heracles' descent was also located here by a contemporary writer, the mythographer Herodorus, himself an inhabitant of Heraclea (*FGH* 31 F 31); cf. also Euphorion fr. 35 Scheidweiler. An etymology of the city name Heraclea is implied. For the entrance to the underworld, cf. also Apollonius Rhodius, *Argonautica* 2.353–6. More commonly, the entrance to the underworld where Heracles descended was located at Taenarum in the southern Peloponnese (Euripides, *Heracles* 23–5; Apollodorus 2.5.12; Pausanias 3.25.4).

140 *harmost*: the Spartan term used for the governors installed in Greek cities by the Spartans after the end of the Peloponnesian War.

since he was not well: the first mention of Chirisophus' illness.

142 *who begin with the gods*: that is, by taking omens and sacrificing. The phrase is proverbial.

cavalry: Timasion is again in charge of the cavalry at 7.3.46, but earlier an Athenian, Lycius, has been the cavalry commander (3.3.20, 4.3.22, 25, 4.7.24). Xenophon does not explain whether Lycius had died or left the army or been demoted for some reason.

144 *Calpe Harbour*: the description that follows hints at the site's suitability for colonization.

145 *Greece*: this account of the motivation of the Greek mercenaries (which strictly refers only to those who had set sail, and not to those recruited in Ionia) seems strongly apologetic (see Introduction, pp. xxvi–xxvii).

148 *Spithridates*: he later revolted from Pharnabazus and joined the Spartans when Pharnabazus wanted to make his daughter a concubine and not a wife (*Hellenica* 3.4.10; *Agesilaus* 3.3); but he was mistreated and left the alliance (*Hellenica* 4.1.20–8).

Everyone agreed that this was a good idea: use of reserves had been uncommon in fifth-century BC hoplite battles; reserves are mentioned at the battle of Amphipolis in 422 BC and the first battle at Syracuse in 415 BC (Thucydides 5.9.8, 6.67.1), but these units were not as mobile as the reserve troops Xenophon sets up here. Xenophon's tactics anticipate future developments in Greek warfare.

149 *the oldest of the generals*: see note to p. 112.

to have our weapons reversed: it would probably have been hard for the hoplite to sling across his back his shield, with its double grip, its diameter of about 3 feet, and its weight of about 15 pounds (some earlier shields shown on Greek vases have a strap around the neck that would have made this possible).

151 *broke off their pursuit early*: rough ground was difficult for cavalry, so it would normally be sought by troops being pursued by cavalry, not by cavalry in flight. Xenophon implies that the Greeks could have inflicted heavier casualties had they kept on with their pursuit.

152 *see these envoys*: Xenophon is stressing either the measures he took to avoid suspicion or the fact that he respected due process by bringing the envoys before assembly.

Dexippus: for his earlier behaviour, see 5.1.15, 6.1.32. If Xenophon's hostile presentation is correct, the fact that he dared to return shows his trust in the power of Sparta and in his own slanders against the Ten Thousand.

155 *in violation of the decree*: see 6.6.2.

155 *Dracontius the Spartiate*: See 4.8.26.

By the Twin Gods: the Tyndarids, Castor and Pollux, who were important deities at Sparta (they were carried on military campaigns by the two Spartan kings, Herodotus 5.75.2). Xenophon characterizes the Spartan speaker by using the Doric form *tō siō*.

156 *to be each other's guest-friend*: *xenoi*, see note to p. 4.

BOOK SEVEN

157 *Anaxibius asked*: the relations that ensue between the Ten Thousand and the Spartan leaders in the Hellespont are confused. First, the Spartans seek to gratify the satrap Pharnabazus by arranging for the Ten Thousand to cross the Hellespont. The Spartans are themselves afraid for the safety of the strategic city of Byzantium, and keen for the Ten Thousand to leave Byzantium and either serve in the Chersonese or else disband (the promise of pay if the Ten Thousand marched to the Chersonese may have been a ruse). Anaxibius makes Xenophon stay with the Ten Thousand, presumably because he wants to use Xenophon's influence over the mercenaries to achieve his own plans. It is only when the Ten Thousand have left Byzantium and his own term of office is over that Anaxibius lets Xenophon accompany him on his journey home. Complications arise when Pharnabazus goes back on his promises to Anaxibius. Xenophon claims that Anaxibius then reverses his policy and tries to keep the Ten Thousand together in the hope that they may be able to harm Pharnabazus' interests. It is because Xenophon lets himself be used by Anaxibius in this move away from official Spartan policy that he incurs the displeasure of the new Spartan governor of Byzantium, Aristarchus. For discussion, see J. Roisman, 'Anaxibios and Xenophon's *Anabasis*', *Ancient History Bulletin*, 2 (1988), 80–7.

Seuthes of Thrace: a Thracian prince who had been brought up by the king, Medocus, and was now seeking to recover land previously controlled by his father (see n. to p. 165). References to Seuthes as a king at this period (Diodorus 13.105.3; Nepos, *Alcibiades* 7.5, 8.3) are anachronistic: it was only later that he established himself as a rival to Medocus. After his death in 383 BC, his son Cotys reunited the Odrysian kingdom. See Z. H. Archibald, *The Odrysian Kingdom of Thrace: Orpheus Unmasked* (Oxford, 1998).

he had recently become: see 6.6.35; for 'harmost', see note to p. 140.

158 *Eteonicus*: a prominent Spartan general in the later stages of the Peloponnesian War, with experience in northern Greece as harmost of Thasos in 410 BC (*Hellenica* 1.1.32) and as an admiral in Thrace (*Hellenica* 2.2.5).

Sacred Mountain: on the north coast of the Propontis, on the immediate route between Byzantium and the Chersonese. Strabo (7 F 55 (56)) calls the mountain 'a sort of acropolis of the country'.

159 *1,000 talents*: at the start of the Peloponnesian War Pericles claimed that the Athenians' income from their allies amounted to 600 talents (Thucydides 2.13.3). As the state also had other sources of income, Xenophon's statement is reasonable.

160 *the first Greek city we've come to*: in fact, Trapezus was the first Greek city the Ten Thousand came to (4.8.22), and they had also been to Cerasus, Cotyora, Sinope, Heraclea, and Chrysopolis. Xenophon's rhetoric separates the Greek cities on the Black Sea coast (which intermingled strongly with the native populations) from Byzantium, closer to mainland Greece and the Greek cities along the shores of the Propontis and along the Aegean coast of Asia Minor.

Coeratadas of Thebes: a military specialist like Phalinus (2.1.7), cf. *Memorabilia* 3.1.1 and Plato, *Laches* 181e–183d for other such military experts. He is probably the same as the Coeratadas who was leader of the Boeotian force helping Clearchus as harmost of Byzantium in 408 BC: in charge of the city at the time of its betrayal to the Athenians, he was taken prisoner, but escaped on landing at Athens (*Hellenica* 1.3.15–22). Later he returned to Thebes and is found on the pro-Spartan side in 395 BC (*Hellenica Oxyrhynchia* 20.1).

Delta: the triangular region between the Black Sea and the Bosporus, to the north of Byzantium.

162 *Neon of Asine . . . Timasion of Dardanus*: an incomplete list. Cleanor has been left out, presumably by mistake. Also missing is Sophaenetus of Stymphalus, who was last mentioned at Calpe Harbour (6.5.13). Phryniscus of Achaea, who is mentioned here for the first time, seems to have replaced Sophaenetus as general, but Xenophon has not mentioned whether Sophaenetus was deposed, left the army, or (if the memoir of the expedition written in his name is a later forgery) died.

asking him to honour their agreement: see the vague formulation at 7.1.1, 'he promised to do anything Anaxibius asked'.

164 *Teres*: the founder of the Odrysian kingdom (see note to p. 165 below). Seuthes was probably his grandson: for a reconstruction of his family tree, see Archibald, *Odrysian Kingdom*, 104.

night-fighting: cf. their night attack at 7.4.14–18; Polyaenus 2.2.6.

165 *he and the Athenians were related*: a bond of kinship forged through myth: the Thracian king Tereus (regarded as an ancestor of Teres) was said to have married Procne, the daughter of the Athenian king Pandion. See Thucydides 2.29.

When things turned bad for the Odrysians: for the Odrysians' former power, see Thucydides 2.97. Their kingdom had been founded by Teres, probably in the 470s BC, after the Persian defeat in Greece; Teres was succeeded by his son Sitalces, who on his death in 424 BC was succeeded by his nephew Seuthes I (died c.410 BC). At its utmost, the kingdom stretched between the coasts of the Black Sea and Propontis to the east and south, the Danube to the north, and the Strymon and the Oescus (Isker) to the west. Towards the end of the fifth century BC the Odrysian king's control over this area became weaker, and local despots like Seuthes became powerful. It is possible, however, that Seuthes is referring only to the Odrysians' loss of control over the area that his father had ruled, a small corner of their kingdom, and that this does not reflect the position in the rest of the kingdom.

166   *in Thrace*: compare Herodotus' account of Thracian marriage customs (5.6.1).

the Sacred Mountain: Xenophon has not previously mentioned that the Spartans wanted the troops to march across this difficult route; his claim here may be devious.

169   *some of your fellow countrymen*: an allusion to the Athenian politician Alcibiades, who gained influence with Medocus and Seuthes (Diodorus 13.105.3) when he was exiled from Athens in 406 BC. His possessions in Thrace are mentioned at *Hellenica* 1.5.17; Nepos, *Alcibiades* 7.4 (Bisanthe and New Fort—two of the places said at 7.5.8 to have been offered to Xenophon—and Orni).

170   *the last drops of wine*: the Thracian custom of sprinkling the last drops of wine on the clothes of other guests is mentioned by Plato, *Laws* 637e2–5 and Suda s.v. *kataskedazein*, where this passage is cited.

like a magadis: a Thracian harp (Duris *FGH* 76 F 28), used for octave concord (M. L. West, *Ancient Greek Music* (Oxford, 1992), 72–3). Xenophon means that the trumpets were played in both a high and a low pitch.

173   *long cloaks*: Thracian patterned cloaks (*zeirai*) are depicted on Greek vases; compare also Herodotus 7.75.1.

attracted to boys: Greek *paiderastēs*—an unusual instance of the Greeks' characterizing a man by his sexual preferences. Xenophon has earlier mentioned another Episthenes who was a lover of boys (4.6.1), from Amphipolis, close to Olynthus: it is possible that this is the same man and that Xenophon made a mistake about his home city. But it should be noted that the earlier Episthenes is named Plisthenes in some MSS.

light shield: the *peltē*, regarded by the Greeks as a Thracian shield in origin.

who had just reached the period of bloom: see note to p. 53.

174   *from these villages either*: it is odd that Seuthes did not simply gather the villagers' food stores and leave. Perhaps he was setting them a trap.

175   *as is their custom*: the Thracians' shields, which could easily be swung behind their backs, by contrast with the less mobile hoplite shields (see note to p. 149).

Hieronymus of Epitalium: this is the Hieronymus of Elis mentioned three times earlier, assuming that the emendation 'of Epitalium' (a town in Elis) is correct.

176 *Teres the Odrysian*: not the same as the Teres mentioned earlier (7.2.22), but a local ruler who had lost control of the area he ruled (note how Xenophon separates it from that of Seuthes' father, who had also lost his domain). He may be the Teres mentioned by a scholion on Aristophanes, *Acharnians* 145, a son of Sitalces and so grandson of the earlier Teres.

177 *written scrolls*: this is the earliest evidence for large-scale trade in books.

to take charge of the war effort: *Hellenica* 3.1.4; the key change in Spartan policy, as the Spartans turned against their former paymasters with the goal of 'liberating' the Greek cities in Asia Minor. Thibron was later banished for maltreating Sparta's allies (*Hellenica* 3.1.8), but he was in command again in 391 BC, when he was killed by the Persian general Struthas (*Hellenica* 4.8.18–19).

178 *panders to their wishes*: the Greek verb is *dēmagōgein*, 'to be a demagogue': the term 'demagogue' evidently had a hostile sense for the anti-democratic Spartans.

179 *to help you*: Xenophon in fact returned because he had been sent back by the Spartans (7.2.8–9), as he acknowledges below.

messages: only two messages have been mentioned earlier (7.1.5, 7.2.10).

180 *let alone the other generals*: referring to the distribution of mules and oxen at 7.5.2–4.

Perinthus: for the Ten Thousand's arrival, see 7.2.11. Xenophon has not mentioned previously that the gates were shut against them.

181 *organized units of cavalry or peltasts*: Xenophon has not previously mentioned that the separate units had disbanded during his absence from the army: the usual unit of forty cavalry is attested at 7.3.46. His claim here is probably a rhetorical exaggeration to make the army's plight seem greater.

182 *trophies*: only two have been mentioned in the narrative (4.6.27, 6.5.32).

183 *put to death by Thibron*: compare the earlier hint of a threat to Xenophon from the Spartans at 7.2.14, and the later hint at 7.7.51.

186 *6,000 men*: they had been 8,600 when counted at Cerasus, but many had been killed or left since then, and 6,000 is in fact an exaggeration of their current numbers, which were probably about 5,300. Isocrates referred to the army as 6,000 in number (4.146).

187 *thirty talents*: this figure suggests that the army numbered about 5,300 at this stage (see above).

190 *everything else I promised you*: Seuthes has earlier promised to make the Greeks his companions, to give them land and oxen, and to give Xenophon his daughter (7.2.36–8).

unfair tactics against you: referring to the night attack described at 7.4.12–24.

who shall I say the talent is from?: Xenophon's worry is that producing any money from Seuthes—even for distribution—would raise suspicions that he had hidden away some of Seuthes' money for himself. He also implies that Seuthes would be laying himself open to suspicion: previously Heraclides has been blamed for not giving out in full the money gained from selling booty, but now Seuthes appears to have some money in reserve himself. One talent was in any case too paltry a sum to meet the troops' grievances. The sum is not mentioned again: it seems that Xenophon did not take it.

190 *to watch out for stones when I leave here*: see 7.6.10.

Thanks to you: see 7.6.39. Xenophon is eager to gratify the Spartans.

officially banished: on the circumstances of Xenophon's exile, see Introduction, p. xv. This sentence need not imply that Xenophon was banished soon after the expedition came to an end.

191 *the murals in the Lyceum*: the Lyceum was a famous sanctuary outside the city walls of Athens, containing a temple of Apollo Lyceius, a gymnasium, and a parade ground; it was frequented by Socrates and other philosophers. Nothing else is known of the painter Cleagoras—if he was indeed a painter: the verb *graphein* can mean 'write' or 'paint', and 'murals' (*entoichia*) is an emendation; some manuscripts read *enupnia*, which gives the sense 'who wrote *The Dreams in the Lyceum*'.

Zeus the Compassionate: Zeus Meilichius, the chthonic (subterranean) Zeus, who was sometimes worshipped in the form of a snake; the most important festival of Zeus at Athens, the Diasia, was held in his honour.

fifty darics: the price (about 1,300 Attic drachmas) suggests an especially fine horse (an ordinary horse would have cost about 300 drachmas).

Hellas: her name means 'Greece'. It has been argued that she was descended from the Athenian general Themistocles and the Spartan king Damaratus (Wiedersich, *Real-Encyclopädie der classischen Altertumswissenschaft*, ed. A. Pauly, G. Wissowa, and W. Kroll, Stuttgart, 1924, Supplement IV, cols. 728–9), both exiles in Persia, but this is implausible.

Gongylus of Eretria: in the *Hellenica* (3.1.6), Xenophon mentions a Gongylus who was given four cities in Asia Minor by the Persian king because he was the only citizen of Eretria (in Euboea) to medize; the medism must refer to his service as commander in Byzantium in the 470s BC, when he collaborated with the medizing Spartan regent Pausanias and sent some noble Persian prisoners back to Persia (Thucydides 1.128.5–6). It is often thought that the Gongylus married to Hellas was the son of this medizing Gongylus, but he is more likely to be the same man (note that Xenophon calls him an Eretrian). His two sons mentioned here went over to the Spartan army in Asia Minor under Thibron.

193 *Damaratus*: see n. on p. 33. Like the two sons of Gongylus, Procles later went over to the Spartans (*Hellenica* 3.1.6). One of his descendants married into the family of Gongylus (an early third-century BC inscription from Delos honours a Damaratus son of Gorgion: W. Dittenberger (ed.), *Sylloge Inscriptionum Graecarum* (3rd edn.; Leipzig, 1915–24), 381).

TEXTUAL NOTES

1.2.9 *Agias*: reading Ἁγίας with Köchly.

1.2.17 *the barbarians*: reading τῶν δὲ βαρβάρων φόβος πολύς, καὶ ἥ τε Κίλισσα with the MSS.

1.2.25 *100 hoplites*: Reading ⟨ἕκαστος⟩ ἑκατόν, with Mather and Hewitt.

1.9.17 *honourable support for*: reading καλῶς ὑπάρχειν with Hug.

1.9.29 *particularly fond*: retaining the MSS reading ὑπ' αὐτοῦ ἀγαπώμενοι.

2.1.12 *Theopompus*: reading Θεόπομπος with the better MSS.

2.3.8 *quickly*: retaining ταχύ with the MSS.

2.6.11 *joy*: omitting ἐν τοῖς ἄλλοις προσώποις with some recent editors.

2.6.28 *young men*: omitting the repeated phrase ἔτι ὡραῖος ὢν, with Jacobs.

3.4.15 *archers*: deleting Σκύθαι with Krüger.

3.4.16 *Persian counterparts*: some words appear to have dropped out of the text, but the sense is clear.

4.7.21 *first men got there*: omitting καὶ κατεῖδον τὴν θάλατταν with some MSS.

4.8.11 *short but deep*: reading ἐπὶ πολλῶν with Disschop.

4.8.12 *enemy phalanx*: deleting οἱ ἔσχατοι λόχοι, with Cobet.

5.4.22 *a little way in front*: reading ὑπολειπομένου with Muret.

5.8.1 *had been elected*: the text is awkward—probably some words have dropped out—but the general sense is plain.

6.4.22 *initiate the sacrifice*: reading προθύεσθαι with Bornemann.

7.4.18 *Epitalium*: reading Ἐπιταλιέα with Schenkl.

7.8.15 *Itabelis*: there is no need to change the text to read 'Itamenes': the name 'Itabelis', attested in several manuscripts, is similar to names found on Babylonian inscriptions.

INDEX OF PROPER NAMES

American Literature

British and Irish Literature

Children's Literature

Classics and Ancient Literature

Colonial Literature

Eastern Literature

European Literature

Gothic Literature

History

Medieval Literature

Oxford English Drama

Poetry

Philosophy

Politics

Religion

The Oxford Shakespeare

A complete list of Oxford World's Classics, including Authors in Context, Oxford English Drama, and the Oxford Shakespeare, is available in the UK from the Marketing Services Department, Oxford University Press, Great Clarendon Street, Oxford OX2 6DP, or visit the website at www.oup.com/uk/worldsclassics.

In the USA, visit www.oup.com/us/owc for a complete title list.

Oxford World's Classics are available from all good bookshops. In case of difficulty, customers in the UK should contact Oxford University Press Bookshop, 116 High Street, Oxford OX1 4BR.

JANE AUSTEN	Emma
	Mansfield Park
	Persuasion
	Pride and Prejudice
	Sense and Sensibility
MRS BEETON	Book of Household Management
LADY ELIZABETH BRADDON	Lady Audley's Secret
ANNE BRONTË	The Tenant of Wildfell Hall
CHARLOTTE BRONTË	Jane Eyre
	Shirley
	Villette
EMILY BRONTË	Wuthering Heights
SAMUEL TAYLOR COLERIDGE	The Major Works
WILKIE COLLINS	The Moonstone
	No Name
	The Woman in White
CHARLES DARWIN	The Origin of Species
CHARLES DICKENS	The Adventures of Oliver Twist
	Bleak House
	David Copperfield
	Great Expectations
	Nicholas Nickleby
	The Old Curiosity Shop
	Our Mutual Friend
	The Pickwick Papers
	A Tale of Two Cities
GEORGE DU MAURIER	Trilby
MARIA EDGEWORTH	Castle Rackrent

A SELECTION OF   **OXFORD WORLD'S CLASSICS**

GEORGE ELIOT

Daniel Deronda
The Lifted Veil and Brother Jacob
Middlemarch
The Mill on the Floss
Silas Marner

SUSAN FERRIER

Marriage

ELIZABETH GASKELL

Cranford
The Life of Charlotte Brontë
Mary Barton
North and South
Wives and Daughters

GEORGE GISSING

New Grub Street
The Odd Woman

THOMAS HARDY

Far from the Madding Crowd
Jude the Obscure
The Mayor of Casterbridge
The Return of the Native
Tess of the d'Urbervilles
The Woodlanders

WILLIAM HAZLITT

Selected Writings

JAMES HOGG

The Private Memoirs and Confessions of a
    Justified Sinner

JOHN KEATS

The Major Works
Selected Letters

CHARLES MATURIN

Melmoth the Wanderer

WALTER SCOTT

The Antiquary
Ivanhoe
Rob Roy

MARY SHELLEY

Frankenstein
The Last Man

TROLLOPE IN OXFORD WORLD'S CLASSICS

ANTHONY TROLLOPE

An Autobiography
The American Senator
Barchester Towers
Can You Forgive Her?
The Claverings
Cousin Henry
Doctor Thorne
The Duke's Children
The Eustace Diamonds
Framley Parsonage
He Knew He Was Right
Lady Anna
The Last Chronicle of Barset
Orley Farm
Phineas Finn
Phineas Redux
The Prime Minister
Rachel Ray
The Small House at Allington
The Warden
The Way We Live Now

THOMAS AQUINAS	Selected Philosophical Writings
FRANCIS BACON	The Essays
WALTER BAGEHOT	The English Constitution
GEORGE BERKELEY	Principles of Human Knowledge and Three Dialogues
EDMUND BURKE	A Philosophical Enquiry into the Origin of Our Ideas of the Sublime and Beautiful Reflections on the Revolution in France
CONFUCIUS	The Analects
ÉMILE DURKHEIM	The Elementary Forms of Religious Life
FRIEDRICH ENGELS	The Condition of the Working Class in England
JAMES GEORGE FRAZER	The Golden Bough
SIGMUND FREUD	The Interpretation of Dreams
THOMAS HOBBES	Human Nature and De Corpore Politico Leviathan
DAVID HUME	Selected Essays
NICCOLO MACHIAVELLI	The Prince
THOMAS MALTHUS	An Essay on the Principle of Population
KARL MARX	Capital The Communist Manifesto
J. S. MILL	On Liberty and Other Essays Principles of Political Economy and Chapters on Socialism
FRIEDRICH NIETZSCHE	Beyond Good and Evil The Birth of Tragedy On the Genealogy of Morals Twilight of the Idols